# Mustang
## America's Favorite Pony Car

## 2nd Edition

NEW YORK
1966 GT

## John A. Gunnell & Brad Bowling

Published by

**krause publications**

700 E. State Street • Iola, WI 54990-0001
Telephone: 715/445-2214

Web: www.krause.com

Please call or write for our free catalog. Our toll free number to place an order or obtain a free catalog is 800-258-0929 or please use our regular business telephone, 715-445-2214.

Library of Congress Catalog Number: 94-77379
ISBN: 0-87341-946-4
UPC: 08322200946-4
Printed in the United States of America

| Front Cover | Back Cover |
|---|---|
| 1) 1966 Shelby GT-350H | 1) 1965 Mustang convertible |
| 2) 1970 Boss 302 | 2) 1976 Cobra II |
| 3) 1966 2+2 | 3) 2000 Cobra R |
| 4) 2001 Bullitt | 4) 1984 SVO |
| **Title Page** | 5) 1968 Shelby GT-350 |
| 1966 GT fastback | |

# Introduction

Because most of my adult life and career have revolved around Mustangs, I am often asked to explain the mystique of Ford's sporty pony car. There are a lot of easy explanations, none of which adequately sum up the world's fascination with a car that started life as nothing more than a spruced-up Falcon.

The Mustang created, defined and dominated the pony car market. One need only look at its competition in 1964 (the now-defunct Corvair Monza) and in 2001 (the soon-to-be-defunct Camaro/Firebird) to realize that the Mustang occupies a unique niche in our culture. It's more than a car, in the same way Route 66 is more than an old highway and Elvis is more than another popular singer.

No, there's no easy way to describe the phenomenon, but this book contains more than a sideways glance at the often triumphant, sometimes troubled, legend of the Mustang.

Chapters 1, 2 and 3 recount the car's introduction and glory years—times of rabid public enthusiasm. In Chapters 4, 5, and 6, you'll read how the horsepower race put the Mustang on top of a crumbling high-performance mountain, leading to the unpopular—but more realistic for the times—Mustang II (Chapter 7). Ford's efforts to capitalize on the success of the first car's formula, including a seven-year attempt to bring a successful turbocharged Mustang to market, are outlined in Chapter 8. Chapter 9 discusses Ford's plans in the late 1980s to turn the Mustang into a four-cylinder, front-drive, Mazda-designed economy car. Chapters 10 and 11 celebrate the arrival of the latest generation—still powered by a V-8 and still driven by the rear wheels. The modified Mustangs of Carroll Shelby and Steve Saleen are the topic of Chapters 12 and 13. For dreamers and schemers, Chapter 14 revisits some of the special one-offs and prototypes that have been considered as new directions for the Mustang over the past 35-plus years. Finally, the first-time Mustang buyer might want to pay particular attention to the helpful tips provided in Chapter 15.

This book is an expansion and updating of an earlier work written by John A. Gunnell for Krause Publications entitled *Mustang: The AfFORDable Sportscar*. Gunnell currently serves as automotive books editor, and has written a number of books on a variety of automotive subjects.

Brad Bowling
Charlotte, N.C.

*Rare 1968 T-5 Mustang. (Owners: Johnnie and Rachel Garner)*

# Foreword

If you've never written a book that spans four decades of an automobile's life, you are blissfully unaware of just how much work can go into such a production—especially when a string of bad luck gets woven into the process.

The first book Brad Bowling edited was my *25 Years of Mustang Advertising*, which was released in time for the marque's silver anniversary in 1989.

Brad was working in California as a p.r. guy for Saleen Autosport when I was hired to write the ad book. Because I had enjoyed his work for *Mustang Times* and *Mustang Monthly*, I asked if he would like to do the editing chores on my new book. He agreed and we set up a meeting to go over the box of color slides and notes he would be molding into a complete book.

The most memorable part of that meeting was how much we laughed about the hardships I had endured in assembling the small mountain of material contained in that box.

A year earlier, just after getting the assignment, I had flown to Detroit to spend a few days with the J. Walter Thompson agency—the company responsible for every Mustang ad ever produced. In other words, this was my one-stop ad shop. Should be pretty simple, right?

My equipment bag was packed with 35mm cameras, lenses, rolls of film and a brand new copy stand. The instructions for the stand were easy enough for a child to use—attach camera to supplied overhead mount, place enclosed sheet of non-glare glass over photo subject (in this case, original ad slicks from the agency's files), focus, shoot.

The Thompson people were very nice to work with and let me have a room to work in that would have been large enough for most office duties, but I had everything spread out and found it necessary to work on the floor. There were boxes and files everywhere. Despite being really careful, after shooting only a few ads, I managed to break my one and only sheet of glass.

I looked through a phone book, located a glass supply store and took off in my rental car. I found the store and purchased two panes of the expensive non-glare glass.

Having killed a whole day with my glass errand, I went to the agency early the next morning and got right to work. Within the first half-hour, I managed to break both pieces of glass and went looking for more. A sympathetic office worker pointed out to me that most of the paintings around the place had non-glare glass in their frames. He also showed me how to remove the glass without harming the print or frame.

I was glad to get back to work until I was looking through a stack of files and backed into the freshly purloined pane, breaking it neatly into three deadly looking shards.

Feeling like an art thief in a cat burglar movie, I surreptitiously removed the glass from another painting and went back to work on my stacks of Mustang ads. Because the glass pieces were different sizes, breakage became even more of a problem as I had to wedge them into place in the copy stand in creative ways. More trips down the hall were necessary.

Eventually, I photographed 25 years worth of Mustang ads and returned the files to the person who had entrusted them to me. Another popular book about America's favorite pony car was on its way to completion.

If there are such acts of desperation and forced resourcefulness behind the creation of Mustang: America's Favorite Pony Car, I haven't heard about them yet. Maybe in a few years, after the statute of limitations has run out, Brad will share them with us.

In the meantime, I'm sure you'll enjoy reading this history of Ford's Mustang—a car so popular that after nearly 40 years of production enthusiasm for the car continues to amaze (and employ) those of us lucky enough to make a living writing about it.

Jerry Heasley
Pampa, Texas

The U.S. Postal Service today (Sept. 5, 1999) unveiled a 33-cent stamp featuring the 1965 Mustang. The wraps came off the Mustang commemorative stamp at the Lone Star Grand National Car Show in Houston, hosted by that city's Mustang Club. The stamp is one of 15 saluting the 1960s as part of the postal service's "Celebrate the Century" program to honor the people, places, events and trends of each decade of this century.

# Acknowledgments

Some passages or facts presented in *Mustang: America's Favorite Pony Car* were originally presented in articles in *Old Cars Weekly*.

Contributors of such information, presented in alphabetical order, are: Roy Ames, Chicago Automobile Trade Association, Phil Hall, Jim Haskell, Jerry Heasley, Tim Howley, Tom LaMarre, Gerald Perschbacher, Peter Winnewisser, Wally Wyss and R. Perry Zavitz.

Photos used in the book were obtained from a variety of sources, including Applegate & Applegate; Autolite Division, Ford Motor Company; Automobiles Intermeccanica; Teresa Bordinat; Brad Bowling; Carolyn Brown (Ford Public Affairs Department); Rick Cole; Dollar Rent-A-Car; Duffy's Collectible Cars; John Eichinger; Ford Division, Ford Motor Company; Frito-Lay Inc.; John A. Gunnell; Tom Gunnell; Phil Hall; (The) Hartford Automobilier; Jerry Heasley; Dave Heise; Harold Hinson, Henry Ford Museum & Greenfield Village; Ross Hubbard; Indianapolis Motor Speedway Corporation (IMSC); Iola Old Car Show, Inc.; Kendall Oil Company; Ron Kowalke ; Bob Lichty; Bill and Mary Mason; Jim MacPherson; Monogram Models Company; Mike Moran (Ford Public Affairs Department); *Old Cars Weekly* (*OCW*); *Old Cars Price Guide (OCPG)*; Ed Pearson; Revell; Jack Rzentkowski; Carroll Shelby (Shelby Automobiles); Dennis Schrimpf; Phil Skinner; Ben Smith; and Wally Wyss.

We greatly appreciate the help of all those listed above, plus car owners whose Mustangs are pictured herein, and others who have, in one sense or another, been involved in the creation of this new work. It could not have been done without all of you.

Help in putting together the second edition of the book came from Jimmy Morrison (Morrison Motor Co., Concord, North Carolina), David and Gina Goff, Jimmy Glenn, Norm and Karen Demers, Liz Saleen and my fiancée Heather Moore. Thanks to Krystal Krause (interior graphic design), Clay Miller (cover design), and Kay Sommerfeld (color section design) of the Krause Publications art and production departments. Editing chores for this second edition were handled by James T. Lenzke, former Krause Publications automotive books editor.

*1968 T-5 Mustang (Owners: Johnnie and Rachel Garner). Most of these cars were exported to Germany.*

# Contents

*1997 Cobra (Owner: Bob Cox)*

# CHAPTER 1

# A 'Bird Begets a Pony
## The Birth of the Mustang I Show Car

In many ways, the 1955 Thunderbird is the closest ancestor to the Mustang. *(Ford)*

*The 1956 Thunderbird, with its rear-mounted "Continental tire" kit, and the 1956 Corvette were both shunned by many imported sports car fans. (Henry Ford Museum)*

*In keeping with the times, tailfins were added to the T-bird for 1957. (Old Cars Weekly)*

Whether for better or worse, World War II changed the lives of millions of people. For the purposes of this book, it is important to consider how it indirectly transformed the American auto industry.

Wartime exposure to automobiles in other parts of the world changed the views and interests of American car enthusiasts who served overseas. Many came back to the United States with a newly-found love of the small, open sports cars they had driven in Europe and Great Britain. By the early 1950s, "dream cars" seen at auto shows began to look like Americanized renditions of the T-series MG or Jaguar XK-120. When the Chevrolet Corvette and Kaiser-Darrin hit the showrooms in 1953 a trend was set for the future.

Ford Motor Company followed the trend with its 1955 two-seat Thunderbird, which it promoted as a "personal car," rather than a sports car. Far more luxurious and weather-tight than an MG, Triumph, Jaguar, or Austin-Healey, the "T-bird" offered such amenities as a detachable fiberglass hardtop, an optional automatic transmission and powerful extra-cost V-8 engines (with a VERY rare option supercharger in some models).

Though far more successful in the showroom than competitor Chevrolet's Corvette, the Thunderbird was an expensive car to build as it shared few components with other Fords. Sales were respectable at 16,155 (for the 1955), 15,631 (1956) and 21,380 (1957); however, the bottom line was always a small loss or a minuscule profit. It was not enough to offset the cost of building an exclusive car line with few production-volume efficiencies.

General Manager Robert McNamara decided to enlarge the Thunderbird into a four-passenger sports/personal model. This "Squarebird" had bucket seats and a center console, like many sports cars, but its larger size, big-car engineering and rich appointments made it more of a luxury vehicle. It had an obvious sporty flavor, but was far from a sports car. It was also a profitable success; one of only two domestic car models to increase sales in 1958.

## THE FALCON GETS SPORTY

During the early 1960s, Ford started adding sporty features to its compact Falcon in an attempt to win some of the former sports car buyers that Chevrolet's Corvair Monza was stealing from imported car dealers.

A 1962 version of the Falcon, called the Futura, got bucket seats and a four-speed floor shift; however, these minor changes did not put it on a par with the radical, rear-engine Monza. It took little away from Chevy's growing market segment, which rose to 350,000 buyers. Ford was getting about one-third as many combined sales from its Falcon Futura and Mercury Comet S-22 sports models.

*Ford's first "Squarebird" was released in 1958 and continued through 1960 virtually unchanged (inset). In addition to a coupe, a convertible was also offered. (Old Cars Weekly)*

*The "golden anniversary" edition of the Indy 500 on May 30, 1961, was paced by a new Thunderbird convertible. (IMSC)*

*The Thunderbird Sports Roadster was a four-passenger convertible with a fiberglass tonneau that snapped on for a two-passenger look. (Old Cars Weekly)*

## MEET THE FAIRLANE GROUP

Lido Anthony Iacocca had started working for Ford Motor Company in the 1950s, where he passed up an engineer's job at the Dearborn, Michigan, factory for a sales job. A successful "$56 per month for a 1956 Ford" campaign caught the eye of Robert S. McNamara, vice president and general manager of Ford Division.

Based largely on the strength of the 1956 promotion, which Iacocca claims helped sell 70,000 extra cars that year, McNamara promoted "Lee" to the new position of truck marketing manager. Iacocca's career rocketed him through the position of car marketing manager and general manager of Ford until 1962, when he became vice president and general manager of Ford.

Iacocca was probably the most influential member of the Fairlane Group, a committee of eight to 10 Ford managers and reps from ad agency J. Walter Thompson. The group met each week at the Fairlane Inn in Dearborn, where they pondered the future directions of various Ford product lines.

*Lee A. Iacocca was the driving force behind the team of people who conceived, designed and marketed the original Mustang. (Old Cars Weekly)*

*"Eugene" Bordinat is one of several men who can claim paternity to the Mustang. (Ford)*

## MUSTANG I

During 1962, Iacocca and friends brainstormed, then built, an all-new prototype sports-competition car as an engineering exercise. The Mustang I was refreshingly different from many of the then-current Detroit experi-mental vehicles due to its ultra-light weight and competi-tion-ready components. It also had a distinctly European flair—no surprise when one realizes it was launched under the direction of Royston G. Lunn, a product plan-ner who was a European transplant.

*Engineer Herb Misch (left) and director of styling Eugene Bordinat (right) view the Mustang I experimental sports car. (Ford)*

*Ford's "Muroc" proposal of the early 1950s had a hint of the Mustang in its compact size, sporty image and four-place seating. (Ford)*

Lunn, whose résumé included time with Aston Martin and AC Cars in England, was given a budget, a clean sheet of paper and the mandate to "build something sporty." Despite the complexity of the project, he did not start with an existing Ford chassis, a fact which helped emphasize its distinction from many other Detroit "dream cars" of the era.

Herb Misch, a former Packard designer, was tapped to be project engineer. During the summer of 1962, Misch helped design and build the Mustang I during an amazingly short period of 100 working days. Under the direction of Eugene Bordinat, sketches of the car were transformed into a clay model in just three weeks. Despite the short turnaround, the impact of his work has stood the test of time. Bordinat had worked his way up through the General Motors' styling studios before moving to Ford in 1947 and over to Lincoln Division in the 1950s. He became vice president and director of styling for the entire company in 1962.

Blessed with the drive of Iacocca, the skills of Lunn and Misch, and the luck of Bordinat, the project sailed along very smoothly that summer. The main factors in the initial concept for the car were drivability, performance, comfort, appearance, feature appeal, and flexibility of application. Though designed as a road vehicle, the Mustang I met all Federation Internationale de l'Auto-mobile (FIA) and Sports Car Club of America (SCCA) competition regulations. It was decided to aim the vehicle at the 1.5-liter engine class, which was mid-range in the small sports car category.

An extremely lightweight machine, the Mustang I had a "space frame" constructed entirely of one-inch tubing, a body skin formed of .060-inch thick aluminum and an integral roll bar. Troutman and Barnes, the California body builders responsible for Lance Reventlow's Scarab race cars, fabricated body panels.

To design a sports car with low-cost potential, an existing driveline had to be utilized. It was determined that either the four-cylinder inline engine used in the English Ford or the German 12M Cardinal V-4 engine could be used. Both engines had over 1,500 cubic centimeters and were attractive for a sports car concept. However, the inline-four's dimensions would have necessitated a conventional, front-engine driveline arrangement, while the V-4 came with a transaxle unit that permitted a rear-drive layout with engine location ahead of the rear axle.

The front-engine approach allowed a shorter overall length and better luggage compartment, while the midship arrangement allowed better drag characteristics and a lower center of gravity. Because a lower mass translated into the best roadability, the V-4 was chosen to power the project car.

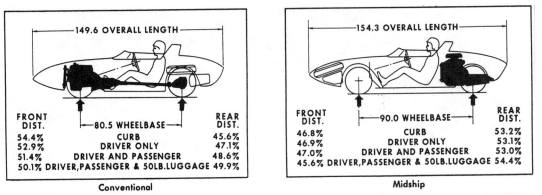

**Conventional**

| | 149.6 OVERALL LENGTH | |
|---|---|---|
| FRONT DIST. | 80.5 WHEELBASE | REAR DIST. |
| 54.4% | CURB | 45.6% |
| 52.9% | DRIVER ONLY | 47.1% |
| 51.4% | DRIVER AND PASSENGER | 48.6% |
| 50.1% | DRIVER, PASSENGER & 50LB. LUGGAGE | 49.9% |

**Midship**

| | 154.3 OVERALL LENGTH | |
|---|---|---|
| FRONT DIST. | 90.0 WHEELBASE | REAR DIST. |
| 46.8% | CURB | 53.2% |
| 46.9% | DRIVER ONLY | 53.1% |
| 47.0% | DRIVER AND PASSENGER | 53.0% |
| 45.6% | DRIVER, PASSENGER & 50LB. LUGGAGE | 54.4% |

*The inline-four drivetrain (left) necessitated a conventional driveline arrangement, while the V-4 (right) came with a transaxle, permitting a rear-drive layout with engine amidships. (Ford)*

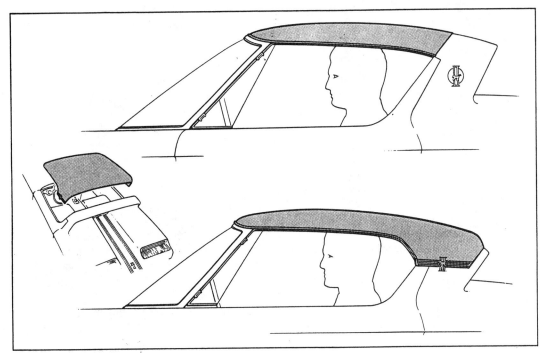

*Optional hard and soft tops were under consideration. All were designed to mate with the Mustang I's integral roll bar. (Ford)*

*An extremely lightweight machine, the Mustang I had a three-dimensional "space frame" constructed entirely of one-inch thick tubing.*

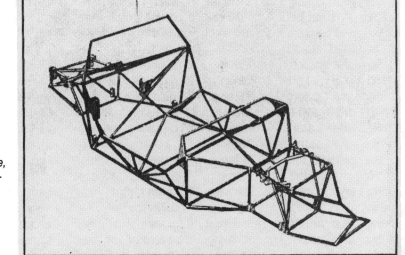

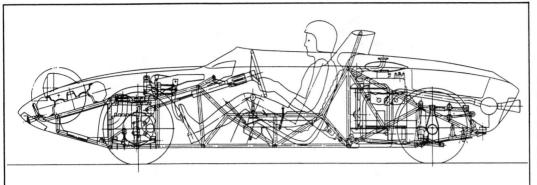

*The final vehicle package used the midship "power pack" location, since the aerodynamic hood (shown clearly in this drawing) could be positioned extremely low over the front wheels. (Ford)*

*In addition to its 1.5-liter engine, the power pack incorporated a four-speed fully-synchronized concentric-drive manual transmission. (Ford)*

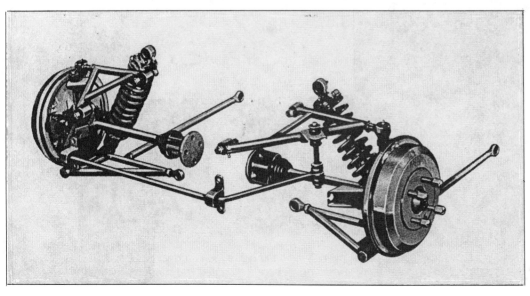

*The front suspension was a short/long arm (SLA) type with welded tubular "A" arms for upper and lower links and ball joints at all pivot points. (Ford)*

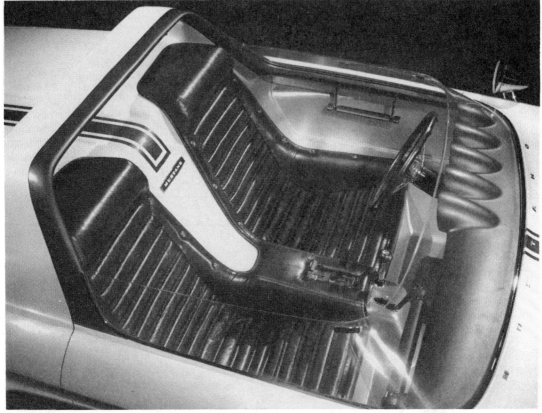

*The Mustang I interior was designed around a fixed-seat and movable-control concept. The seats were part of the body structure, making it stronger. (Ford)*

*The interior had an easily accessible gear-change lever, fly-off hand brake, horn, turn signals, and choke control located in the console. Large, easy-to-read gauges were mounted in a padded dash with a built-in grab handle. (Ford)*

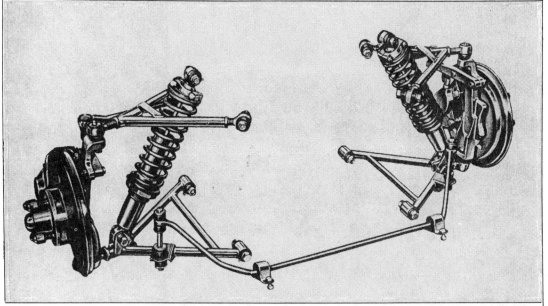

*Independent link rear suspension was used. It featured an upper "A" frame, an inverted "A" lower arm and a trailing link for fore-and-aft stability.(Ford)*

Bordinat was given a 90-inch wheelbase platform to build on and a 48-inch front and 49-inch rear track. Overall length worked out as 154 inches. Overall width was 61 inches. The spare wheel, gas tank, and battery sat up front, while a drop-in luggage carrier was designed for the rear deck lid opening. Inside, the seats were fixed in place and driving controls were adjustable. Foldaway head-lamps made the aerodynamic front possible.

The body skin was a one-piece "pod" riveted to the space frame where possible. It included the inside surface of the floor and toe board and the seat pans. All attachment brackets for the mechanical units were welded to the space frame. Built-in wheel arches, headlamp cans, and other forms strengthened the body pod.

*The low hood created a more aerodynamic package than anything on American highways at the time. (John Gunnell)*

When Ford spent $250,000 on this experimental car, they weren't about to cut corners on the oil filter. So they used an Autolite filter. Like you buy. Under $4.

The Mustang I sports car concept was seen in an Autolite/Ford ad that said it cost $250,000 to build. The hand-formed aluminum body ran over $50,000 and the tab for the movable control panel was $10,000. Of course, the high-quality Autolite oil filter cost only $4. (Ford/Autolite)

Including the seats as part of the body skin made the car stronger and allowed use of a clean, lightweight seat trim and built-in headrests. Safety belts were rigidly attached to the structure and could be made easily retractable; and a composite, central console was constructed to provide easily accessible controls. Also, less floor trim was required and seat attaching and adjusting hardware was eliminated.

In addition to clutch/brake/accelerator pedals with four inches of adjustment, the interior featured an easily accessible gear-change lever, a fly-off hand brake, a horn, turn indicators and choke control—all located in the console. Large, easy-to-read instruments were mounted in a padded dash with a built-in grab handle.

While the prototype had a competition-type windshield, a road-going unit and several optional hard and soft tops were under consideration. All were designed to mate with the integral roll bar, which had a hinged or pivoted backlight.

In a paper on the car, Lunn described the engine/transaxle as the "power pack" and noted that it was the larger displacement version of a unit designed for the 12M German Cardinal. It consisted of the 1,500cc, 60-degree V-4 balance-shaft engine, a four-speed fully-synchronized concentric-drive manual transmission combined in a common housing with an axle unit and conventional clutch.

Changes made to upgrade performance of the production engine included a high-lift camshaft: high-pressure springs; a larger single-throat carburetor; an electric fuel pump; installation of a vacuum and centrifugally actuated distributor: and use of a gauze-type air cleaner. For competition applications, a new manifold with twin-throat Weber carburetors could be installed. A special gear-shift mechanism was fabricated, but a close-ratio transmission could not be developed

within the 100-day deadline; widely-spaced standard gear ratios were used.

A two-radiator cooling circuit was designed for the car, with interior heating provisions. The side-mounted radiators had electric fans controlled by a thermostat.

The front suspension was a short/long arm (SLA) type and independent link rear suspension was used. The mid-engine configuration contributed greatly to good weight distribution, which enhanced the car's handling characteristics. Brakes were adapted from the Ford Consul model (built by Ford of England) and consisted of 9.5-inch discs up front and 9-inch diameter rear drums. The Mustang was designed for tires in the 5.30x13 to 5.50x13 size range.

Road versions of the engine generated 89 hp, which was good for a top speed of about 112.9 miles per hour. The Weber-carbureted track version produced 109 hp at the same 6,500-rpm maximum and about 13 more miles per hour of top speed.

The Mustang I made its first appearance at the United States Grand Prix, in Watkins Glen, New York, on Oct. 7, 1962. On October 20, it was seen at the Laguna Seca Pacific Grand Prix, in Monterey, California.

It set the enthusiast world on its ear and whet an appetite for things to come.

Under McNamara, Ford had made many profitable products, but few really exciting ones had been seen since the two-seat Thunderbird. European automotive journalists especially found the Mustang I refreshing. France's Bernard Cahier wrote, "The Mustang could put on a convincing performance (as a sports car)."

Eventually, the prototype served out its useful life. It was given to the Henry Ford Museum and Greenfield Village for safekeeping. Today, millions of visitors see it there, as part of the museum's "The Automobile in American Life" exhibit.

## Falcon XT-Bird

Prior to initiating the T-5 project, Ford had toyed with a concept called the "Falcon XT-Bird." Budd Body Co., which manufactured bodies for the original Thunderbird, suggested this low-cost way to revive a two-passenger sports car. Budd proposed supplying modified Thunderbird bodies for around $400. The firm estimated the complete car, made with many Falcon drivetrain components, could go out the door for less than $3,000. Production and tooling costs would be amazingly low because of the shared componentry.

In the end, the Falcon XT-Bird went no further than the drawing board. It was not pursued because it lacked eye appeal and was limited to a two-passenger configuration only. The Fairlane Group had researched lots of numbers telling them what postwar "baby boomers," who were just reaching car-buying age, really wanted and what they could afford to pay for it. The Falcon XT-Bird did not seem to match their buyer profiles.

TWICE-A-YEAR (or 6,000-mile) MAINTENANCE. The '64 total performance cars from Ford go 36,000 miles or 3 years* between major chassis lubes; 6,000 miles or 6 months between oil changes and minor lubes. In fact, every '64 car built by Ford needs so little service it's just good sense to see that it gets the best—at your Ford Dealer's. His factory-trained mechanics and special tools add up to a great service combination you can get nowhere else! Other '64 Ford service savings include: engine coolant-antifreeze, installed at the factory, good for 36,000 miles or two years; self-adjusting brakes; aluminized mufflers; and galvanized vital underbody parts to resist rust and corrosion.

Try TOTAL PERFORMANCE
For A Change!

# FORD

Falcon · Fairlane · Ford · Thunderbird

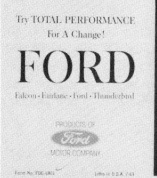

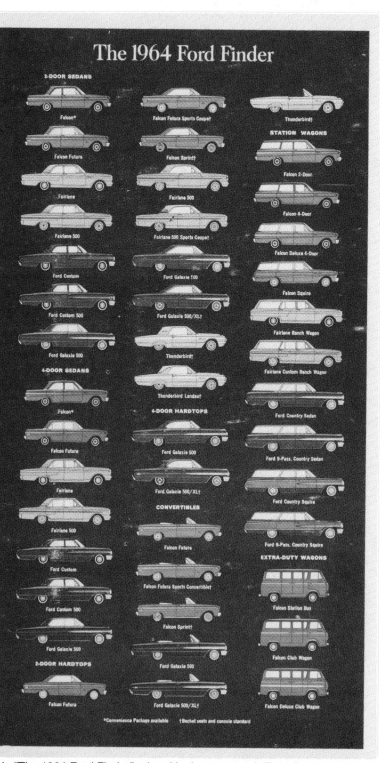

*The Mustang did not show up in "The 1964 Ford Finder" printed in the company's* Total Performance Cars for 1964 *sales catalog. There was a good reason—all Mustangs had 1965 vehicle identification numbers. (Ford)*

# CHAPTER 2

## The Mustang Generation Boomed in 1964

*On April 17, 1964, the official introduction of the Mustang took place at the New York World's Fair. The previous evening, the car had been unveiled to 29 million television viewers in commercials on all three major networks. Notice this non-production model does not have the horizontal bars in the grille. (Ford)*

When the original Mustang was introduced in the spring of 1964, the economy was booming. With plenty of jobs and few social concerns, America was experiencing a youth movement as the "baby boomers" of the 1950s became young adults. In Ford's lingo, this was the "Mustang Generation," a phrase coined to express the enthusiasm of the time and the car that captured its excitement.

"This generation wants economy and sportiness, handling and performance, all wrapped up in one set of wheels," went the sales pitch. "There is a market out there searching for a car. Ford Motor Company committed itself to design that car. It carries four people, weighs under 2,500 pounds and costs less than $2,500."

The production Mustang came close to matching those lofty design parameters. Admittedly, it was a few pounds over the target weight, and rear passengers needed to be on the short end of the spectrum to fit comfortably. Still, four seats there were, and Ford did a great job of hyping that and all of the Mustang's other attributes. Not since Henry Ford introduced the Model A had such a keen publicity campaign been concocted by the Ford Motor Company.

In March, a full month before the Mustang's public introduction, the company had a member of the Ford family drive a black pilot model to a luncheon in downtown Detroit. There, the *Detroit Free Press* snapped "spy" photos and sent pictures out on the news wires, where *Newsweek*, among others, picked one up and ran it.

America's affair with the Mustang officially began April 16, 1964, when all three networks ran commercials showcasing the new pony car to nearly 29 million viewers. The following day, spectators attending the New York World's Fair saw the car up close and personal at a special unveiling ceremony. On the first sales day, more than 22,000 orders were taken; within a year, Mustang sales reached 417,000 units.

Introducing the car in April as a "midyear" model was Lee Iacocca's idea. He had successfully launched other performance cars, such as the Falcon Futura and the Galaxie 500XL, outside the traditional fall schedule. While playing with the schedule had the desired effect of shining a stronger spotlight on the Mustang, it has led to the idea that Ford produced a "1964-1/2" model—there's simply no such animal.

The economy was booming when the original Mustang was introduced in the spring of 1964 and there were plenty of jobs. Ford pictured members of the "Mustang Generation" in publicity photos like this one. It shows a young housewife driving her youthful, business executive husband to the train station. (Ford)

A pre-production model, lacking final trim, appears on the design studio turntable. Ford's goal was to design a car that carried four people, weighed under 2,500 pounds and cost less that $2,500. The production version came very close to those design parameters. (Ford)

Surprisingly spacious trunk

*"A surprisingly spacious trunk" was promoted as a 1965 Mustang feature. While its sporty-looking "short" rear deck did limit load-hauling capacity to some degree, it was big enough to make the Mustang a good grocery-getter. (Ford)*

*Another member of the "Mustang Generation" seems happy with her Wimbledon White hardtop. This car is wearing 1963 Florida license plates and is probably an early, pre-production model. (Ford)*

## New Ford Mustang
### $2368* f.o.b. Detroit

This is the car you never expected from Detroit. Mustang is so distinctively beautiful it has received the Tiffany Award for Excellence in American Design ... the first time an automobile has been honored with the Tiffany Gold Medal.

You can own the Mustang hardtop for a suggested retail price of just $2,368—f.o.b. Detroit.

* This does not include destination charges from Detroit, options, state and local taxes and fees, if any. Whitewall tires are $33.90 extra.

Every Mustang includes these luxury features unavailable—or available only at extra cost—in most other cars: bucket seats, wall-to-wall carpeting, all-vinyl upholstery, padded instrument panel, and full wheel covers. Also standard: floor shift, courtesy lights, sports steering wheel, front arm rests, a 170 cu. in. Six, and much more.

That's the Mustang hardtop. With its four-passenger roominess and surprisingly spacious trunk, it will be an ideal car for many families. Yet Mustang is designed to be designed by you. For instance, the trip to the supermarket can be a lot more fun when you add convenience options like power brakes or steering, Cruise-O-Matic transmission, push-button radio, 260 cu. in. V-8.

Or, you can design Mustang to suit your special taste for elegance with such luxury refinements as air conditioning, vinyl-covered roof, full-length console, accent paint stripe, and convertible with power top.

If you're looking for action, Mustang's the place to find it, with a 289 cu. in. V-8, 4-speed fully synchronized transmission, Rally-Pac (tachometer and clock) and other exciting options.

For an authentic scale model of the new Ford Mustang, send $1.00 to Mustang Offer, Department A-1, P.O. Box 35, Troy, Michigan. (Offer ends July 31, 1964.)

### TRY TOTAL PERFORMANCE FOR A CHANGE!

## FORD

Mustang · Falcon · Fairlane · Ford · Thunderbird

*The Mustang had flair. It was very stylish, with its clean and dramatic lines. It had a long hood and a short rear deck. Advertisements stressed the low price of $2,368 for the hardtop. This ad announced that the Mustang received the Tiffany Award for Excellence in American Design. Other ads invited people to ride Walt Disney's "Magic Skyway" in Ford Motor Company's "Wonder Rotunda" at the New York World's Fair. A scale model of the car was offered for $1. (Ford)*

*The Mustang was the best-selling new car in history and Ford moved fast to increase its output. (Ford)*

# Company is:

The introduction of the '65 Mustang gave whole families a license to be young.

Now, everywhere you look, we're serving up more young ideas in our '65 cars: new disc brakes, livelier engines, 3-speed automatic transmissions across the line, new fresh air ventilation with windows closed—even *reversible* keys.

Our cars not only look, feel, and act young—they'll stay young.

Because of one old idea we never forget: quality.

The young ideas come from... 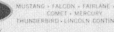 MUSTANG · FALCON · FAIRLANE · FORD
COMET · MERCURY
THUNDERBIRD · LINCOLN CONTINENTAL

MOTOR COMPANY

Desmond was afraid to let the cat out...until he got his Mustang. Mustang! A car to make weak men strong, strong men invincible. Mustang! Equipped with bucket seats, floor shift, vinyl interior, padded dash, full carpeting, more. Mustang! A challenge to your imagination with options like front disc brakes, 4-on-the-floor, big 289 cu. in.V-8, you name it. Desmond traded in his Persian kitten for an heiress named Olga. He had to. She followed him home. (It's inevitable...Mustangers have more fun.)

Best year yet to go Ford

MUSTANG!
MUSTANG!
MUSTANG!

*While the under-34 age bracket was Mustang's best, 16 percent of the buyers were in the 45 to 55 category. The Mustang seemed to bridge the generation gap. (Ford)*

*The Henry Ford Museum is home to the very first production Mustang. (John Gunnell)*

Two models were marketed originally, a spunky-looking little hardtop coupe and a convertible. Both had 108-inch wheelbases and overall lengths of 181.6 inches. The hardtop weighed 2,449 pounds and the convertible weighed 2,615 pounds. They were priced at $2,368 and $2,614, respectively. The closest competitors already on the market were the Corvair Monza Spyder coupe, at $2,599, the Corvair Monza Spyder convertible, at $2,811, and the two-week-old 1964 Plymouth Barracuda fastback, at $2,365.

Standard engine for the Mustang was a 170-cid inline-six that generated 101 hp. By comparison, the Monza Spyder had a 150-hp "pancake" six, and the Barracuda offered a 225-cid "slant" six with 145 hp. However, the Mustang's secret weapon was a "cheap" V-8 that was part of a long list of options and accessories. The V-8 used in early Mustangs was the 260-cid version with 164 hp. While this was less powerful than the Barracuda's 273-cid 180-hp, extra-cost V-8, the Mustang had an appearance that more buyers preferred at the time. In a "beauty contest," the Mustang won out over the Barracuda.

The Mustang's performance look was an instant hit. Its appeal was so strong that Ford was quickly pumping out ponies from its Dearborn, Michigan, San Jose, California, and Metuchen, New Jersey, plants.

Ford did an exceptional job of keeping the Mustang ahead of its direct competitors in the horsepower race. When *Road & Track* tested Mustangs in its May 1964 issue, available engines were the 170-cid 101-hp six, the 260-cid 164-hp V-8 with two-barrel carburetor and the 289-cid 210-hp V-8 with four-barrel carburetor. For real speed freaks, the 271-hp "Hi-Po" 289-cid V-8, introduced in the Indy Pace Cars, had a four-barrel carburetor, solid valve lifters and 10.5:1 compression. Later in the year, a 200-cid 120 hp six became the base engine, and the 170-cid six and the 260-cid V-8 were dropped.

By the end of calendar year 1964, the Mustang had scored 263,434 sales. Despite its late start, only a handful of established people-movers from Chevrolet (Impala, Bel Air, and Chevelle) and Ford (Galaxie 500) had outsold it. It even surpassed the Falcon, from which it was partly derived.

Interestingly, most early Mustangs were not plain-janes or base models. Only 27 percent had the base six-cylinder engine. Nearly half had automatic transmissions and nearly 20 percent had optional four-speed manual transmissions—a manual three-speed was standard. Other creature comforts included radios (77.8%), heaters (99%), power steering (31%), whitewall tires (88%), windshield washers (48%), back-up lights (47%), tinted windshields (22.4%), full tinted glass (8%), and air conditioning (6.4%).

# Ford Motor

600 horses and a wild little pony

*The truck included a two-man cabin with television, stove and refrigerator and could travel 600 miles between fuel stops. (Ford)*

# Company is:

**Husky ideas. Frisky ideas.**

Our engineers keep trotting them out. From the brash little Mustang that nuzzled its way into America's heart, to a huge workhorse of a truck designed for tomorrow's superhighways.

This super-hauler is our experimental 600 h.p.

Gas Turbine Truck. It will cruise at turnpike speeds and swallow up 600 miles between refuelings. The two-man cabin has TV, stove and refrigerator.

It's a big hauler. In fact, only one thing carries more weight at Ford Motor Company—our insistence on top-notch quality in everything we build.

**The bold engineering comes from...** *Ford* MOTOR COMPANY

MUSTANG · FALCON · FAIRLANE · FORD
COMET · MERCURY
THUNDERBIRD · LINCOLN CONTINENTAL

*Ford made clever use of an early Mustang to drive home the idea that its "concept vehicles" can become production line realities. This suggested that the company's "Super Hauler," a 600 hp gas turbine truck, might follow the Mustang into production.*

*The Mustang was a very popular car at the beach or anywhere else young people traveled. By its first birthday on April 17, 1965, the Mustang set a new model sales record of over 418,000 units. (Ford)*

In terms of demographics, the Mustang's surprisingly large success can be understood by looking at the age of buyers. While more than half of them fit into the under-34 year old bracket, where great popularity had been anticipated, a sizable 16 percent of the customers fell into the 45-to-55 year old category.

To steal even more buyers away from the Barracuda, Ford introduced a new fastback body style on Oct. 1, 1964. Called the "2+2," it was not a hardtop in the sense of having pillarless styling, because it had no rear side windows. In the area where such windows are normally expected, there was a set of louvers used as outlets for the flow-through ventilation. On April 17, 1965, the Mustang celebrated its first birthday and took the cake by setting a new sales record of over 418,000 units. It exceeded the previous record set by the Falcon in 1960 by about 1,000 units. It is interesting to think that both of these achievements came from the same company that gave us the Edsel in 1958.

## THE FIRST MUSTANG INDY 500 PACE CARS

The Mustang's performance theme was further driven home by its selection as "Official Pace Car" for the 1964 Indianapolis 500. Ford assembled approximately 230 pace car Mustangs, including 35 convertibles and about 190 hardtops. The convertible pace cars were sold to dealers after the race who then sold them to the public. The hardtops were distributed to the winners of two contests.

The "Checkered Flag" and "Green Flag" contests were Ford Division-sponsored dealer incentives designed to promote the new Mustang and its selection as the Indy 500 pace car. Checkered Flag winners qualified for a free trip to Dearborn, to participate in ceremonies awarding them a free hardtop pace car. Green Flag winners had to pay for their cars, albeit at a $500 reduction from the normal price.

Both contests were run simultaneously during the month of April 1964. Every Ford dealership had the opportunity to participate in at least one of the contests.

Each domestic district (there were 37 at the time) arrayed the dealers in its district into groups, which were based on sales volumes for the preceding 12 months. A sales objective (number of units) was established for each dealer in each Checkered Flag and Green Flag group. Winning dealers were those who exceeded their sales objectives by the highest percentages.

Dearborn was shooting for a roughly even split between Checkered Flag and Green Flag winners and was making plans to bring about 100 Checkered Flag winners to Dearborn for the ceremonies. In mid-April, prior to conclusion of the contests, 185 hardtop pace cars (five per district) were assembled. Each car carried the standard-order DSO (district sale office) number for its respective district.

A slight problem arose when some districts wound up with more than five total winners of the two contests, while others wound up with less than five winners. Dearborn saw, through reports from its districts, that it needed a few more hardtop pace cars to distribute to winning dealers. On May 1, 1964, a small number of additional hardtop pace cars was assembled. Each carried a DSO number of 84, which meant "Home Office Reserve." Other than this code, the May 1 cars were identical to the first 185 pace cars.

In all, 105 dealers won the Checkered Flag contest and were invited, along with their wives, to the "Checkered Flag Winners' Day in Dearborn" on May 14. There they received the royal treatment, with Ford picking up the tab for everything. Events planned for the winners included a cocktail party with Ford brass, a tour of the company's facilities, the award ceremonies, picture-taking sessions with Lee Iacocca, a dinner in Windsor and other functions. The dinner speaker was race driver Eddie Sachs (who would perish two weeks later in an accident during the Indy 500).

The Checkered Flag winners left for home the next day with most driving their brand new Mustang pace cars. Meanwhile, the 85-odd Green Flag cars were being shipped to Ford's 37 district offices to be paid for and claimed by their winners. Although a few winning dealers from each contest kept their cars, most displayed them in their showrooms, then sold them.

In appearance and equipment, the hardtop pace cars were all exactly alike. They had the 260-cid V-8 engine with two-barrel carburetor, automatic transmission and power steering. All were painted Pace Car White (not Wimbledon White) and all had white vinyl interiors with blue appointments. Of course, they all carried the distinctive stripes and lettering made for Ford by 3M to trim the Indy Pace Cars.

The 37 Mustang pace car convertibles were assembled during the middle of April and 35 of them were shipped to Indianapolis Motor Speed-

*1964 Mustang Indianapolis 500 Pace Car.*

way by May 1. The two "actual" pace cars (one led the race cars around the parade lap, and the other was for back-up) arrived there at a later date.

Traditionally, various track officials and others drive so-called "festival" pace cars, prior to race day, to promote "the greatest spectacle in racing" and the pace car itself. In 1964, however, Ford could not build Mustangs fast enough to meet this tradition. In an attempt to pacify the Indy 500 officials, Ford sent 35 LTDs to Indianapolis in March. These were replaced with Mustang convertible pace cars on May 1, 1964.

One of these pace cars was used by Josephine Hauk, executive director of the Indianapolis 500 Festival Committee. Another was used by the queen of the 1964 Indianapolis 500 parade and race. The remaining 33 convertibles were used by members of the Indianapolis 500 Festival Board of Directors.

The convertibles were equipped somewhat differently than the hardtop pace cars. The two

"actual" pace cars featured the 289-cid high-performance "K" engine (not available to the public until June 1964) and had four-speed manual transmissions. Their powerplants were not modified in any way. However, their suspension systems were bolstered to more confidently handle the high-speed turns during the pace laps. The remaining 35 festival pace car convertibles had 289-cid "D" engines with four-barrel carburetors.

Normally, the Indy 500 Festival Committee members have an opportunity to purchase the cars they are using once the race is over. Not in 1964, though. Again, because of the very strong public demand for Mustangs, Ford decided to market the 35 pace cars through its dealers. They were shipped to Louisville, Ky. (the Indianapolis district's accounting location in 1964), soon after the Indy 500. They were then sold to dealers who bid the highest for them. Successful bidders were required to go to Louisville to pick up the cars.

*Pace car at Indy museum.*

*This 1965 convertible features the 271-hp V-8 that debuted with the Indy 500 Pace Cars. (Ross Hubbard)*

# CHAPTER 3

## One Million Mustangs in Two Years! (1965-66)

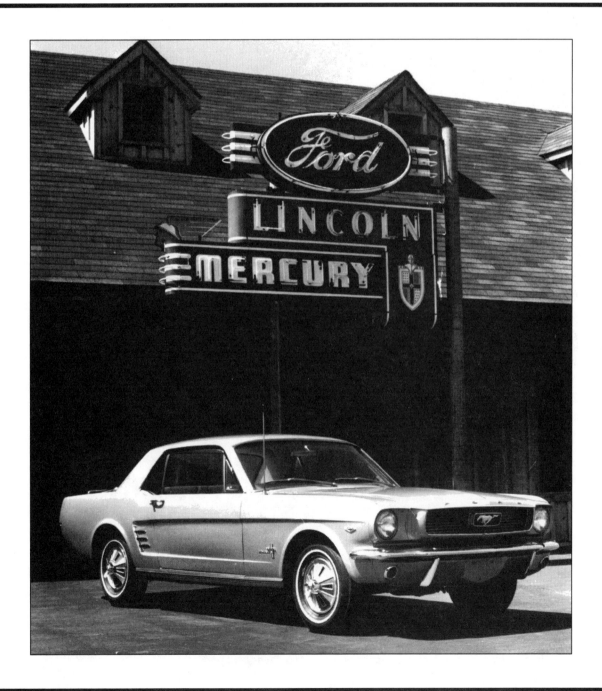

# Dress your Mustang from top to bottom with Ford Total Performance Kits

Whether you want to add some personal style touches to your Mustang or put more power under the hood, your Ford Dealer—"Your Total Performance Headquarters"—is the place to shop. The items shown here are just a sample of the accessories and performance kits he has for you.

**RALLY PAC:** A must for performance enthusiasts, this Rally Pac is a unique illuminated twin-pod cluster with a 6000-rpm tach and precision clock. Has hooded cover with "camera case" finish. Mounts on steering column. Part No. C5ZZ-10B960-C. $75.95*

**COBRA TWO 4V INDUCTION KIT:** Here's a great way to boost horsepower for hot performance. Kit includes two 4-barrel carburetors on a cast-aluminum intake manifold, special air cleaners, hardware. Easy to install on all Mustang V-8 blocks. Part No. C4OZ-6B068-E. $243.00*

**LAKE PIPES:** Use these Lake Pipes on your Mustang V-8 to cut back-pressure and give more power. Chromed pipe ends have removable caps for a rich, resonant tone. In sets of two. Part No. C4AZ-5C246-A. $57.00*

**STYLED STEEL WHEELS:** Add a distinctive touch of elegance to your car with this beautifully designed and chromed accessory. Quality engineered for precision fit . . . easy to install. Wheel with cap and lugs—$44.50*

**COBRA DRESS-UP KIT:** Adds exciting "Cobra" look to your engine. Includes finned, polished aluminum valve covers; dipstick, radiator cap, master cylinder cap, oil filler cap, air cleaner cover and filler—all in gleaming chrome. Part No. C4OZ-6980-A. $82.85*

*Manufacturer's suggested retail price. Installation charges and state and local taxes, if any, are extra.

PRODUCTS OF (Ford) MOTOR COMPANY

See your Ford Dealer—"Total Performance Headquarters"

*Promotions for 1965 tied into Lee Iacocca's full embrace of "youthful thinking" at the company. He pushed performance and motorsports involvement like never before. (Ford)*

*Attractive louvers on the 1965 Mustang 2+2 (top) were exhausts for the Silent-Flo ventilation system. Styled steel wheels (bottom right) were optional. Rear seats (bottom left) folded flat to increase 2+2's cargo space. (Ford)*

## 1965

Industry trade journals list Oct. 1, 1964, as the beginning of model year 1965 for Fords—the midyear-introduced Mustang being the only exception. Actually, the 1965 Mustang series was simply continued with a number of minor changes, and the fastback 2+2 model was added. Several additional options were seen such as front disc brakes, luxury interiors, and a GT package.

An alternator replaced the generator used on early cars. Otherwise, engine options remained the same, except that the small Falcon-derived six-cylinder (the 170-cid unit) was replaced with the 200-cid "big car" six. Some minor changes that collectors have associated with the transition from early-production cars to "regular" 1965 Mustangs are door handles attached with Allen screws (rather than C-clips); 1/4-inch longer Mustang nameplates (approximately five inches total length) on the fenders; and chrome-plated (instead of colored) inside door lock buttons.

Promotions for 1965 were tied into Lee Iacocca's full embrace of "youthful thinking" at the company, pushing performance and motorsports like Robert S. McNamara never had done. New options were promoted with slogans like "Another 'unexpected' from Mustang . . . new GT" and "Mustang Unique Ford GT stripe—badge of America's greatest total performance cars!" The new option packages allowed buyers to "design" a luxury Mustang or a sports Mustang.

Any Mustang hardtop, convertible or 2+2 could be made friendlier by ordering the luxury interior option. It included an instrument panel with wood-grained vinyl trim, new bucket seats with handsome, embossed inserts, a sports-steering wheel with chromed "rivets," and more little niceties like integral door armrests and door courtesy lights. The embossed bucket seats became known as the "pony" interior, as the embossment showed "herds" of stylized wild mustangs.

For buyers who wanted to "design" a Mustang GT, the package included the 225 hp V-8; three-speed fully-

Wolfgang used to give harpsichord recitals for a few close friends. Then he bought a Mustang. Things looked livelier for Wolfgang, surrounded by bucket seats, vinyl interior, padded dash, wall-to-wall carpeting (all standard Mustang)...and a big V-8 option that produces some of the most powerful notes this side of Beethoven. What happened? Sudden fame! Fortune! The adulation of millions! Being a Mustanger brought out the wolf in Wolfgang. What could it do for you?

Best year yet to go Ford

MUSTANG!
MUSTANG!
MUSTANG!

*For Wolfgang, it was a dark green 1965 Mustang hardtop that "brought out the wolf" in him. His lady friend doesn't seem too impressed by his sudden fame. Such themes were later repeated in 1994 Ford television commercials. (Ford)*

*Several additional options were introduced in 1965 such as front disc brakes, luxury interiors, and a GT package. (Ford)*

synchronized stick shift; special GT grille with built-in fog lamps; GT front fender insignia; a GT five-dial instrument cluster; a GT paint stripe (which could be deleted); a dual exhaust system with "trumpet" extensions; front wheel disc brakes and a special handling package. For more money, the 27-1 hp, solid-lifter, high-performance V-8 and four-speed stick shift could be substituted.

Also available for Mustangs (and other Fords) from the FoMoCo Genuine Parts division were a series of "Cobra Kits" that could be installed for better perfor-

mance. Kits for the 221-, 260-, and 289-cid Ford V-8s were marketed. They included extras from simple packages (such as chrome dress-up parts and a Cobra distributor kit) to harder-to-install engine performance kits, dual exhaust kits, cam kits, heavy-duty clutch kits, and induction kits with single four-barrel, dual four-barrel, and triple two-barrel carburetor setups.

Ford did a fabulous job selling the Mustang as a car that could be "factory-customized" to suit the individual buyer's needs. A series of "Walter Mitty"-themed advertisements was printed in leading

*The 2+2 body style, introduced shortly after the Mustang's debut, suggested high-speed, long-distance cruising. (Ford)*

magazines, recounting tales of how a bashful Midwest schoolteacher became a society darling after buying a Mustang or how Wolfgang (a harpsichord player) had his life changed after he purchased the sporty Ford. In almost all cases, the cars depicted were hardtops with full wheel covers, whitewall tires and V-8 badges. Not surprisingly, these options all had high-installation rates in 1965.

Along with a much-publicized Tiffany Gold Medal for excellence in American design during 1964, the 1965 Mustang was honored with a Bronze Medal Award from the Industrial Design Institute. The public loved the car as much as the design critics. For calendar year 1965, the Mustang racked up a total of 518,252 registrations, making it second only to the Chevrolet Impala and very nearly equal to Dodge's entire line of cars in sales volume.

*Ford's ads often suggested that the Mustang was an elegant car suitable for people who were accustomed to the finer things in life. (Ford)*

*This cowgirl seems protective of her Wimbledon White "Total Performance" Mustang GT hardtop. The red stripes on the body side, patterned after those of Ford's LeMans race cars, were in the GT package, but could be deleted. (Ford)*

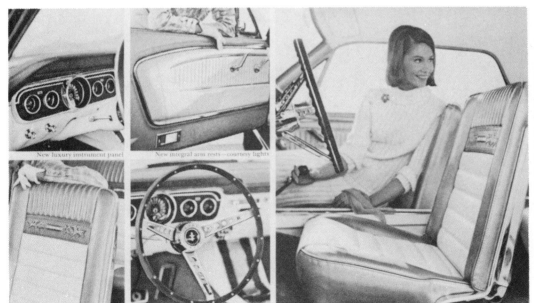

*Any 1965 Mustang hardtop, convertible or 2+2 could be made friendlier by ordering the luxury interior option including (clockwise from top left): comprehensive instrument panel, integral arm rest and courtesy lights, "pony" interior, sports steering wheel, and embossed seat backs. (Ford)*

Ford Mustang Hardtop with Vinyl-Covered Roof

# Presenting the unexpected... new Ford Mustang!
## $2368* f.o.b. Detroit

This is the car you never expected from Detroit. Mustang is so distinctively beautiful it received the Tiffany Award for Excellence in American Design . . . the first time an automobile has been honored with the Tiffany Gold Medal. Mustang has the look, the fire, the flavor of the great European road cars. Yet it's as American as its name . . . and as practical as its price—just $2,368 f.o.b. Detroit.

\* That's the suggested retail price for the basic Mustang Hardtop. It does not include, of course, destination charges from Detroit, options, state and local taxes and fees, if any. Whitewalls are $33.90 extra and the vinyl roof covering is $75.80 extra.

It does include, however, at no extra cost, a padded instrument panel and full wheel covers, which cost extra on most other cars...

See the Mustang and ride Walt Disney's Magic Skyway at the Ford Motor Company's Wonder Rotunda, New York World's Fair.

as well as bucket seats; floor-mounted shift; wall-to-wall carpeting; vinyl upholstery; arm rests; cigarette lighter; room for four; sensibly sized trunk; sports steering wheel; courtesy lights; a 170-cu. in. Six . . . and more!

The basic Mustang is an eminently practical and economical car, yet it was designed to be designed by you. You can make your Mustang into a luxury or high performance car by selecting from a large but reasonably priced group of options.

For added luxury choose such options as air conditioning, push-button radio, vinyl roof covering, 3-speed Cruise-O-Matic, power brakes, power steering—you name it.

Or, for sports car performance add the big 289-cu. in. V-8 engine (the same basic V-8 that powers the famous Cobra), 4-speed stick shift (synchro in all forward speeds), and Rally Pac (tachometer and clock).

Ford Mustang Convertible

TRY TOTAL PERFORMANCE
FOR A CHANGE!

# FORD

Mustang · Falcon · Fairlane · Ford · Thunderbird

For an exciting, authentic scale model of the new Ford Mustang, send $1.00 to Ford Offer, Department L, P.O. Box 35, Troy, Michigan. (Offer ends July 31, 1964)

*This shot shows an early, non-production car, as can be seen by the grille's missing horizontal bars. (Ford)*

*Ford replaced its rather small 170-cid inline six-cylinder with this peppier 200-cid unit. (Brad Bowling)*

*Although this convertible sports a tag proclaiming it to be a 1964-1/2 model, Ford never recognized such a designation. The first Mustangs were considered 1965s. (Brad Bowling)*

*Is it a pony car or a pointy car? This unusual Mustang fastback illustrates just how quickly the aftermarket responded to the car's success. The fiberglass nosepiece replaced all stock sheetmetal from the A-pillar forward. (Brad Bowling)*

*Also available for 1965 Mustangs (and other Fords) from the FoMoCo Genuine Parts division was a series of "Cobra Kits." Kits included simple packages like chrome dress-up parts and a Cobra distributor kit and induction kit with dual four-barrel carburetor setup. (Ford)*

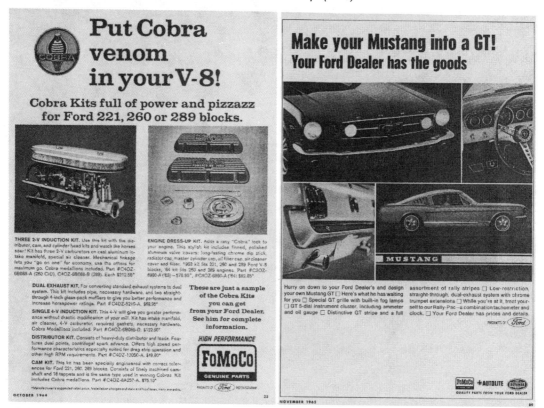

*Cobra Kits gave better performance to Mustangs. Kits for the 221-, 260-, and 289-cid Ford V-8s were marketed. In addition to Cobra kits, the Ford Parts Division sold the parts needed to make any Mustang into a GT. (Ford)*

If they're still waiting for Agnes down at the Willow Lane Whist and Discussion Group, they'll wait a long time. Agnes hasn't been herself since she got her Mustang hardtop (with its racy lines, bucket seats, smooth, optional 3-speed automatic transmission and fire-eating 200 cu. in. Six). Mustang is more car than Willow Lane has seen since the last Stutz Bearcat bit the dust. (And Agnes has a whole new set of hobbies, none of which involves cards.) Why don't you find out if there's any truth in the rumor–Mustangers have more fun?

Best year yet to go Ford
**MUSTANG!**
**MUSTANG!**
**MUSTANG!**

*In another 1965 Ford advertisement, a red Mustang hardtop gave Agnes, a mild-mannered member of the "Willow Lane Whist and Discussion Group," a "whole new set of hobbies." (Ford)*

*When the GT package was ordered for (or added to) the 1966 Mustang, the grille came with fog lamps that had horizontal divider bars stretching to them from the "corral." (Brad Bowling)*

*The rear of the GT package included a special gas cap and exhaust cut-outs in the valance panel. This restored example is missing the "trumpet" exhaust tips. (Brad Bowling)*

## 1966

In 1966, little change was needed—or made—to the popular Mustang. A revised instrument panel, designed to look less like the Falcon's, was used. The grille retained its now-familiar shape, but had the Mustang horse emblem running in a floating "corral" with a background of horizontal metal strips. The 1966 side cove received more ornate trim with what many describe as a "three-toothed comb." Federally mandated safety features including seat belts, a padded instrument panel, emergency flashers, electric windshield wipers (with washers), and dual padded sun visors were made standard.

Prices increased $44 for the hardtop, $18 for the 2+2 and $49 for the convertible. Ford wasn't alone in hiking prices that year. Tags on just about all kinds of products rose as the American cost of living jumped 3.7 percent. Wages and income rose, too, but not enough to offset higher prices. Teamed with interest rates that jumped to a record 5.5 percent, all these factors pushed Americans' purchasing power downwards a full percent. Car sales, zooming at the start of the season, fell drastically in the second half of the year. This, combined with a shortage of V-8 engines, motivated Ford's sales push for six-cylinder Mustangs.

Installations of V-8s slipped to 58 percent as Ford placed ads with headlines like "Six and the single girl" or "Now don't forget to wave when you pass your gas station. . . ." If the war-weakened economy didn't start a trend toward sixes all that quickly, at least Ford's timing was just right to take advantage of the economic downturn that started to be felt around midyear.

In the April 15 issue of *Life* (and in many other magazines) Ford ran a beautiful three-panel advertisement that trumpeted "One million Mustangs in two years!" An interesting aspect of this announcement is that it noted the three best-selling new cars of all-time were all Fords: the Model A, the Falcon and the Mustang. It also set the stage for another six-cylinder promotion.

"What do you do after you build a million Mustangs? Start on the second million!" joked an advertisement for the "Millionth Mustang Sale!" This promotion offered buyers a personalized nameplate for purchasing any Mustang during the time period. They could also get a special price on a specially equipped Limited Edition Mustang with the 200-cid six, special wheel covers, a distinctive accent stripe, a center console, an engine decal, and a chromed air cleaner.

Also continued in 1966 were the effective "Walter Mitty" ads, such as one showing a "harried accountant"

*Rocker panel stripes and a special "GT" emblem adorned the side of Mustangs ordered with the GT package. (Brad Bowling)*

The standard 1966 grille retained its now-familiar shape, but had the Mustang horse emblem "floating" in the center of the "corral." It had horizontal, but no vertical dividing bars. The side cove had new wind split moldings. (Ford)

The 1966 Mustang gas filler cap was solid metal, unlike the standard 1965 unit, which featured a plastic disc over a "running pony" emblem. The 1966 GT cap (shown) told everyone following the Mustang that its owner paid a little extra for performance feature (Old Cars Weekly)

A trunk rack was optional for all 1966 Mustangs. (Ford)

These 1966 wheel covers have the popular "knock-off" feature. (Old Cars Weekly)

The 2+2's sloping roof was a nod toward a science that was still in its infancy for cars in the 1960s—aerodynamics.
(Brad Bowling)

who changed his life-style to that of a relaxed-looking convertible owner through the purchase of a red Mustang ragtop. Another promotion of the year offered a motorized Mustang GT toy car, which was available from Ford dealers for $4.95. Ford even took out a full-page ad showing a young boy pushing the car under his Christmas tree.

Despite the slowing economy, production of Mustangs peaked at 607,568 in 1966. By the end of the year, there had been a total of 1,288,557 Mustangs built since the middle of 1964. That was quite an amazing number!

This 1966 fastback was ordered with a few special options, such as the woodgrain steering wheel, air conditioning and "pony" interior.
(Brad Bowling)

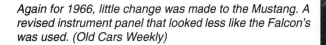

*Again for 1966, little change was made to the Mustang. A revised instrument panel that looked less like the Falcon's was used. (Old Cars Weekly)*

*The fastback's back seat was a clever device. Now you see it . . . (Brad Bowling)*

*. . . now you don't. Notice the panel at the rear that folds up to accommodate long items. (Brad Bowling)*

*The 2+2 was unmistakably a Mustang, but with a sporty, European flair. (Brad Bowling)*

Notice the "pony" inserts in the seat vinyl and special-order side-mounted speaker. (Brad Bowling)

This car is wearing the stock wheel covers for 1966. (Brad Bowling)

This rare air conditioning system and short console make the 1966 Mustang coupe very luxurious. (Brad Bowling)

Here's another example of Ford's attempt to bring women customers into the Mustang family. It must have worked. (Ford)

*The early Mustangs, such as this 1966 convertible, were great travel cars. (Brad Bowling)*

*Ford's drive to put customers in Mustangs powered by its six-cylinder engine resulted in the Springtime Sprint. (Brad Bowling)*

*The 1966 Mustang's grille was less busy than in the previous model. (Brad Bowling)*

## What do you do after you build a million Mustangs?

## Start on the second million!

# Millionth Mustang Sale!

### On specially equipped, specially priced Mustangs. Limited time only.

Mustang! Fastest first million a new car ever had. And here's the sale to kick off the second million. Hardtops, convertibles and fastbacks, V-8's or sixes . . . all with your personalized nameplate. Also included are specially priced, specially equipped Limited Edition Mustangs with a lively 200 cubic inch six, special wheel covers, distinctive accent-stripe, center console, engine decal, chromed air cleaner. Want to talk horse sense? Come in and talk Mustang!

**You're ahead in a Ford all the way!**

*The "Millionth Mustang Sale" offered buyers a choice of any body style with either type of engine and a personalized nameplate or a special price on a specially-equipped Limited Edition Mustang with the 200-cubic-inch six. (Ford)*

It really isn't surprising that a million drivers became Mustangers...not when they discovered they could design a car to be just what they always wanted! Mustang can be a sports car, a luxury car, a practical family car ...but it gets off to a wonderful head start with the equipment that comes standard.

Just look at what you get on even the lowest priced Mustang.
- 200-cu in. Six
- bucket seats
- pleated vinyl trim
- 3-speed manual floor shift
- full carpeting
- front and rear seat belts
- windshield washers & electric wipers
- backup lights
- sports steering wheel
- courtesy lights
- padded dash
- sun visors
- outside mirror
- 5-dial instrument cluster
- low-profile tires
- full wheel covers

Start with that and you're starting with a car that was born with all the advantages. Now consider the options... because Mustang is a car that was designed to be designed by you!
- AM Radio Stereo-Sonic Tape System
- 4-speed manual transmission
- 3 V-8 engines (up to 271 hp!)
- power steering
- power brakes
- front disc brakes
- vinyl roof covering
- T-Bar Cruise-O-Matic Drive
- Ford Air Conditioner
- interior décor group
- wire style wheel covers
- deluxe seat belts with reminder light
- night lighted Rally Pac
- accent stripe
- tinted glass
- woodlike deluxe steering wheel

*In the April 15, 1966 issue of* Life, *Ford ran a beautiful three-panel advertisement that trumpeted "One million Mustangs in two years!"*

- convertible with power-operated top
- white sidewall tires
- luggage rack
- special handling package
- brake warning light
- compass
- and more than 50 other options!

Whatever you ever dreamed of in an automobile—looks, performance, economy—Mustang's got it. So why don't you stop in at your Ford Dealer's during his Special Millionth Mustang Sale? He's offering specially equipped, specially priced Mustangs. Try one. Get the feel of a millionaire. One million Mustangers can't be wrong!

**Mustang**

# One million Mustangs in two years!

A million Mustangs! This makes the fastest first million a new car ever rolled up! In its first year, Mustang outdistanced Falcon's astonishing sales record. And now our two-year-old Mustang nudges out the all-time automotive record breaker, Ford's Model A, to establish itself as the most popular newcomer ever to hit the American road.

*An interesting aspect of this announcement is that it noted the three best-selling new cars of all time were Fords: the Model A, the Falcon and the Mustang. What a coup for Dearborn's prettiest coupe! (Ford)*

### Should a harried Public Accountant drive a relaxed private fun car like Mustang?

It figures. If anything will get a frazzled figure-wrestler away from his worries in one great glorious hurry, it's Mustang. The '66 version is enhanced in a dozen subtle, significant ways. A new grille. Gleaming new trim. A great new Safety Package, and a sporty Six, standard. New options like the AM Radio/Stereo-sonic Tape system that gives you over 70 minutes of music on each easy-to-load tape cartridge. The array of luxury and performance options goes on and on—it'd take an accountant to sort out the whole list, from air-conditioning through power brakes and steering, vinyl-covered hardtop, special handling package, Cruise-O-Matic transmission, big 289 cubic-inch V-8 and much more. Adds up to quite a lot, doesn't it? If you've been feeling a little driven lately, maybe it's time to drive a Mustang '66.

America's Favorite Fun Car

MUSTANG
MUSTANG
MUSTANG

*Also continued in 1966 were the "Walter Mitty" ads, such as one showing a "harried accountant" who changed his life-style to that of a relaxed-looking convertible owner through the purchase of a red Mustang soft top. (Ford)*

# CHAPTER 4

# Birth of the Big-Block
# Pony (1967-68)

This 1967 Mustang sports the Interior Decor Group option (and what looks like a really scared child in the back seat). Bucket seats, a floor-mounted shifter, and vinyl trim were standard again. A full-width front bench seat with pull-down armrest was optional. (Ford)

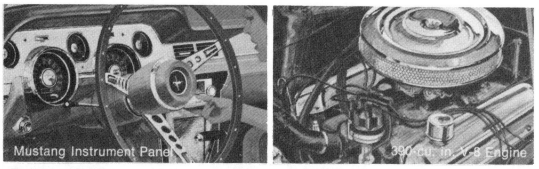

The 1967 model factory stereo tape system fit in the instrument panel. A 390-cid "big-block V-8" was new. (Ford)

Ford was hard-pressed to improve on the "classic" Mustang it had introduced in 1964, but it had to. The competition was getting very keen, indeed. Iacocca and company did a great job updating the Mustang theme for 1967. (Ford)

*The 1967 Mustang got a new body (hardtop on top and 2+2 fastback bottom left), a wider track for better traction and a wider range of engines. Option choices were also widened and included (bottom right) Tilt-Away steering. (Ford)*

## 1967

By 1967, competition had come to the Mustang in the so-called sports-compact market. Plymouth's Barracuda had been the Mustang's only real competitor since 1964, and the Dodge Charger was considered a fringe, youth-market threat that did not really go head-to-head with Ford's pony car.

Ford's success had caught other companies unprepared in 1964, but now they were poised to catch up. Mercury introduced its fancy version of the Mustang—the more luxurious Cougar—in 1967. Chevrolet, which had made little effort to respond to the Mustang through its dying Corvair, chose to create the entirely new Camaro for 1967, with Pontiac's sister act Firebird following six months later.

*The Exterior Decor Group for 1967 added functional hood louvers with integral turn signals (top). Several wheel and tire options were available. (Ford)*

*Carryover GT Equipment Group for 1967 included (clockwise from upper left) GT gas cap, disc brakes, and quad exhausts with 289- and 390-cid V-8s. (Ford)*

In 1967, Ford's optional "Fingertip Speed Control" system allowed Mustang drivers to set cruising speeds between 25 and 80 miles per hour. At all times, the driver could override the control by braking or accelerating. Afterward, a built-in "memory" automatically returned the car to the pre-set cruising speed. (Ford)

Styling for 1967 followed the same theme as the first two years, just larger. That was a wise move. A big change in appearance could have hurt the classic Mustang's eye appeal, especially since there were now other pony cars to pick from. (Ford)

*The roofline of the 1967 Mustang 2+2 had a clean, unbroken sweep downward to a distinctive, concave rear panel. Functional air louvers in the roof rear quarters are thinner than previous models. (Ford)*

The 1967 Mustang received a jazzy new body, a wider track for better road grip, a more diverse range of engines and a longer options list. Must-haves for the big-budget crowd now included a Tilt-Away steering wheel; a built-in heater/air conditioner; an overhead console; a Stereo-Sonic tape system; a SelectShift automatic transmission that also worked manually; a bench seat; an AM/FM radio; Fingertip speed control; custom exterior trim group; and front power disc brakes.

Styling followed the same "more is better" theme, with a decidedly muscular appearance. On the exterior, the 1967 Mustang was heftier and more full-fendered. Especially low and sleek was the new 2+2 fastback, featuring all-new sheetmetal. The roofline had a clean, unbroken sweep rearward to a distinctive, concave rear panel. Functional air louvers in the roof rear quarters became thinner. The wheelbase was unchanged, but overall length grew by nearly two inches. Front and rear tread widths went up by 2.1 inches and overall width was 2.7-inches wider at 58.1 inches.

Sculpting was more obvious, with lots of rounded contours. "Hairy" was how many enthusiasts described it back then. The larger, snout-like grille looked ready to take a bite out of all the "Johnny-come-lately" sporty cars. Fake, but prominent, air scoops placed just ahead of the rear tires suggested the Mustang might be more fighter plane than pony car—in later years, they were known as "cheese graters."

The hot performance news for 1967 was the debut of a big-block Mustang V-8, a 390-cid 320-hp powerplant that provided neck-snapping street performance and some drag strip success for only $264.

*Cars with automatic transmission and GT equipment were known as GTAs in 1967 only. This convertible has GTA rocker panel insignias. (Old Cars Weekly)*

The same three body styles were offered for 1967, but the Mustang did not really have different "models" like the Mercury (Cougar RX-7); Chevrolet (Camaro Rally Sport and/or Super Sport and Z28);

*and Pontiac (Firebird Sprint, H.O. and 400) pony cars did. The GT option was still available. (Ford)*

*In the days before Mustang performance options such as the Boss 302 and Mach 1, a well-optioned GT was the hot ticket. (Ford)*

The small-bore/long-stroke engine was a member of the Ford "FE" family, introduced way back in 1958.

All the 1966 engines were carried over, and a 1967-only GTA option indicated the GT package was ordered with an automatic transmission.

As always, Ford's advertisements for the pony car touted all of the new features. "The Mustang Pledge," where owners promised not to brag too much about their new cars, was the theme that seemed to be hit the hardest. One advertisement, headlined "Strike a blow for originality," showed a giant boxing glove with the galloping pony badge and a red hardtop, pushing the concept that Mustang was the lowest-priced car of its kind with bucket seats. Another advertisement, aimed

*A "Sports Sprint" was advertised in the spring of 1967. (Ford)*

*An attractive 1967 sales catalog promoted "Three new ways to answer the call of the Mustang." (Old Cars Weekly)*

*To pump up sales, auto makers upgraded warranties, even on their most popular 1967 offerings, like this Mustang convertible. (Ford)*

at women, showed a blue car and a blonde taking the pledge. "I will not sell tickets to all the people who want to ride in my 1967 Mustang," was among her promises. "Bred first ... to be first," was another slogan used in several color ads.

Ford deserves some credit for promoting safe driving in its 1967 advertising program. Marque experts will recall that Ford launched the first auto safety thrust in 1956 and the move failed from a marketing standpoint. Nevertheless, while blatantly pushing "Total Performance," the automaker showed some responsibility by backing a Safe Driving Incentive Program. This program offered 40 grand prizes (Ford Mustangs or Mercury Cali-

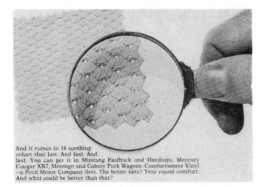

And it comes in 14 soothing colors that last. And last. And last. You can get it in Mustang Fastback and Hardtops, Mercury Cougar XR7, Montego and Colony Park Wagons. Comfortweave Vinyl —a Ford Motor Company first. The better idea? Year round comfort. And what could be better than that?

*One of Ford's "better ideas" for 1967 was Comfortweave Vinyl upholstery, which was available in Mustangs in 14 colors. (Ford)*

entes) to five Ford employees and 35 winners from dealers' contests, plus other awards. In all, 3,200 young drivers, who demonstrated their safety consciousness, were selected as winners. Twenty winners appeared in one ad with a Mustang hardtop.

American automakers had predicted another hot, nine-million-unit sales season, but 1967 ended with the industry losing one million sales from 1966 levels due to a slowing economy.

The Mustang Sports Sprint that came out in the springtime was another effort to shore up sales. Available in hardtop and convertible styles, it was offered in a "Ford's better ideas for sale" promotion that pitched "1968 ideas at 1967 prices." For a special price, Sports Sprint buyers got sporty hood vents with recessed turn indicators; whitewalls; full wheel covers; bright rocker panel moldings; a chrome air cleaner; and a vinyl-covered shift lever (if SelectShift Cruise-O-Matic transmission was ordered). In addition, Sports Sprint buyers were tempted with a special price on factory-installed SelectAire air conditioning.

Model year production of Mustangs wound up at 472,121. This was a drop of 135,447 cars from 1966. Dealer sales totaled just 377,827 units. Ford managed to increase V-8 production by 20 percent. At the same time, the special promotions boosted air conditioning installations to 16 percent, a 6.5 percent upwards bump.

The 1967 hardtop had a base price of $2,461. It weighed 2,578 pounds, without extras. Production of this body style totaled 356,271 units, including 22,228 with Luxury Decor option and 8,910 with bench seats. (Ford)

The 1967 convertible had a base price of $2,698. It weighed 2,738 pounds, without extras. Production of this body style totaled 44,808 units, including 4,848 with Luxury Décor and 1,209 with bench seats. (Ford)

## Strike a blow for originality!
### (Take the Mustang Pledge.)

Still the original and lowest-priced car of its kind with bucket seats. MUSTANG *Ford*

*Ford's 1967 "Strike a blow for originality" ad showed a giant boxing glove with the galloping pony badge and a red hardtop, pushing the concept that Mustang was the lowest-priced car of its kind with bucket seats. (Ford)*

*The 1967 2+2 fastback had a base price of $2,592. It weighed 2,605 pounds, without extras. Model year production of this body style totaled 71,042 units. This included 17,391 with Luxury Décor option. (Ford)*

*1967 Ford Musttang Fastback (Richard Seiverling)*

You'd love to answer the call of Mustang? Good! There are three new ways: hardtop, fastback and convertible! Standard for '67? Bucket seats, carpeting, floor shift, Ford Motor Company Lifeguard-Design safety features, more. Now what? Options that say you!

Stereo-Sonic Tape System, SelectShift automatic transmission that also works manually, V-8's up to 390-cu.-in., power front disc brakes, bench seat, tiltaway steering wheel, AM-FM radio, air conditioning. Smitten? Great! May we pronounce you "Man and Mustang?"

## '67 MUSTANG
Bred first...to be first

*"Bred first . . . to be first," was another slogan used in several color ads for 1967. It was a tough year, though. America's love affair with the sporty Mustang was summed up by the Plymouth-like use of a heart in the center of the ad layout. (Ford)*

*Ford backed a Safe Driving Incentive Program in 1967, offering 40 grand prizes (Ford Mustangs or Mercury Comet Calientes) to five Ford employees and 35 winners from dealers' contests. (Ford)*

# Ford's better ideas for sale—

Your Ford Dealer has ideas for sale right now that other cars won't have until next year—if then. Ideas like: SelectShift Cruise-O-Matic transmission, the automatic that works as a manual, too, even on 6-cylinder cars. Tilt-Away steering wheel swings aside, adjusts 9 ways. Convenience Control Panel warns if fuel is low or door's ajar. Lots more. Get these exclusives on hot-selling '67s like the Mustang Sports Sprint!

Mustang Sports Sprints, hardtop and convertible, come with special equipment at a special low price:
• Sporty hood vents with recessed turn indicators
• Whitewalls
• Full wheel covers
• Bright rocker panel moldings
• Chrome air cleaner
• Vinyl-covered shift lever—if you choose SelectShift
• Plus Mustang's long list of standard features
No wonder Mustang resale value is so high . . .
no wonder it outsells all its imitators combined!

# 1968 ideas at 1967 prices!

## NOW! Special Savings on SelectAire Conditioner!

Here's an air-conditioning unit that isn't just "hung on." It's handsomely built into the instrument panel. So it saves space . . . and looks as good as it keeps you feeling. You can get SelectAire right now at a special low price on a Mustang Sports Sprint or special Ford Galaxie models.

Also special savings on Galaxie 500 2- and 4-door hardtops.

**SEE YOUR FORD DEALER TODAY!** FORD

MUSTANG · FALCON · FAIRLANE · FORD
THUNDERBIRD · CORTINA

23

*The Mustang Sports Sprint came out in the spring of 1967. Available in hardtop and convertible styles, it was offered in a "Ford's better ideas for sale" promotion that pitched "1968 ideas at 1967 prices." (Ford)*

# 1968

Ford invited 1968 car shoppers to "Turn yourself on, switch your style and show a new face in the most exciting car on the American road," in reference to the Mustang. Often, the ad copywriters stressed a "Great Original" theme, highlighting the Mustang's role as America's original pony car. Another slogan, "designed to be designed by you," emphasized the buyer's ability to "customize" a car with many options.

"Get hip to the great transformer," bragged Ford, in its continuous push to associate its pony car with a youthful lifestyle. "Mustang makes dull people interesting, interesting people absolutely fascinating!" Another ad related how Sidney, a white-shirt-and-tie type, spent his Sundays "seashelling at the seashore" before he purchased a red Mustang 2+2. A time-sequence photo shows him being "transformed" into a lifeguard with three bathing beauties clinging to his muscular arms. "Only Mustang makes it happen!" says another slogan.

Only subtle changes were actually made to the 1968 model. Bucket seats, a floor-mounted stick, a sports steering wheel and rich, loop-pile carpeting remained standard. Minor trim updates included a front end with the Mustang emblem "floating" in the grille, script-style (instead of block letter) Mustang bodyside nameplates and cleaner-looking bright metal trim on the cove (replacing the previous "cheese graters").

*Minor trim updates for 1968 included a front end with the Mustang emblem "floating" in the grille, script-style (instead of block letter) Mustang bodyside nameplates and cleaner-looking bright metal trim on the cove. (Tom Gunnell)*

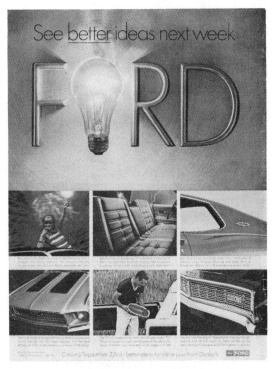

*There was a new two-tone hood for the 1968 Mustang (featured lower left). (Ford)*

*Time-sequence photo shows 1968 Mustang owner Sidney "transformed" into a lifeguard with three bathing beauties on his muscular arms. (Ford)*

MUSTANG CONVERTIBLE

*Only subtle changes were actually made for 1968. Bucket seats, a floor-mounted stick, a sports steering wheel and rich, loop-pile carpeting remained standard. (Ford)*

There was a new two-tone hood that predicted the more radical coloring to come on the 1969 Mach 1s and Bosses. Despite minimal changes in the product, prices rose substantially, averaging about $140 more per model.

The most obvious feature to be had by ordering the $147 GT option was a choice of stripes; either the rocker panel type or a reflecting "C" stripe could be specified. The latter widened along the ridge of the front fender and ran across the door, to the upper rear body quarter. From there, it wrapped down, around the sculptured depression ahead of the rear wheel, and tapered forward, along the lower body, to about the mid-point of the door.

*Ford invited 1968 car shoppers to "Turn yourself on, switch your style and show a new face in the most exciting car on the American road," in its advertising for the 1968 Mustang. (Ford)*

*The High Country Special was a rare model that combined the styling of a coupe with several items found on the more expensive Shelby Mustang, such as the driving lights, rear brake scoop, twist-down hood locks, and sequential taillights. As the name suggests, they were built for Colorado customers. (Brad Bowling)*

Other GT goodies included auxiliary lights in the grille, a GT gas cap and GT wheel covers. The extra lights no longer had a bar separating them from the "corral" in the grille. Front disc brakes were usually an extra-cost, but became standard equipment when big-block V-8s were ordered. A total of 17,458 GTs were assembled in 1968.

Many new engine options were offered in 1968, and some reflected midyear changes. The same size six and V-8 were standard, but their ratings dropped to 115

*The $147 GT option for 1968 included a choice of stripes. Either the rocker panel type or this reflecting "C" stripe could be specified. Other GT goodies included auxiliary lights in the grille, a GT gas cap, and GT wheel covers. (Ford)*

*The High Country Special gave a performance look to the 1968 coupe.*

and 195 hp, respectively. There were no options with the base 289-cid V-8. Ford offered a 302-cid V-8 instead. This was initially seen with a four-barrel carburetor and 230 hp output rating. Later on, a 220-hp version, with a two-barrel carburetor, was released.

A 390-cid V-8 with 320 hp and a 427-cid 390-hp V-8 were two new "FE" family engines offered in the Mustang for 1968. Starting in April 1968, a new 428 Cobra-Jet V-8, with 335 hp, was put into about 2,817 Mustangs. Cars with four-speed transmissions included strengthened front shock absorber towers and revised rear shock absorber mountings.

About 5,000 GT/CS "California Special" Mustangs were produced in 1968. Their features included a Shelby-style deck lid with a spoiler, sequential taillights and a blacked-out grille (minus Mustang identification). The wheel covers were the same ones used on 1968 GTs, but without GT identification.

In the 1968 season, production fell again. With 317,404 units built, the Mustang accounted for just 3.8 percent of total industry output. It had slipped from second place in domestic auto production in 1965, to seventh place in 1968. However, it was still the best-selling pony car.

*The High Country Special shared taillights with the 1968 Shelby GT-350 and GT-500, which lifted them from the 1965 Thunderbird. (Brad Bowling)*

*The High Country Special's brake scoop advertised its high-altitude attitude. (Brad Bowling)*

*The Mustang slipped from second place in domestic auto production in 1965, to seventh place in 1968; however, it was still the best-selling pony car. The hard-top (pictured here) was the best seller with 249,447 units produced. (Ford)*

*A total of 17,458 GTs were made in 1968. This is a 2+2 fastback with GT fender badges and the new accent stripe. (Applegate & Applegate)*

*In the 1968 season, production fell again. With 317,404 units built, the Mustang accounted for just 3.8 percent of total industry output. The base six-cylinder convertible listed for $2,814 and 25,376 were made. (Ford)*

# CHAPTER 5

## Diversity to the Extreme (1969-70)

# MUSTANG GRANDE

GRANDE

PHOTO NO. PRD 51

New for 1969, the Mustang Grande is a super-luxury hardtop with the custom touch. It is aimed towards the car buyer who prefers the handling and feel of a sports car with the bonus features of a high series model.

Four features in particular distinguish the Grande model . . . a special insulation package, a modified rear suspension system, elegant interior appointments – including cloth-trimmed seats offered for the first time in a sports-type car – and classic exterior trim. Standard features for the Mustang Grande include:

## SPECIAL INSULATION PACKAGE

Available with the Grande, this special sound package contains an additional 55 pounds of sound insulation and deadener materials.

## UNIQUE REAR SUSPENSION SYSTEM

Grande's luxury ride characteristics result from the use of voided rubber bushings in the front spring eyes. These bushings permit a slight rearward movement of the springs to absorb impact when the wheels strike a bump. "Iso-Clamp" rubber-cushioned mounts eliminate any metal-to-metal contact between the rear springs and the axle housing.

## ELEGANT INTERIOR APPOINTMENTS

Luxury appointments in the Grande include • Hopsack Cloth and Vinyl Seat Trim • Simulated Teakwood-Grained Instrument Panel and Cluster Applique • Deluxe Three-Spoke Steering Wheel (Includes Simulated Teakwood Rim and "Rim-Blow" Horn) • Molded Door Panels with Safety/Courtesy Lights •

Padded Interior Quarter Trim Panels with Armrests • Electric Clock with Sweep Second Hand • Bright-Trimmed Pedal Pads.

## CLASSIC EXTERIOR TRIM

Exterior trim items included on the Grande are • Grande "C" Pillar Script • Dual, Color-Keyed Racing Mirrors (Remote Operation for Driver's Side) • Wire-Style Wheel Covers • Bright Wheel Lip and Rear Deck Moldings • Special Two-Toned Narrow Paint Stripe Below Fender Line.

## RUGGED 200-C.I.D. SIX-CYLINDER ENGINE

GRANDE

PHOTO NO. PRD 52

*Four groups of standard features that characterized the new-for-1969 Mustang Grandé ranged from a special insulation package to a 200-cid inline-six engine. (Ford)*

*1969 Mach 1s featured dual color-keyed racing mirrors and a handling suspension. The fanciest Mustang interior with high-back buckets; black carpets; a Rim-Blow steering wheel; center console; a clock; insulation; and teakwood trim on the doors, dash, and console was used. (Ford)*

## 1969

"Diversity is a good thing," goes an unattributed quote, "unless there's too much of it."

It seems like a paradox, but it's arguable that the years 1969-70 had too many different overlapping Mustang models and packages. In the automotive industry, market segments are sacred ground where manufacturers tread lightly and respectfully, yet there was a two-year period when Ford Motor Company sold its Mach 1, GT, Boss 302, Boss 429, Shelby GT-350 and Shelby GT-500 with a wild array of high-performance engines that could confuse even the most enthusiastic buyer.

During those years there were no fewer than nine V-8 powerplants available, including an "economy" 302-cid unit, the awesome 302-cid Boss motor, a 351-cid "Windsor," a 351-cid "Cleveland," a final-year 390-cid, a 428-cid Cobra Jet, a 428-cid Super Cobra Jet, a 429-cid in "wedge head" form and the ground-pounding 429-cid Boss plant.

Whether the base 200-cid inline-six or Boss 429, all engines were wrapped in a new, body that retained the original's long-hood/short-deck theme in a package that was now 3.8-inches longer than the original—although it retained the 108-inch wheelbase.

The windshield was more sharply raked in—keeping with the longer/lower/wider trend of the times. Quad round headlamps were used for the first (and only) time on a production Mustang in 1969. The outer lenses were deeply recessed into the fender openings, while the inboard units were set into the grille ends.

Missing for the first time in Mustang history was the indented scoop (or cove) that had visually "pinched" the waist of the earlier pony cars. This styling gimmick was

*For model year 1969, the Mustang got its third major restyling. A new body for 1969 kept the Mustang image—not drastically changed, but in overall length it grew 3.8 inches. (Ford)*

Bonneville Salt Flats, September 19, 1968

# 1969 Mustangs shatter 295 speed and endurance records.

**All-new Mustang runs 24 hours nonstop at 157.663 m.p.h.**

No American production car has ever gone so far so fast. In a single 24-hour run—the engine never stopped turning—the specially prepared and modified canary yellow 1969 Mustang SportsRoof screamed its way around the rutted 10-mile course at an average of 157.663 miles per hour. Driven by professional record-breaker Mickey Thompson and co-driver Danny Ongais, the sleek new Mustang, powered by a 302-cubic inch Ford V-8, went a distance of 3,783 miles in the 24 hours. Thompson's average speed was 17 miles per hour *faster* and the distance driven was 405 miles *farther* than the previous record. In the 24-hour period the yellow 1969 Mustang set over 100 American stock car records in the Class "C" Division for engines between 183 and 304 cubic inches as prescribed by the United States Auto Club. In another specially prepared 1969 Mustang SportsRoof, Thompson went on to break all standing and flying start records from 25 to 500 miles in Class B (305 to 488 cubic inch displacement). All these records make an undeniable statement about the new 1969 Mustang . . . never before has any car combined the performance to go so fast and the durability to do it for so long. What this means to you: The 1969 Mustangs are winners—at the track or on the turnpikes. See them in your Ford Dealer's Performance Corner.

### NEW MUSTANG RECORDS
— (Partial listing) —

**Class B** (305 to 488 cu. in. displacement)
Flying Start—25, 50, 75, 100, 200, 250, 300, 400 and 500 kilometers
Flying Start—25, 50, 75, 100, 200, 250, 300, 400 and 500 miles

Standing Start—25, 50, 75, 100, 200, 250, 300, 400 and 500 kilometers
Standing Start—25, 50, 75, 100, 200, 250, 300, 400 and 500 miles

**Class C** (183 to 305 cu. in. displacement)
Flying Start—25, 50, 75, 100, 200, 250, 300, 400, 500, 1000, 2000, 3000, 4000, 5000 kilometers
Flying Start—25, 50, 75, 100, 200, 250, 300, 400, 500, 1000, 2000, 3000, 4000 miles

Standing Start—25, 50, 75, 100, 200, 250, 300, 400, 500, 1000, 2000, 3000, 4000, 5000 kilometers
Standing Start—25, 50, 75, 100, 200, 250, 300, 400, 500, 1000, 2000, 3000, 4000 miles

Flying Start—1-hour, 3-hour, 6-hour and 24-hour endurance
Standing Start—1-hour, 3-hour, 6-hour and 24-hour endurance

FORD
IT'S THE GOING THING!

USAC    MUSTANG    *Ford*

**The place you've got to go to see what's going on-your Ford Dealer!**

*At the Bonneville Salt Flats on September 19, 1968, all-new 1969 Mustangs shattered 295 speed and endurance records. (Ford)*

*1969 convertibles (top) and hardtops (center) had a rear-facing, simulated air vent in front of the rear wheel opening. On fastbacks (bottom), the feature line led to a C-shaped air scoop above the main feature line. (Ford)*

Though the styling theme remained Ford-like, the Mustang adopted a GM-like marketing program with distinctive "models" to suit the tastes of different buyers. Mustangs now came in basic, luxury, sporty, and high-performance formats, like a Camaro or Firebird. To a degree, this may have reflected the influence of Semon "Bunkie" Knudsen, a long-time GM executive who became president of Ford Motor Company after resigning as a General Motors executive vice president.

Knudsen was hired on February 6, 1968. While he didn't have enough time to change long-range product development for model year 1969, it's just about certain he went to work on the marketing thrust immediately. After all, Knudsen was famous for his 11th-hour transformation of the 1957 Pontiac from an "old maid's" car into a youth-oriented machine, which he accomplished in a matter of weeks. At Ford, part of his Mustang marketing strategy involved hiring GM designer Larry Shinoda and turning him loose to create what became the racetrack-inspired Boss 302.

A new model for 1969 was the Grandé, a dressed-up edition of the notchback hardtop, sporting a vinyl roof, plush interior, deluxe two-spoke steering wheel, color-keyed racing mirrors, full wheel covers, electric clock, bright exterior body moldings, dual outside paint stripes, and luxury foam bucket seats. The Grandé was priced $231 above the normal hardtop with comparable equipment.

The GT Equipment Group could be added to the base models for $147 when teamed with specific options. "Mustang's all-new GTs come in three sporty shapes—hardtop, convertible and Sports-Roof," announced Ford's *1969 Performance Buyer's Digest*. "And all of them have a big slice of the all-out performance that has made our specially prepared Mustangs the big Trans Am gun over many a rough road course."

Mustang GT equipment was not available with Grandé coupes, with sixes or the 302-cid V-8. Only 4,973 Mustang GTs were sold in 1969, so the package was a lot less popular than it had been in the past. Base engine in the GT was a 351-cid "Windsor" V-8 with 250 hp. GT buyers also received a special handling package; lower body racing stripes; dual exhausts; pin-type hood lock latches; simulated hood scoop with integral turn signal indicators (shaker scoop with the "428CJ Ram Air" V-8); three-speed manual transmission; four-wheel drum brakes; glass-belted white sidewall tires; styled steel wheels with Argent Silver trim; and GT hubcaps.

replaced with a feature line that ran from the tip of the front fender to just behind the rearmost door seam, at a level just above the front wheel opening. Convertibles and hardtops sported a rear-facing, simulated air vent just in front of the rear wheel opening on both sides of the body. On fastbacks, the feature line led to a backwards C-shaped air scoop above the main feature line.

The 2+2 was renamed the SportsRoof and was designed to feature a 0.9-inch lower roofline than earlier fastbacks. Beginning with 1969 models, Mustang fastbacks became true hardtops with a small window abutting the door glass.

*The most luxurious Mustang available in 1969 was the Grandé. (Brad Bowling)*

The Mach 1 was a model option based on the Sports-Roof. "Mustang Mach 1—holder of 295 land speed records," said the *1969 Performance Buyer's Digest*. "This is the one that Mickey Thompson started with. From its wide-oval, belted tires to its wind tunnel-designed SportsRoof, the word is 'go.'" The copy pointed out that the production car had "the same wind-splitting sheetmetal as the specially modified Mach 1 that screamed around Bonneville clocking over 155, hour after hour, to break some 295 USAC speed and endurance records."

"Bunkie" Knudsen's background included a heavy emphasis on high-performance cars. He personally liked the look of the SportsRoof. Consequently,

*This Grandé came equipped with the 351-cid V-8 and four-barrel carburetor. (Brad Bowling)*

# MUSTANG STANDARD FEATURES

Highlighting Mustang's formidable list of standard equipment for 1969 are an all-new instrument panel, ventless side glass, and dual headlamps set in a new plastic grille. Standard features include:

CONVERTIBLE                    PHOTO NO. PRO 61

## DUAL HEADLAMPS

In a distinctive horizontal design, the five-inch inboard lamps are mounted in the recessed area of the new grille with the outboard pair on the adjacent swept-away area of the fenders.

## PLASTIC GRILLE

Mustang's new injection-molded plastic grille is lightweight and corrosion-resistant. The grille is an egg-crate design with a black matte finish, highlighting Mustang's tri-color emblem mounted in an off-center position.

HARDTOP                        PHOTO NO. PRO 62

## VENTLESS SIDE GLASS

New for Mustang in 1969, the ventless side windows are mounted on a tube-in-shoe guidance system for positive window positioning. This new style window eliminates the vent window, latch and division bar and provides an improved appearance and increased driver/passenger visibility.

D-6

## IMPROVED WEATHER STRIPPING

The windshield in the 1969 Mustang is bonded to the body opening, offering a marked improvement in the sealing quality. An additional reduction in wind noise is achieved through the use of new hollow-section door weather stripping.

## NEW ACCELERATOR LINKAGE

The accelerator assures smoother, more precise control by utilizing a cable-type linkage. The flexible cable isolates the pedal from engine movements and provides improved throttle opening characteristics.

## HEATING AND VENTILATION

A new heating and ventilating system is standard equipment for the 1969 Mustang. A new blower motor and a larger air rotor provide increased air flow and improve heater and defroster performance. The cowl side ventilation system uses three sets of vanes, mounted on the cowl side trim panels to provide uniform distribution of air to all parts of the vehicle. Individual slide controls are located in each panel.

PHOTO NO. PRO 63

## FASTBACK QUARTER WINDOW

A new design for the Mustang fastback, the flipper-type, rear-quarter window provides increased rear passenger visibility and excellent air-extraction ventilation, and adds a sporty flair to the fastback styling.

*Although the concept of "customer customizing" was essential to the Mustang sales program, the base-level 1969 cars still came with a large assortment of standard equipment. (Ford)*

*The fastback, formerly known as the 2+2, became known as the SportsRoof model for 1969. It had a 0.9-inch lower roofline than earlier fastbacks. (Ford)*

*A kicked-up rear treatment gave 1969 Mach 1 SportsRoofs their racy looks and a 428 Cobra Jet V-8 was a scorcher that could be ordered for under the hood. (Ford)*

*Beginning with 1969 models, Mustang fastbacks were true hardtops. The rear quarter louvers were gone and a small window abutted the door glass. (Ford)*

*Ford published this 1969 Performance Buyer's Digest.*

*1969 was the final year for the GT package, a $146.71 premium that could be added to any hardtop, convertible or fastback. (Ed Pearson)*

this body style became the basis for a series of hot-performing "buzz bombs" like the Mach 1 and the CJ 428/SCJ 428, plus the soon-to-be-released Boss 302 and Boss 429.

Standard on all Mach 1s was a matte black hood, a simulated hood scoop, and exposed NASCAR-style hood lock pins, which could be deleted. A spoiler cost extra. A reflective side stripe and rear stripes carried the model designation just behind the front wheel arches, and above the chrome pop-up gas cap. Chrome styled steel wheels and chrome exhausts tips (when optional four-barrel carburetors were ordered) were other bright touches. Also featured were dual color-keyed racing mirrors and a handling suspension. Mach 1s also had the fanciest interior appointments with high-back bucket seats; black carpets; a Rim-Blow steering wheel; center console; a clock; sound-deadening insulation; and teakwood-grained trim on the doors, dash, and console. Base engine was a 351-cid two-barrel Windsor V-8. This was essentially a stroked 302-cid Ford V-8 with raised deck height, which created a great street performance engine.

*A 1969 Mustang Mach 1 set 295 speed records at Bonneville. The late Mickey Thompson drove the record holder across the salt flats. Thompson was familiar to Bunkie Knudsen, who supplied the four engines for Thompson's Pontiac-powered "Challenger I" World Land Speed Record car of the 1950s. (Phil Hall)*

*The lock-down hood pins were a nice touch to the Mach 1 performance package. (Brad Bowling)*

Options included the 351-cid 290-hp four-barrel V-8 and a 390-cid 320-hp V-8.

Another option available to enthusiast buyers was a Cobra Jet 428 engine with either the GT or Mach 1 package. This motor had become Ford's big-block performance leader on April 1, 1968. It came in Cobra Jet (CJ-428) or Super Cobra Jet 428 (SCJ-428) versions. The former was referred to as the "standard Cobra engine" in the *1969 Performance Buyer's Guide*. It generated 335 horsepower at 5,200 rpm and 440 lb.-ft. of torque at 3,400 rpm. The latter

*The muscular body, scoops and racing stripes probably contributed to quite a few speeding tickets among 1969 Mach 1 drivers. (Brad Bowling)*

*This 1969 Mach 1 has all of the go-fast appearance goodies, including front air dam, rear spoiler and shaker hood scoop. (Brad Bowling)*

was the same engine with Ram Air induction, a hardened steel cast crankshaft, special "LeMans" connecting rods and improved balancing for drag racing. It had the same advertised horsepower. After one drag strip test, *Hot Rod* called this machine "the fastest running pure stock in the history of man."

A total of 81.5 percent of 1969 Mustangs came equipped with V-8s. In the other 19.5 percent, there were two six-cylinder options, including a new 250-cid six with 155 hp. Automatic transmission installations ran just over 71 percent, but four-speed manual gearboxes (wide- or close-ratio) were found in nearly 11 percent. Power brakes were added to 31.5 percent of production and 66 percent featured power steering. While option installation rates were rising, total production was down to 299,824 units.

*By 1969 air conditioning was considered a necessity by many Mustangers. (Brad Bowling)*

1969 Mustang Mach 1 with 428 CID 4V Cobra Jet Ram-Air V-8

Ford's Exclusive "Shaker" scoop actually protrudes through the hood—rams air directly into the carburetor under full throttle.

**Mach 1 Specifications**—*Standard engine:* 351 CID 2V V-8. Bore and stroke, 4.00 x 3.50 in. 9.5:1 compression, regular fuel. 250 hp at 4600 rpm. Torque 355 lbs-ft at 2600 rpm *Optional engines:* 351 CID 4V V-8, compression 10.7:1, premium fuel, 290 hp at 4800 rpm. Torque 385 lb. at 3200 rpm. 390 CID 4V V-8, compression 10.5:1, premium fuel, 320 hp at 4600 rpm. Torque 427 lb. at 3200 rpm. 428 CID 4V V-8. All 4V engines have dual exhausts. *Transmissions:* Std. 3-speed fully synchronized floor shift, ratios 2.42:1, 1.61:1, 1.00:1. Optional 4-speed floor shift, ratios 2.78:1, 1.93:1, 1.36:1, 1.00:1. SelectShift, ratios 2.46:1, 1.46:1, 1.00:1. *Brakes:* 10.0 in. drums, lining area 173.3 sq. in. *Wheelbase:* 108.0". Overall length 187.4". Weight 3473 lb. *Wheels:* Chrome styled steel, 14 x 6 with wide-oval belted white side-wall tires. Optional FR70 radial ply *Suspension:* GT handling with 351 & 390 CID V-8's, competition HD with 428 CID V-8. **Mustang GT Specifications**—*Standard engine:* 351 2V V-8 (see Mach 1 specifications). *Optional engines:* 351 4V V-8, 290 hp, 390 CID 4V V-8, 320 hp, 428 CID 4V V-8, 335 hp (see page P2). 428 CID Cobra Jet Ram-Air 4V V-8, 335 hp with through-the-hood functional air scoop (see page P2). All 4V engines have dual exhausts. *Transmissions:*

Standard 3-speed fully synchronized floor shift. Ratios 2.42:1, 1.61:1, 1.00:1. Optional 4-speed floor shift, ratios 2.78:1, 1.93:1, 1.36:1, 1.00:1. SelectShift, ratio 2.46:1, 1.46:1, 1.00:1. *Brakes:* 10.0 in. drums, lining area 173.3 sq. in. *Wheelbase:* 108.0". Overall length 187.4". *Weights:* Hardtop—3243 lb., SportsRoof—3267 lb., Convertible—3353 lb. *Wheels:* Styled steel, 14 x 6 with wide-oval belted white sidewall tires. Optional FR70 radial ply tires. *Suspension:* GT handling with 351 & 390 CID V-8's, competition HD with 428 CID V-8. **Mach 1 and Mustang GT Options:** 351 CID 4V V-8 (290 hp); 390 CID 4V V-8 (320 hp); 428 CID 4V V-8 (335 hp) (390 and 428 CID require Cruise-O-Matic or 4-speed manual transmission; 428 CID 4V Cobra Jet Ram-Air V-8 (335 hp) (requires Cruise-O-Matic or close ratio 4-speed manual transmission and F70x14 wide-oval belted tires) • SelectShift Cruise-O-Matic Transmission—351 2V or 4V V-8 • 390 4V, 428 4V or 428 Cobra Jet V-8 • Four-Speed Manual—351 2V or 4V V-8—390, 428 and 428 CID Cobra Jet V-8 engines (includes tach & trip odometer) • Power Steering • Traction-Lok Differential • Power Front Disc Brakes • F70x14 Wide-Oval Belted Black Sidewall Tires with raised white letters to look like a performer.

*The Mach 1 was a model option based on the SportsRoof. "Mustang Mach 1—holder of 295 land speed records," said the* 1969 Performance Buyer's Digest.

### Mustang Mach 1—Holder of 295 land speed records.

This is the one that Mickey Thompson started with. From its wide-oval, belted tires to its wind tunnel designed SportsRoof, the word is "go." There's just one body — the same wind-splitting sheetmetal as the specially modified Mach 1 that screamed around Bonneville, clocking over 155, hour after hour, to break some 295 USAC speed and endurance records. Underneath that sleek, new shape is more Mustang than ever before. Standard are a new lightweight, free-breathing 2V 351 CID V-8, rated at 250 hp; handling suspension, simulated hood scoop, exposed lock pins and matte black hood, chrome styled steel wheels, and wide-oval belted white sidewall tires. In the high back bucket seat you sit behind a Rim-Blow deluxe steering wheel with integral horn rim switch, and look in dual color-keyed racing mirrors. Check the complete instrument cluster mounted in the simulated teakwood-grained panel. Shift the fully synchronized manual transmission from the center console. Then and only then, you'll begin to realize what kind of great machine you have.

### Mustang GT—Stack extra performance on the Mustang you fancy.

Mustang's all-new GT's come in three sporty shapes—hardtop, convertible and SportsRoof. And all of them have a big slice of the all-out performance that has made our specially prepared Mustangs the big Trans Am gun over many a rough road course. The GT Equipment Group includes styled steel wheels, wide-oval belted white sidewall tires, simulated hood scoop and locking pins, special handling package, racing stripes, and more. Performance comes on strong with the new, lightweight 351 CID 2V 250-hp V-8.

1969 Mustang GT Hardtop

P5

*"This is the one that Mickey Thompson started with." (Ford)*

1969 Mustang Mach 1. See your Ford Dealer for all the facts about the 1969 Ford, Mustang, Torino, Fairlane, Thunderbird, Falcon.

The original Mustang. Gave so many people
so many beautiful memories.

*Standard on 1969 Mach 1s was a matte black hood, simulated hood scoop and NASCAR-style hood lock pins, which were deletable. (Ford)*

If you haven't
got a past yet...
get a Mustang.

Now.

Let the good times roll. Take off in a new Mustang Mach I that's down-to-earth light-
ning. Comes with a 351-cu. in. V-8 that comes on. Comes with the works; GT suspension
to put you in a groove on curves, fully synchronized 3-speed manual transmission, styled
steel wheels, wide-tread tires, external hood latches, built-in rear deck spoiler, high-
backed buckets, faired side mirrors. And lots more like that. Or consider life in a Grandé,
the most luxurious Mustang of them all. All 5 Mustangs for '69 have been redesigned to
be roomier, wider, longer, lower, racier. Start there and design your own Mustang.
Sporty, cool, hot or what-not. There are options
for whatever you have in mind. Start living an
action story. Go Mustang! And get a past. Fast.

MUSTANG   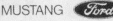 Ford

It's the going thing!

*A reflective side stripe and rear stripes carried the Mach 1 model designation just behind the front wheel
arches, and above the chrome pop-up gas cap in 1969. (Ford)*

*A reflective side stripe carried the model designation just behind the front wheel arches. (Ford)*

Mustangs, raw and rare.

Rare luxury: Grandé.
Most elegant of the longer,
wider, roomier new Mustangs.
With pre-packaged luxuries,
inside and out. From special
soft-ride suspension to thick
buckets trimmed in vinyl and
hopsack cloth. Grandé. Most
refined sport known to man.

Raw power: Mach I.
For people with a burning
desire for action, it's all here.
GT suspension. Wide oval
belted tires. Rear deck spoiler.
5 hot V-8's. Up to optional 428
Cobra Jet ram-air with through-
the-hood "shaker." Shake up
your world...in a new Mach I.

Started first. Still first.
Nothing moves like a Mustang!

FORD
It's the going thing!

*Chrome styled steel wheels and chrome exhausts tips (with optional four-barrel carburetors) were other bright touches. (Ford)*

*As you can see, the "Shaker" hood scoop is just the tip of the Cobra Jet iceberg. (Brad Bowling)*

*"Power seekers, your Mustang Mach 1 is ready," said 1969 Ford ads. "Power to pass, power to climb, power to play with. Five big engines including the 428 Cobra Jet V-8 option. See all the powers that be at your Ford dealers." (Ford)*

*Base power in 1969 Mach 1s was a 351-cid two-barrel Windsor V-8. Essentially a stroked 302 with raised deck height, it made a great street engine. (Duffy's)*

*From its wide-oval, glass-belted tires to its wind tunnel-designed roofline, the word for the 1969 Mach 1 was "go." (Ford)*

*1969 Mach 1 (Brad Bowling)*

*Rear louvers, a factory option, kept direct sunlight out of the steeply raked backlight. (Brad Bowling)*

MUSTANG

*With the popularity of the sporty Mach 1, we sometimes forget that the SportsRoof could be ordered with minimal options. (Ford)*

## MUSTANG GENERAL SPECIFICATIONS

| All dimensions are in inches unless otherwise specified | Hardtop | Convertible | 2+2 Fastback |
|---|---|---|---|
| **GENERAL** | | | |
| Wheelbase | 108 | 108 | 108 |
| Tread—Front | 58.5 | 58.5 | 58.5 |
| —Rear | 58.5 | 58.5 | 58.5 |
| Height—Overall | 51.2 | 51.2 | 50.3 |
| Width—Overall | 71.3 | 71.3 | 71.8 |
| Length—Overall | 187.4 | 187.4 | 187.4 |
| **ENTRANCE ROOM** | | | |
| Door Opening Width | 55.0 | 55.0 | 55.0 |
| Door Opening Height | | | |
| (scuff plate to windcord) | 32.8 | 32.8 | 32.2 |
| Foot Clearance—Front | 15.1 | 15.1 | 15.2 |
| Entrance Height (seat to windcord) | | | |
| "H" point) | 29.2 | 29.1 | 29.3 |
| **FRONT SEAT ROOM** | | | |
| Head Room (effective) | 37.4 | 38.2 | 37.1 |
| Maximum Leg Room to Accelerator | 41.1 | 41.1 | 41.1 |
| Hip Room | 55.6 | 55.6 | 55.6 |
| Shoulder Room | 56.0 | 56.0 | 56.0 |
| Cushion Height | | | |
| (from floor to crest front) | 10.3 | 10.3 | 9.5 |
| Cushion Depth | 13.2 | 13.2 | 13.1 |
| Steering Wheel to Thigh Clearance | 2.9 | 2.9 | 2.7 |
| **REAR SEAT ROOM** | | | |
| Head Room (effective) | 35.8 | 35.9 | — |
| Minimum Leg Room | 29.5 | 29.5 | — |
| Hip Room | 51.3 | 43.6 | — |
| Shoulder Room | 54.7 | 43.2 | — |
| Cushion Height | | | |
| (from floor to crest at front) | 11.3 | 11.3 | 7.8 |
| Cushion Depth | 11.2 | 11.2 | — |
| **LUGGAGE CAPACITY (CU. FT.)** | | | |
| Usable Luggage Capacity | 9.8 | 8.0 | 5.3 |
| **GLASS AREA** | | | |
| Side Glass Exposed Surface Area | 1072 | 1074 | (N.A.) |
| Windshield Exposed Surface Area | 1138 | 1127 | (N.A.) |
| Backlight Exposed Surface Area | 678 | 779 | (N.A.) |
| Total Glass Exposed Surface Area | 2888 | 2980 | (N.A.) |
| **CURB WEIGHT (POUNDS)** | | | |
| Six Cylinder Manual | 2838 | 2948 | 2862 |

*General specifications for the 1969 Mustangs.*

*Ford built 14,746 Mustang convertibles in 1969. (Ford)*

*Coupe production for 1969 totaled 128,458, plus 22,182 Grandés. (Ford)*

# MUSTANG POWER TEAMS

### ENGINES

The popular 200-c.i.d. six-cylinder engine continues its role as the standard power plant for the Mustang line. In offering Ford customers a maximum choice in total equipment, however, two new engines have been designed for 1969 and are included in the growing Mustang option lineup.

These include:

### 4.1 LITRE (250-C.I.D.) SIX-CYLINDER

This engine is designed to develop nearly 25% greater horsepower than the standard six . . . at the same time reacting almost as economically in fuel consumption.

### 351-C.I.D. V-8

Available in two-barrel or four-barrel versions, it is extremely compact, lightweight and provides excellent performance and good handling characteristics. The lightness in itself reduces the total weight of the vehicle, thus producing greater accelerating power.
(Refer to Power Team Section for additional data.)

### TRANSMISSIONS

Ford's proven three-speed manual transmission is the standard selection for the five Mustang models. The fully-synchronized, constant-mesh design means dependable performance and easy shifting. Optional transmissions include:

### SELECTSHIFT CRUISE-O-MATIC

The popular Ford transmission offers manual shifting or a completely automatic operation.

### FOUR-SPEED MANUAL

A favorite with the sporting crowd, this sturdy transmission provides "take-off and go" qualities unsurpassed in the industry.
(Refer to Power Team Section for additional data.)

### 1969 MUSTANG POWER TEAM SELECTIONS

| ENGINES | TRANSMISSIONS | | | REAR AXLE RATIOS | | | | | |
| | 3-Speed Manual | 4-Speed Manual | Cruise-O-Matic | 3-Speed Manual Std. | 3-Speed Manual Option | 4-Speed Manual Std. | 4-Speed Manual Option | Cruise-O-Matic Std. | Cruise-O-Matic Option |
|---|---|---|---|---|---|---|---|---|---|
| **HARDTOP, FASTBACK AND CONVERTIBLE** | | | | | | | | | |
| Std. 200 Six | Std. | N.A.** | Option | 3.08 | N.A.** | N.A.** | N.A.** | 2.83 | 3.08 |
| Opt. 250 Six | Std. | N.A.** | Option | 3.00+ | 2.79 | N.A.** | N.A.** | 2.79 | 3.00+ |
| Opt. 302 2v V-8 | Std. | Option | Option | 2.79 | 3.00+ | 3.00+ | 2.79 | 2.79 | 3.00+ |
| Opt. 351 2v V-8 | Std. | Option | Option | 2.75 | 3.00 3.25+ | 3.00 | 3.25+ | 2.75 | 3.00 3.25+ |
| Opt. 351 4v V-8 | Std. | Option | Option | 3.00 | 3.25+ | 3.00 | 3.25+ 3.91* 3.50+ 4.30* | 3.00 | 2.75 3.25+ |
| Opt. 390 4v V-8 | N.A.** | Option | Option | N.A.** | N.A.** | 3.00 | 3.25+ 3.50+ 3.91* 4.30* | 2.75 | 3.00 3.25+ 3.50+ 3.91* |
| Opt. 428 4v V-8 (Non-Ram-Air) and 428 4v V-8 CJ (Ram-Air) | N.A.** | Option | Option | N.A.** | N.A.** | 3.50+ | 3.25+ 3.91* 4.30* | 3.50+ | 3.25+ 3.91* 4.30* |
| **HARDTOP, FASTBACK AND CONVERTIBLE WITH GT EQUIPMENT GROUP OPTION** | | | | | | | | | |
| Opt. 351 2v V-8 | Std. | Option | Option | 3.00 | 3.25+ | 3.00 | 3.25+ 3.91* 3.50+ 4.30* | 3.00 | 2.75 3.25+ |
| Opt. 351 4v V-8 | Std. | Option | Option | 3.25+ | 3.00 | 3.25+ | 3.00 3.91* 3.50+ 4.30* | 3.25+ | 3.00 |
| Opt. 390 4v V-8 | N.A.** | Option | Option | N.A.** | N.A.** | 3.25+ | 3.00 3.50+ 3.91* 4.30* | 3.25+ | 3.00 3.50+ 3.91* 4.30* |
| Opt. 428 4v V-8 (Non-Ram-Air) and 428 4v V-8 CJ (Ram-Air) | N.A.** | Option | Option | N.A.** | N.A.** | 3.50+ | 3.91* 4.30* | 3.50+ | 3.91* 4.30* |

+Also available with optional limited-slip differential.  *Available only with limited-slip differential.  **N.A.—Not available.

*1969 Mustang power teams*

For 1969, Mustangs were loaded with more sporty features than ever, such as wall-to-wall carpeting, bucket seats and a floor-mounted shifter. (Old Cars Weekly)

Of all 1969 Mustang convertibles made 3,439 had deluxe equipment. (Ford)

**Every Ford can be a winner with Ford performance parts**

*Ford performance parts were again cataloged for Mustangs.*

If you've already got a Ford, Torino, Fairlane, Cobra, Mustang, or Falcon, and you want to add to its muscle and maneuverability, come to the Performance Corner at your Ford Dealer's. Don't worry about fit or fitness, this is the same parts bin that Dan Gurney, A. J. Foyt and Dave Pearson use. We don't have nearly enough space to show you all the high performance parts Ford makes, but here are a few of the most wanted items. If you don't see what you need, look in the Parts Catalog at your Ford Dealer's. He'll be glad to help you select the right pieces for your engine.

**351 CID V-8.** Light weight, short stroke, precision cast. Bore and stroke—4.00" x 3.50". 250 hp at 4600 rpm and 355 torque at 2600 with 2V carb and 9.5:1 compression. 290 hp at 4800 rpm, and 385 torque at 3200 with 4V carb and 10.7:1 compression. See your Ford Dealer for the proper parts number to fit your model and transmission.

**Cam and Lifter Kit.** A relatively mild grind for street or strip.

Ideal for conversion of 289 and 302 blocks complete with hydraulic lifters. C8DZ-6A257-A.

**Induction Kit 4V.** Includes 4V carburetor and intake manifold. Fits all 260, 289, 302 CID V-8's. Carburetor, low restriction air cleaner. C6AZ-6B068-A or C8DZ-6B068-A for 1968 models with emission control.

**289 CID High Performance Cylinder Head & Gasket.** This head utilizes screw-in valve studs and includes eight heavy-duty springs with damper, eight valve spring retainers and seals. C7OZ-6049-E.

**Distributor Kit.** Dual point centrifugal advance unit giving high efficiency at high rpm operation. Fits 260, 289, 302. C4DZ-12050-A.

**Connecting Rod.** This is the forged, spot-faced rod used in the 289 high performance engine. Recommended for high rpm operation on 260 and 289 engines. C3OZ-6200-C.

**Exhaust Manifold.** Header type, high efficiency cast iron manifolds effectively relieve back pressure in high performance applications. Fit most Fairlane and Mustang 260 and 289 equipped vehicles. C5ZZ-9430-B (right hand), C3OZ-9431-A (left hand).

**Clutch Kit.** Especially engineered for high performance engines. Consists of clutch disc with heavy-duty facing, and pressure plate with heavy-duty springs. Will fit 1963 through 1968 Fairlane, Falcon, Mustang with 3- or 4-speed or overdrive transmissions. C8DZ-7A537-A.

*Twenty-nine 1969 Mustang convertibles were given away as second prizes in the "Frito Bandito" Under-the-Hat Sweepstakes run by the makers of Frito-Lay potato chips.*

## BOSS 302 AND 429

In a year filled with exciting performance options, packages, and models, the big news for 1969 Mustang fans was the introduction of the Boss twins—the 302 and 429. *Hot Rod* reported that the Boss 302, when introduced early in the year, outclassed "most of the world's big-engined muscle cars." The Boss 302 was Ford's answer to the Camaro Z28 on the Sports Car Club of America's Trans-American racing circuit and a worthy competitor on the showroom floor.

The main asset of a Boss 302 is the high-performance engine beneath the hood, essentially the ultimate evolution (at the time) of the 260- and 289-cid Mustang V-8 introduced in 1964. The Boss 302 had special cylinder heads that gave it a performance advantage over the previous small-block Mustang V-8s. Sometimes called "Cleveland" heads (because of their similarity to those used on the 351-cid engine made in Ford's Cleveland, Ohio, foundry), they used canted intake and exhaust valves that permitted bigger ports and valves to fit. Another benefit of the head design was a straighter-flowing fuel/air mixture, giving better volumetric efficiency, especially with a little "improvement" to the stock exhaust system.

On the 1969 model, the intake valves measured a massive 2.23 inches, and exhaust valves are a large 1.71 inches—incredibly large for a production-type small-block engine. The combustion chambers of the Boss 302 engine were also different from those of the earlier small-blocks, with an advanced wedge-shaped design that resembled the shape of the chambers in the Ford "427" racing engine. They're sometimes called a "semi-hemi" design.

The Boss 302 engine used a lopey camshaft with 290-degrees of duration for both intake and exhaust cycles and a .290-inch lift. The crankshaft, balanced both statically and dynamically (with the rods and pistons in place), was made of forged steel to stand up to high rpms. It was anchored in place by five main bearings, of which the three center units had four-bolt caps. Forged steel connecting rods were used.

The Boss 302 engine also featured a high-rise, aluminum intake manifold with a single 780-cfm four-barrel Holley carburetor; pop-up type pistons; a dual-point distributor; a high-pressure oil pump; lightweight, stamped rocker arms; screw-in rocker arm studs and pushrod guide plates (with specially hardened pushrods); an oil pan windage baffle; and screw-in freeze plugs.

Ford determined that an automatic transmission would be out of character and a detriment to such a purpose-built performance car; shifting was handled through one of two four-speed manuals

*Standard equipment for the 1969 Boss 302 included black tail lamp bezels; a black chrome backlight molding; black headlamp castings; color-keyed, dual racing mirrors, and a black-finished hood, rear deck lid and lower back panel. (Ford)*

through a floor-mounted Hurst shifter. Surprisingly, the four-speed best-suited for use with the Boss 302, for street performance and dragstrip use, was the wide-ratio type. The close-ratio option was better utilized for road racing.

Some performance magazines of the era claimed that a slightly modified Boss 302 engine would keep increasing power clear up to 8,000 rpm. There was an rpm limiter that began working at around 5,800 rpm. It randomly cut spark to the cylinders to keep the revs under about 6,150 rpm. However, it could easily be disconnected and often was. Suffice it to say that Ford's peak horsepower rating of 290 at 5,800 rpm was conservative, although it was convenient for advertising, as the Camaro Z28 advertised that number.

Ford equipped the Boss 302 with three different rear axle ratios: a standard 3.50 non-locking version, plus the Traction-Lok 3.50 and 3.91. Also available was a No-Spin axle with a 4.30 ratio built by Detroit Automotive. With each of these ratios, Ford installed fully-machined axle shafts that helped prevent buildup of stress points via larger axle shaft splines, an extra-strength cast nodular iron center section and larger wheel seals. This axle is another one of the "goodies" that performance buffs are quick to buy from a wrecked Boss 302.

Ford also gave the Boss 302 special attention when it built the suspension. The front suspension used high-rate (350 inch-pounds) springs with

*A "C" stripe identified the 1969 Boss 302. (Old Cars Weekly)*

heavy-duty, direct-acting Gabriel shock absorbers and a special steel stabilizer bar with specifically-calibrated rubber mounts.

The rear suspension was of the Hotchkiss type, with 150 lbs./in. leaf springs, and it used a staggered shock absorber arrangement. The left shock absorber was bolted behind the axle and the right one was ahead of the axle. Wheel hop, bounce and the tendency of the tires to break tread were substantially controlled with this setup. Ford also added a rear stabilizer bar for improved cornering. This induced a little oversteer, but helped keep the rear end from swaying.

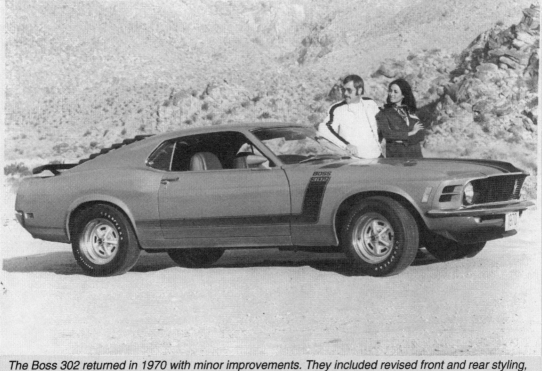

*The Boss 302 returned in 1970 with minor improvements. They included revised front and rear styling, new Grabber colors and a "hockey stick" stripe with the words "Boss 302" above and on the "blade" of the hockey stick. (Ford)*

*Even while sitting still, the Boss 429 leans forward as though it's ready to charge. (Brad Bowling)*

Power front disc brakes were standard in Boss 302s. The stock manual steering had a quick 16:1 ratio and power steering was optionally available. This option is desirable with the fat F60-15 tires.

Additional standard equipment for the small-block muscle machine included black taillamp bezels; a black chrome backlight molding; black headlamp castings; color-keyed, dual racing mirrors; a black-finished hood, rear deck lid, and lower back panel; dual exhausts; hub caps with trim rings; black tape identification on the front fender and front spoiler; a 45-ampere battery; and a Space-Saver spare tire.

On the inside, the Boss 302 used the basic layout of other Mustangs. Circular gauges were used, with "idiot lights" to monitor oil pressure and electrics. A tachometer was provided and easily visible. Although the car was fairly well loaded in standard format, two very desirable options were an adjustable rear deck lid spoiler and rear window SportSlats.

Ford was required to produce a minimum of 1,000 Boss 302 Mustangs to qualify it as a "production" car for competition in the Trans-Am racing series. The model proved to be more popular than anyone at Ford had anticipated with 1,934 of the 1969 editions cranked out.

In a similar vein, Ford wanted to qualify its new-for-1969 429-cid "semi-hemi" big-block V-8 for NASCAR racing by offering it in a street-performance car and building at least 500 copies. Although the Mustang wasn't used in stock car racing, the strong sales of the Boss 302 indicated that it would be easier to sell 500 big-block Mustangs than to sell that many Torino Talladegas with the 429.

Ford contracted with an aftermarket firm called Kar Kraft, in Brighton, Michigan, to build Boss 429s. It was not an easy job to squeeze the big engine into the little Mustang. Kar Kraft did many suspension changes and chassis modifications to achieve its goal.

*The Boss 429 (1970 model shown) was the most brutally powerful Mustang ever built. (Brad Bowling)*

*This big-block was the heart of the Boss 429. (Brad Bowling)*

*The SportsRoof was the basis for "buzz bombs" like the Mach 1, CJ 428/SCJ 428, Boss 302, and Boss 429. Mickey Thompson had several Boss 429 drag cars. (Phil Hall)*

Speed ace Mickey Thompson poses with another of his 1969 Boss 429 Mustang funny cars. Many of these cars got into the hands of professional race car builders and drivers like Thompson and Smokey Yunick. (Phil Hall)

Parnelli Jones (inset) was the driver of this Boss 302, shown on its way to winning a Trans-Am race in Seattle, Wash. He took five of 11 wins in the 1970 series and Seattle clinched the Trans-Am title for him. (Ford)

*George Follmer also won a Trans-Am race for Mustang.* (Old Cars Weekly)

A total of 1,358 Boss 429s were constructed during the 1969 calendar year. This included 857 of the 1969 models made in early 1969 and 499 of the 1970 models built late in the summer.

Body alterations for these cars included engine bay bracing, inner wheel well sheetmetal work and flared wheel housings (to accommodate a widened track and the use of seven-inch Magnum 500 wheel rims). A huge, functional scoop was installed on the hood and a special spoiler underlined the front bumper. Power steering and brakes, a Traction-Lok axle with 3.91 gears, and a Boss 302 rear spoiler were also included. All of the cars had the fancy Decor Group interior option, high-back bucket seats, deluxe seat belts, the wood-trimmed dash and console treatment, and the Visibility Group option. Automatic transmission and air conditioning were not available, but the $4,932 price tag included all of the above. Horsepower for the Boss 429 was advertised as 375, although real ratings were rumored to be much higher.

The Boss 302 continued as a 1970 model, also with minor improvements. They included the Mustang's revised front and rear styling, new Grabber paint colors and a "hockey stick" striping treatment, with the name "Boss 302" above and on the "blade" of the hockey stick on the upper front fender. Wide 15x7-inch steel wheels with hubcaps and trim rings were standard, while the shaker hood became optional. High-back bucket seats were added to the standard features list. Smaller diameter valves and a new crankshaft were used in the small-block performance V-8 and most Boss 302s used finned aluminum valve covers. A rear sway bar was added to the suspension and the front one was thickened.

*Hot Rod* claimed, in its January 1970 edition, that the new Boss 302 was "definitely the best handling car Ford has ever built." *Motor Trend* called the Boss Mustang, "The word of our time. Good, only better, fuller, rounder and more intense." The words suggested supercar qualities even above those of the GTO, Road Runner, and Chevelle. On the other hand, the practical-thinking *Consumer Guide* labeled it "uncomfortable at any speed over anything but the smoothest surface."

The passing of the Boss 302 at the end of the 1970 model year was mourned by the performance crowd, even though an all-new Boss 351 replaced it. They knew that the years of the high-compression, high-performance Detroit muscle cars were drawing to a close. A writer in the March 1971 issue of *Speed and Supercar* called the Boss 302, "probably the most advanced non-hemi (engine) design ever to emanate from Detroit."

*The SportsRoof remained one of the basic 1970 models. With the redesign of the Barracuda that year, a real fastback was now a choice that no other muscle car could offer. It was a Mustang exclusive. (Ford)*

## 1970

For 1970, the Mustang was a gradual continuation of the 1969 editions designed before "Bunkie" Knudsen arrived at Ford. The new models were introduced in September 1969. Knudsen would not be at Ford long enough to see the 1970 introductions. Chairman Henry Ford II fired him, on short notice, in August 1969.

"HFII" never explained his firing of Knudsen. Some observers believed it was related to his desire to move away from muscle cars and motorsports, which Knudsen favored. (Ford pulled out of factory racing in 1970). Others guessed that Knudsen had too rapidly built up a power base in an operation that preferred family-centralized power. They said he had tried to overstep the limits of his power too often.

*The shaker hood scoop on this 1970 Mach 1 is a sign that there's serious power under there. (Jack Rzentkowski)*

*Somehow, the 1970 coupe didn't have the sporty style of the fastback or convertible models. (Ford)*

*Speed belongs on the track or the strip, not on the street. Your Ford Dealer urges you to drive safely.*

FORD

it's the going thing!

*The 428-cid Cobra Jet V-8 (top left) was among Ford's factory speed equipment offered in 1969 and 1970.*

*This 1970 Mustang still competes in nostalgia*

*Ford touts its winning lineup for 1970.*

Knudsen was initially replaced by three executives: Lee Iacocca was made executive vice president and president of North American Operations; Robert L. Stevenson held the same titles for International Operations; and Robert J. Hampson was executive vice president and president of Non-Automotive Operations. Within a year, though, Iacocca would become Ford's overall president.

The biggest change to the 1970 model Mustangs was the return to single headlamps, which were located inside a larger, new grille opening. Simulated air intakes were seen where the outboard headlights were on the 1969 models. The rear end was also slightly restyled.

The 1970 Mach 1 featured the new front end, taillights recessed in a flat panel with honeycomb trim between them, ribbed aluminum rocker panel moldings (with big Mach 1 call-outs) and a cleaner upper rear quarter treatment minus simulated air scoops at the end of the main feature line. A black-striped hood with standard fake scoop replaced the completely matte-black hood. New twist-in pins held the hood down, and a shaker hood scoop was available with the 351 V-8. A redesigned steering wheel was the big interior change. A larger rear stripe, larger rear call-out mag-type hubcaps, wide 14x7-inch wheels, and bright oval exhaust tips were also new. Black-painted styled wheels were a no-cost option.

With new competition from the Dodge Challenger, plus totally redesigned Barracudas, Camaros and Firebirds, the Mustang lost around 100,000 sales in 1970. A total of 190,727 Mustangs were built, including 13,581 Grande coupes, 7,673 convertibles (1,474 with deluxe equipment), 40,970 Mach 1s and 6,319 Boss 302s.

A low-gloss grille with fog lamps, a striped hood and dual body-colored racing mirrors were features of the 1970 Mustang Mach 1. This one has hood call-outs for the Cobra Jet 428 engine. (Ford)

MUSTANG

The biggest change for 1970 was the return to single headlamps. They were located inside a larger, new grille opening. Simulated air intakes were seen where the outboard headlights were on the 1969 models. (Ford)

The 1970 Mustang engine lineup caused some confusion. This factory photograph shows a convertible with a 390-cid V-8, which was discontinued that year. It may be a mock-up, a prototype or a rarity. (Ford)

The 1970 Grandé offered a standard three-quarter landau-style vinyl roof and luxury houndstooth upholstery. Both the aluminum rocker panel moldings and lower back panel molding came with "camera case" vinyl inserts.

A total of 190,727 Mustangs were built in 1970. This included 13,581 Grande coupes (shown here), 7,673 convertibles (1,474 with deluxe equipment), 40,970 Mach 1s and 7,013 Boss 302s. (Ford)

*The 1970 Mach 1 had the taillights recessed in a flat panel with honeycomb trim between them, ribbed aluminum rocker panel moldings (with big Mach 1 call-outs) and a cleaner upper rear quarter treatment. (Ford)*

*The "Twister Special" was a limited-edition option for the 1970 Mustang Mach 1 ordered by the Kansas City sales district office for Ford's "Total Performance Day." All 1996 Mustangs were to be equipped with the 428-cid Cobra Jet V-8, but some cars were shipped with 351-cid four-barrel V-8s. (Old Cars Weekly)*

## '70 Mustang Facts

"Five years ago, Mustang started a whole new idea in sporty cars," said one advertisement. "And Mustang's been first ever since." The ad listed "sporty facts" that made the Mustang favored in its market segment:

Fact. Six great Mustang models. They include the hot Mach 1, luxurious Grandé, and the race-bred Boss 302. (Three rooflines, too. hardtop, convertible and a SportsRoof, a choice no one else can give you.)

Fact. Power your Mustang your way. With nine Mustang engines to pick from (the lineup was the same as 1969, except that the 390-cid V-8 was discontinued). Economical 200-cid six all the way up to the 429-cube V-8.

Fact. Loaded with sporty features. Mustang standards: Wall-to-wall carpeting. Bucket seats. Belted bias-ply tires. Locking steering column. Full synchronized manual transmission. Sporty floor-mounted shift. Rear deck spoiler on SportsRoof models.

Fact. You can design it yourself. With more options than ever. Power front disc brakes. Functional hood scoop. Rear window louvered Sport Slats. Vinyl roof. Hurst Shifter. SelectAire Conditioning. Stereo system. Tachometer. Drag Pack. 'Grabber' exterior paint colors.

# CHAPTER 6

## The Really Big Chill (1971-73)

*1971 Mustangs bowed Sept. 18, 1970. The convertible had increased rear seat room, a neater interior and more convenient top operation. (Ford)*

## 1971

The biggest news for Mustangers in 1971 was, well, size. While the winning proportions of the 1965 were retained, the cars now looked like bigger, more muscular distant cousins to the original design. Some new features were apparent in this evolutionary step, such as the flatter roof shape of the SportsRoof models and the "tunnel backlight" (basically a recessed rear window) built into hardtop coupes. All models featured flush door

*The 1971 Mustang Mach 1s had the base 302 V-8; the sportlamp grille; competition suspension; small hubcaps with trim rings; a black, honeycomb-textured back panel appliqué; E70-14 whitewalls; and a pop-open gas cap. This example sports the no-cost optional NASA-style hood. (Ford)*

*A Dual Ram Air induction option was $65 for 1971 Mustangs with 351 V-8s (standard on 429CJ-R Mustangs). Included was a functional NASA hood with black or Argent Silver two-tone paint, hood lock pins and Ram Air decals. Shown is the NASA-style hood, minus other equipment. (Ford)*

handles and hidden windshield wipers. The closed cars had thinner roof sections for a more open look.

The 1971 Mustangs had a slightly longer wheelbase (109 inches) and gained 2.1 inches of length over the 1970 model. They measured 190 inches bumper-to-bumper, 7.9-inches more than the original 1965 model. They were also 2.4-inches wider than the 1970 Mustang and 5.9-inches wider than the 1965 version. Weights were up an average of 500 pounds from the previous year.

Why the weight and size increases?

*This 1971 convertible has the standard chrome bumper and chrome hood and front fender moldings with the plain hood. The sportlamp grille was optional. (Old Cars Weekly)*

*A "corral" returned to the standard chrome grille. The plain hood was standard. (Ford)*

The answer lies in Ford's desire to evolve the Mustang into a platform capable of creating a high-performance supercar or a luxurious and spacious mode of daily transportation for sporty young families. With the help of an outside assembly line, Ford had managed to shoehorn the Boss 429 big-block V-8 into the 1969-70 platform, but the new Mustang's engine compartments could accommodate such iron without a problem. The longer body gave designers precious inches needed to create passenger seating that was more comfortable than the original pony car.

*The standard 1971 SportsRoof had a tape stripe on the rear panel with M-U-S-T-A-N-G spelled out across the lip of the deck lid. Full wheel covers were $26 extra on standard models. (Ford)*

*This 1971 Mustang convertible has the standard bumper and grille with the plain hood. (Old Cars Weekly)*

*A restyled body with a different-looking front end appeared on the larger 1971 Mustangs. The new design broke from Mustang tradition most with the unique, flatter Kammback-style roof shape of the SportsRoof models. (Ford)*

*Hardtops had what Ford called a "tunnel backlight" (recessed rear window). All models, including this 1971 Grandé coupe, had flush door handles and hidden windshield wipers. Closed cars had thinner roof sections for an airier look. (Ford)*

When this "fourth-generation" Mustang was in the planning stages (roughly 1968-70), car companies and the American public were willing partners in a horsepower escalation that seemed to have no end. By the time the all-new 1971 hit the showrooms, high insurance premiums and increasing government safety and emissions regulations were putting the brakes on all that enthusiasm.

The same basic models were available: hardtop, SportsRoof and convertible. The Grandé, Mach 1 and Boss models were back, too; however, a new Boss 351 replaced the Boss 302 and Boss 429. Its 351-cid 330-hp "Cleveland" engine became the Mustang's small-block, high-performance V-8.

A full-width grille incorporated the headlights at each end. On standard models the famous "corral" returned to the center of the grille. It had a large, chrome pony inside it. Optional was a honeycomb-textured grille insert with sportlamps. It did not have a "corral," but instead the center had a smaller galloping pony emblem on a red, white and blue bar. A chrome bumper and chrome fender and hood moldings were standard, except on Mach 1s and Boss 351s.

Standard equipment for Mustangs included color-keyed nylon carpeting; floor-mounted shift lever; high-back bucket seats; steel door guard rails; DirectAire ventilation; concealed wipers with cowl air inlets; a mini-console

*Chrome block letters said M-U-S-T-A-N-G on the rear of 1971 hardtops and convertibles. Grandés had dual accent stripes, color-keyed racing mirrors, rocker panel moldings, vinyl roof, wheel covers and wheel lip moldings. (Ford)*

*Other 1971 Grandé features were bright pedal pad surrounds, deluxe cloth high-back buckets and dash trim, deluxe two-spoke steering wheel, electric clock, molded trim panels with integral pull handles and armrests and a rear ashtray. (Ford)*

with ash tray; arm rests; courtesy lights; a cigar lighter; a heater and defroster; an all-vinyl interior; a glove box; the 250-cid six; E78-14 fiberglass-belted black sidewall tires; and—on convertibles—a power top.

Grandés came with the same basic equipment as Mustangs, plus bright pedal pad surrounds; deluxe cloth high-back bucket seat trim; deluxe instrument panel trim; a deluxe two-spoke steering wheel; an electric clock; molded trim panels with integral pull handles and arm rests; a rear ash tray in the right quarter trim panel; dual accent paint stripes; color-keyed dual racing mirrors (remote-controlled left-hand mirror); rocker panel moldings; vinyl roof; full wheel covers; and wheel lip moldings.

Mach 1s included all the basic equipment, plus a color-keyed spoiler/bumper with color-keyed hood and front fender moldings. Also color-keyed were the dual racing mirrors, with the left-hand mirror featuring remote-control operation. Mach 1s also had the unique grille with sportlamps; competition suspension; hubcaps and trim rings; a black, honeycomb-textured back panel applique, a pop-open gas cap; a deck lid paint stripe; black or Argent Silver lower bodyside finish with bright moldings at the upper edge; E70-14 whitewalls and the base V-8. NASA-style hood scoops were optional at no extra charge.

The greater weight of the new body necessitated the end of the 200-cid six; the 250-cid six became the smallest Mustang engine. The standard V-8 was a mild version of the 302-cid motor with 210 hp. Other small-block options included 240- and 285-hp versions of the 351-cid V-8, plus the Boss 351 powerplant.

*1971 Mustang instrument panels had all instruments grouped in front of the driver with a large glove box to the right. There were two large dials and a small center dial with the warning lights and gauges. (Ford)*

*Introduced as exclusive standard equipment on 1971 Boss 351s, this stripe treatment was later made optional for Mach 1s. This Mach 1 has black striping—Argent Silver stripes were another choice. (Ford)*

For Mustang buyers who demanded big-block muscle, there was a new 429 Cobra Jet (429CJ) engine for $372 more than the cost of the base V-8. A 429 Cobra Jet Ram Air (429CJ-R) option was $436 above the base V-8. Both were rated at 370 hp. A 429 Super Cobra Jet with Dual Ram Air induction and a 375-hp rating was available for $531 over the base V-8.

The 429CJ-R had hydraulic valve lifters, four-bolt main caps, dress-up aluminum valve covers and a GM Quadrajet four-barrel carburetor. The 429SCJ-R featured mechanical lifters, adjustable rocker arms, a larger Holley four-barrel carburetor, and forged pistons.

Mustangs with the 429CJ-R engine came with a competition suspension; Mach 1 hood; 80-ampere battery; 55-ampere alternator; dual exhausts; extra-cooling package; bright engine dress-up kit with cast-aluminum rocker covers and a 3.25:1 ratio, non-locking rear axle. It was not available with air conditioning combined with the Drag Pak option or with the Dual Ram induction option. A C-6 Cruise-O-Matic or close-ratio four-speed manual transmission was required, along with disc brakes. Power steering was required on air-conditioned cars. The 429SCJ engine required the Drag Pak option and a 3.91:1 or 4.11:1 high rear axle.

The new 429s were not the same as the Boss 429, which had been derived from Ford's "semi-hemi" NASCAR racing engine. Instead, they were actually destroked versions of the "wedge head" 460-cid V-8 used in Thunderbirds and Lincolns. They were available in all three body styles, and the 1971 version was much more tractable for daily driving.

Desirable options for 1971 included the Magnum 500 chromed-styled steel wheels, which cost $120 for Mach 1s and Boss 351s, $129 for Grandés, and $155 for other Mustangs. This package included an F78-14 Space-Saver spare tire and required F60-15 raised white-letter tires and the competition suspension. A Dual Ram Air induction option was also offered for the Boss 351 at $65. It included appropriate Ram Air decals. A rear deck lid spoiler was available for SportsRoof, Mach 1, and Boss 351 models for $32.

A Decor Group interior was $97 for the Boss 351 and the Mustang convertible and $78 for all other Mustangs, except Mach 1s and Grandés. It included a choice of knitted vinyl or cloth and vinyl high-back bucket seats (knitted vinyl was required for convertibles); a rear ashtray; deluxe left- and right-hand black instrument panel appliqués; a deluxe two-spoke steering wheel; molded door trim panels on convertibles and Boss 351s; color-keyed racing mirrors (left-hand remote-control), if not standard; and rocker panel and wheel lip moldings (except on the Boss 351).

In 1971, *Sports Car Graphic* magazine tested both a CJ-powered Mach 1 and a Boss 351. The big-block car was only marginally faster. It won zero-to-60 miles per hour at 6.3 seconds versus 6.6 and did the quarter-mile in 14.6 seconds at 99.4 miles per hour against 14.7 seconds and 96.2 miles per hour. Considering the 351's

*Here's another 1971 Mach 1 with optional black Boss 351-style striping. (The Keystone chromed-styled steel wheels and modern radials are not original equipment.) A deck lid stripe and black or Argent Silver lower body finish with moldings at the upper edge were standard. (Old Cars Weekly)*

fewer cubes and 330 advertised horsepower, it performed quite well against the nose-heavy Mach 1 with the big-block.

With the high-performance era winding to a close and the government and insurance companies ganging up on muscle cars, Ford discontinued factory involvement in racing this year. Mustang production for 1971 continued to decline, dropping to 149,678. Of this total, about 1,800 were made with 429 Cobra Jet V-8s—the last of the big-block Mustangs ever built.

## Meet the New Boss

The Boss 351 was the car with most appeal to street performance buffs, and it was a better-balanced car than the big-block Fords.

Standard equipment included all of the Mustang basics, plus a functional NASA-style hood with black or Argent Silver full hood paint treatment, hood lock pins, and Ram Air engine decals.

Also featured were the racing mirrors; the unique grille with sportlamps; hubcaps and trim rings; black or Argent Silver bodyside tape stripes (these also became optional on Mach 1s late in the year); color-keyed hood and front fender moldings; Boss 351 nomenclature; dual exhausts; power front disc brakes; a Space-Saver spare tire; a competition suspension with staggered rear shocks; a 3.91:1 axle ratio with Traction-Lok differential; a functional black spoiler (shipped "knocked-down" inside the car for dealer installation); an 80-ampere battery; Ford's Instrumentation Group option; an electronic rpm-limiter; high-back bucket seats; a special cooling package; a wide-ratio four-speed manual transmission with Hurst shifter; the 351-cid H.O. (high-output) V-8 with 330 hp; and F60-15 belted blackwall tires. A chrome bumper was standard on Boss 351s, while the Mach 1-style color-keyed bumper was an option.

The 1971 Boss 351 appealed to street performance buffs. It was better balanced than big-block cars. Standard was a chrome bumper, functional NASA hood with black or Argent Silver paint, hood lock pins and Ram Air decals. (Ford)

A decal on the lip of the deck lid said "BOSS 351." Also featured were racing mirrors, black or Argent Silver tape stripes, dual exhausts, a competition suspension with staggered rear shocks and a 3.91 Traction-Lok rear axle. (Ford)

The 1971 Boss 351 had the sportlamp grille and color-keyed hood and front fender moldings. Optional on some cars, in place of a chrome bumper, was a color-keyed bumper. The spoiler was black in all cases. (Ford)

The 351-cid H.O. (high-output) V-8 with 330 hp, a wide-ratio four-speed manual transmission with Hurst shifter and F60-15 belted blackwall tires were standard on 1971 Boss 351s. Magnum 500 wheels (shown) were optional. (Ford)

*The Boss 351 SportsRoof was discontinued in 1972, but this publicity photo shows such a car. It's either a pilot model, or a picture of a 1971 Boss 351 with "1972" air-brushed on the rear license plate. (Ford)*

## 1972

Despite its enormous size (by today's standards) Ford promoted the 1972 Mustang as a "sports compact." There were very few appearance changes from 1971. Two grille treatments were available again, plus the choice of chrome or color-keyed front bumpers, depending on models and options. On the rear of base models, the Mustang name in block letters was changed to a chrome script on the upper right-hand corner of the deck lid. Some models had decals instead.

Five basic models were offered for 1972: hardtop, SportsRoof, convertible, Grandé and Mach 1. Convertibles had a new, standard interior package that included ComfortWeave knitted vinyl upholstery, an instrument panel appliqué and molded door trim panels. (The Boss 351 was dropped, although a factory photograph of a pilot model for a 1972 version does show up in some places. Apparently, the decision to drop this model was a late one.)

A new Sprint Decor option was released at midyear for Mustang hardtops and SportsRoofs, Mavericks and Pinto Runabouts. A press release dated Feb. 24, 1972, described it as a "red, white and blue" paint trim package, although most people viewing it would probably say it was "white, blue and red;" the bulk of the body was white with light medium-blue paint all around the lower perimeter. Two wide blue stripes decorated the hood. The lower back panel was also blue. A red pinstripe ran along the lower body, emphasizing the color break. The interior was also two-tone white and blue. Each Sprint included dual white racing mirrors, color-keyed seats and carpets and white sidewall tires with color-keyed hubcaps and trim rings. A flag-like decal commemorating the 1972 Olympics was on the rear fender. A second "B" Sprint package, for Mustangs only, substituted mag-type wheels, F60-15 raised white-letter tires and a competition suspension.

There were small changes in the list of Mustang features for 1972. Standard equipment for all hardtops, SportsRoofs and convertibles included concealed wipers; rocker panel and wheel lip moldings; a lower back panel appliqué with bright moldings; color-keyed dual racing mirrors; recessed exterior door handles; "bottle cap" hubcaps; DirectAire ventilation; a heater and defroster; high-back bucket seats; and bonded door trim panels with pull handles and arm rests (in closed body styles). All Mustangs also included a mini-console; carpeting; courtesy lights; a deluxe two-spoke steering wheel with wood-tone insert; E78-14 bias-ply blackwall tires; a three-speed floor-mounted transmission; and the 250-cid six (rated at 95 SAE net horsepower).

SportsRoofs also had fixed rear quarter windows (except cars with power windows) and a tinted glass backlight. Convertibles added a five-ply power-operated top; a color-keyed top boot; a tinted windshield; a glass backlight; a bright upper back panel molding; knit-vinyl seat trim; molded door handles; and black instrument panel appliqués.

*There were few appearance changes for 1972 Mustangs. This is a standard hardtop with an optional vinyl top, sportslamp grille and color-keyed hood and fender moldings. It was the most popular body style with 57,350 assemblies. (Old Cars Weekly)*

Grandés came with the same basic equipment as standard Mustangs, plus a vinyl roof with Grandé script; unique bodyside tape stripes; unique full wheel covers; a trunk floor mat; Lambeth cloth and vinyl upholstery; bright pedal pads; deluxe instrument panel trim with black camera case and wood-tone appliqués; a panel-mounted electric clock; and a rear ashtray.

On Mach 1s, buyers got all the basic SportsRoof equipment plus a competition suspension; a choice of a hood with or without NASA-style scoop (with 302-cid V-8 only); a color-keyed front spoiler bumper; color-keyed hood and fender moldings; a black honeycomb grille with integral sportslamps; a black back panel appliqué; black or Argent Silver lower body finish; front and rear valance

*On 1972 Mustang hardtops and convertibles, a chrome script with the Mustang's "signature" appeared on the right edge of the deck lid, in place of chrome block letters across the deck lid. (Ford)*

*Classic long hood/short deck styling continued to characterize Mustangs. The 1972 Grandé coupe accented luxury with a standard vinyl top, color-keyed racing mirrors, full wheel covers and a deluxe interior. (Ford)*

*The Mach 1 SportsRoof for 1972 was almost a match for the 1971 model. It featured a black honeycomb grille, color-keyed front bumper/spoiler and hood scoops. This one has the black decal and lower body finish. (Ford)*

*Mach 1 production dropped to 27,675 cars in 1972. The biggest and hottest powerplant was the 351 H.O. V-8. This car has the Argent Silver decal and lower body perimeter. The white-letter Firestone Wide Ovals were extra. (Ford)*

*The basic, plain-Jane coupe for 1972 still offered a good list of standard equipment. (Ford)*

panels; a rear tape stripe with Mach 1 decals; hubcaps and wheel trim rings; a 302-cid two-barrel V-8 (with 136 net hp); and E70-14 bias-ply belted white sidewall tires.

The Mach 1 interior included knit-vinyl high-back bucket seats with accent stripes; an electric clock; triple instrument pod gauges; door trim panels with integral pull handles and armrests; deep-embossed carpet runners; the deluxe instrument panel with black appliqués and a wood-tone center section; and a rear seat ashtray. This could be added to other fastbacks at extra cost.

*The hot engine for 1972 was this 351-cid V-8 with Ram Air option. (Brad Bowling)*

*Mach 1 graphics for the 1971-72 models (1972 shown) were much more subtle than in previous years. (Brad Bowling)*

Three V-8s of 351-cid were optional in Mustangs—the regular two-barrel version, the regular four-barrel version and the four-barrel H.O. option offering 168, 200 and 275 hp, respectively. (If all the 1972 engine output figures seem like a massive drop from 1971 horsepower ratings, it's because the new numbers were expressed in SAE net horsepower.)

There were no big-block options for the 1972 Mustang and the options list was smaller. Some choices that appealed to enthusiast buyers included Color Glow paints ($34.90 extra); the instrumentation group with tachometer, trip odometer and three-pod gauge cluster ($55.24 on Grandés and $70.83 on other Mustangs); front disc brakes ($62.05); AM/FM stereo ($191.01); Sport Deck rear seat

*The top-line Mustang for 1972 was a Mach 1 with the 351-cid V-8 and Ram Air. This example is so equipped, plus it is dressed up with air dam and rear spoiler. (Brad Bowling)*

*This 1972 Mach 1 is "dressed down." (Brad Bowling)*

for SportsRoofs, which included a Space-Saver spare, folding rear seat and load floor ($75.97); a black or Argent Silver bodyside tape stripe for Mach 1s and Mustangs with Decor Group trim ($23.23); Magnum 500 chrome wheels ($107.59 to $138.67 not including the required competition suspension and F60-15 tires); Dual Ram induction ($58.24 with any 351 V-8 including a NASA hood with black or Argent Silver two-tone paint, hood lock pins and Ram Air engine decals); and the Mach 1 Sports Interior package ($115.44 for standard SportsRoofs).

Only two Mustangs went up in popularity in 1972. The Grandé attracted about 600 additional buyers and the convertible drew an additional 280+ orders. All other models saw substantial drops and total output was just 125,093 units.

*This one is "dressed up" with stripes, spoilers, and "competition" gas cap. (Brad Bowling)*

*Convertibles had a new, standard interior package for 1972. It included ComfortWeave knitted vinyl upholstery, an instrument panel appliqué, and molded door trim panels. (Ford)*

MUSTANG

*Convertibles added a five-ply power-operated top to the standard equipment list for 1972. A color-keyed top boot, tinted windshield, and glass backlight were also featured. Decorating the back was a bright upper panel molding. (Ford)*

*A 1972 Mustang hardtop with the midyear Sprint Decor option appears on the upper left. The Maverick (upper right) and the Pinto Runabout (foreground) were also offered with Sprint Decor trim honoring the Olympics. (Ford)*

## 1973

The 1973 Mustangs were mildly face-lifted and suffered from another weight and size increase. The cars grew four-inches longer, because a new impact-resistant front bumper was required to meet federal safety regulations. On some 1973 Fords, the "safety bumpers" were exceedingly ugly, but the Mustang's color-keyed bumper was the most attractive of the lot.

Two grille designs were optional again, but neither was exactly the same as 1971-72. Both had parking

*The 1973 Mustangs were mildly face-lifted. The cars grew four-inches longer this year, because a new impact-resistant front bumper was required to meet federal safety regulations. The convertible listed for $3,102 with a six-cylinder engine. (Ford)*

*Convertible production climbed to 11,853 in the body style's "last" year. This 1973 convertible has the factory-optional slotted mag wheels. Buyers thought the end was coming for convertibles. Some decided to "stock up." (Bob Lichty)*

lights mounted vertically at each end of the grille opening. The standard design featured an egg crate-style insert with a corral and the large chrome pony. However, sportier models substituted a smaller, freestanding pony badge without a corral.

Standard equipment was about the same as in 1972. The list included a 250-cid six or 302-cid V-8; E78-14 bias-belted black sidewall tires; rocker panel and wheel lip moldings; a lower back panel appliqué with a bright molding; a chrome rectangular left-hand rearview mirror; all-vinyl upholstery and door trim; a front mini-console; color-keyed loop-pile carpeting; a deluxe two-spoke steering wheel with wood-tone insert; a cigarette lighter; a seatbelt reminder system and door courtesy lamps. SportsRoofs added a tinted back window and fixed rear quarter windows. Convertibles also had under-dash courtesy lamps; a power-operated convertible top; a color-keyed top boot; a glass backlight; ComfortWeave knit-vinyl seat trim; and power front disc brakes.

The Grandé hardtop model returned. In addition to the standard features, it gave buyers color-keyed dual racing mirrors; a vinyl roof; bodyside tape striping; special wheel covers; a trunk mat; Lambeth cloth and vinyl seat trim;

molded door panels with integral arm rests; bright pedal pads; a deluxe instrument panel; and an electric clock.

A new bodyside tape stripe was seen on the 1973 Mach 1 SportsRoof. The model name was just ahead of the rear wheel opening. It featured a standard 302-cid 136-hp V-8. In addition to base equipment, Mach 1s had a competition suspension; a choice of a NASA or plain-style hood; E70-14 whitewall Wide-Oval tires; color-keyed dual racing mirrors; a black grille; a black back panel appliqué; hubcaps with wheel trim rings; a tinted back window; all-vinyl upholstery and door trim; and high-back front bucket seats.

There were some safety refinements made to the instrument panel, primarily to eliminate protruding objects and glare. Larger brakes were used, too. New, flame-retardant interior fabrics were required. The emissions system also received some attention. Engine choices were virtually identical to 1972.

In its final year, the big Mustang saw a jump in sales, owing largely to Ford's news that 1973 would be its last year of convertible production (1973 convertible sales doubled to more than 11,000). When it was all said and done, the count stood at 134,267 units for the model year.

*A new bodyside tape stripe was seen on the 1973 Mach 1 SportsRoof. The model name was just ahead of the rear wheel opening. It was base-priced at $3,088 with a 302-cid 136-hp V-8. Production rose to 35,440 for model year 1973. (Ford)*

*Collectors snapped up the 1972 (behind) and 1973 Mustang convertibles due to Ford's announcement that it would cease production of open cars with the 1973 model year. (Brad Bowling)*

*A NASA-style scooped hood was optionally available again in 1973. This convertible also has the optional sportslamp grille without a corral and with a smaller Mustang emblem in its center. It does not have the Sport-type mirror. (Ford)*

*Prices for the 1973 Mustang Grandé coupe started at $2,946. With a base V-8, the standard price was $3,088. Its popularity increased and a total of 25,674 were built. It was the Grandé's final appearance. (Ford)*

# CHAPTER 7

## II Little, II Late (1974-78)

*Ford wisely elected to stay with long hood/short deck styling, a slightly protruding nose with a mostly oval-shaped grille and single headlamps for the all-new 1974 Mustang II. (Ford)*

*The 1974 Mustang II was obviously shorter than any previous model. Its 96.2-inch wheelbase was seven inches shorter than that of the original Mustang and more than a foot less than the 1973 model. (Ford)*

# 1974

The most controversial decision Ford ever made concerning its legendary Mustang was introduced in the middle of 1973 as the "Mustang II." While Mustang purists have bashed Ford's "luxury compact" for being too slow, uncomfortably small, and strangely proportioned, this pint-sized pony car recorded an impressive increase in popularity, with 338,136 assemblies counted for calendar year 1974. (Compare that to 193,129 units for the "big" Mustang in calendar-year 1973.)

It earned 4.75 percent of the industry's total output, a piece of the pie the Mustang had not enjoyed since 1967. Just like the 1965, the fact it enjoyed an 18-month introductory model year helped close the books on a positive note despite sluggish initial sales.

Promoting the car as a luxury model backfired to a degree, but the II quickly found its real niche as an economy car. Viewed in this light, and considering the impact of the 1973 OPEC oil embargo, its timing was perfect. Ford advertised it as "the right car at the right time"—a slogan that proved more truthful than the company first thought. Customers were more attracted to the cheaper models, with the low-end hardtop and 2+2 accounting for 252,470 of all first-year Mustang IIs made.

The new car was a timely reaction to America's changing life-style trends. The previous Mustangs had been slowly moving away from their original role as small, sporty and low-priced vehicles that many American families purchased as second cars. The brief Bunkie Knudsen era had pushed the Mustang to new heights as a high-performance car; however, as the 1970s unfolded, small bodies replaced big engines as items car buyers wanted the most.

The Mustang II was certainly shorter than its predecessor. Its 96.2-inch length was seven inches less than that of the original Mustang and more than a foot down from the 1973 wheelbase. It also seemed a lot more economical, with a 2.3-liter (140-cid) inline-four as base engine. A 2.8-liter V-6 was available, but there was not even one optional V-8 in 1974. In retrospect, exclusive use of a four and a V-6 was probably a mistake. With a V-8, sales would probably have gone even higher. By the time 1975 models bowed Ford had rectified this miscue.

Far from a mistake was the decision to stay with long hood/short deck styling, a slightly protruding nose with a mostly oval-shaped grille and single headlamps. Though changed more than ever before, the basic Mustang image was still preserved in the new car, although it had many modern touches.

Models included a notchback coupe (often referred to as a "hardtop" and, in one press release, a "two-door sedan") and a 2+2 hatchback (also referred to as a "fastback" or "three-door"). The former came with an optional fancy Ghia package and the latter a Mach 1 performance group.

Prices for 1974 Mustang IIs were $3,081 to $3,621. Ford kept production costs to the bare minimum by using the same trick it employed for the original Mustang: spinning the new car off an existing one. In this case, the Pinto was the base vehicle, with which the Mustang II shared many components. To Ford's credit, many of those components were upgraded and installed in such ways that their characteristics were more in keeping with the more expensive Mustang.

Window stickers were up from those of the 1973 Mustangs on a model-for-model basis. For instance, the 1973 Mach 1 V-8 listed for $3,088 versus $3,674 for a 1974 Mach 1 with V-6. Economy didn't come cheap!

Mustang II styling represented a blending of the work of Ford's top stylists (like Eugene Bordinat, Al Mueller, L. David Ash and Dick Nesbitt) with the ideas of Italian designers who worked at Ghia. Ford had acquired a controlling interest in that Italian design firm in 1970.

Long-time Mustang features like a floor shifter (four-speed), bucket seats (low-back), vinyl upholstery and carpeting were standard in Mustang IIs. Even full wheel covers returned to the regular equipment list to emphasize the link to the past. A long equipment list now included such modern niceties as solid-state ignition; front disc brakes; a tachometer; steel-belted whitewalls; simulated burled walnut interior appliqués; and Euro-styled armrests. The 2+2 models also included a folding rear seat and styled wheels.

The Mustang II's base engine was a 2.3-liter "Lima" four (named for its production plant in Ohio), which was sluggish, noisy, and rough running. It did give up to 23 miles per gallon, which was considered quite economical for an American car at that time. The optional 2.8-liter V-6 was pirated from the German-built Mercury Capri of that era. It delivered 105 hp and, in many cases, mechanical headaches. Problems with engine valves, piston rings, and the cooling system were typical. Many buyers who spent $229 extra for this engine were sorry they had.

Ghia model upgrades were deluxe color-keyed seat belts and door mirrors (remote-controlled); a Super Sound package; shag carpeting; wood-tone door panel accents; a digital clock; spoke-style wheel covers; a super-soft color-coordinated vinyl roof covering; and a choice of super-soft vinyl or Westminster cloth interior trims. The Ghia was the second-most popular individual model with 89,477 assemblies.

Mach 1s added the following to standard 2+2 equipment: 2.8-liter V-6; dual color-keyed remote-control mirrors; Wide-Oval steel-belted black sidewall radial tires; black lower bodyside paint; deck lid striping; and styled steel wheels with trim rings.

About the hottest option available for 1974 Mustang IIs (except Ghias) was the Rallye package, which required the 2.8-liter V-6. It included a Traction-Lok differential; raised white-letter steel-belted tires; an extra-cooling package; a competition suspension; dual color-keyed remote-control door mirrors; styled steel wheels; a Sport exhaust system; a digital clock; and a leather-wrapped steering wheel.

*There were no changes in features of the 1975 Mustang II Ghia hardtop. Its upgrades included color-keyed seat belts and door mirrors; a Super Sound package; shag carpets; wood-tone door panel accents and more. (Ford)*

*There was a new Ghia Silver Luxury Group package for 1975 with Silver metallic paint; a silver half-vinyl top; hood ornament; body stripes; silver moldings; Cranberry velour interior; color-keyed headliner and sun visors and console. (Ford)*

## 1975

There was very little change in the 1975 Mustang II, except for the addition of a 302-cid (5.0-liter) V-8 to supplant the V-6 as the top performance engine. V-8s all came with a SelectShift automatic transmission ($227), while V-6s were manually shifted. The standard 2.3-liter four came with both kinds of transmissions. The only styling change was a larger grille opening, necessitated by the V-8's need for more fresh air. A new steering wheel was also used. It again had a two-spoke design, but the spokes bent downwards at each end.

There were no changes in standard equipment or in the ingredients of the Ghia or Mach 1 package. There was a new Ghia Silver Luxury Group package that cost $151. It included Silver Metallic paint; a silver, Normande-grain, half-vinyl roof; a stand-up hood ornament; Cranberry body striping; silver bodyside moldings; an all-Cranberry interior in Media velour cloth; and a color-keyed headliner, center console, and sunvisors.

Midyear brought a new MPG model and a plainer Ghia. The Rallye package was available again for 2+2s ($218) and Mach 1s ($168). Likewise, the 5.0-liter V-8 was $172 in Mach 1s and $199 in other models. This 122-hp two-barrel engine was often described as "thirsty," as it got only 13.7 to 15.9 miles per gallon. It could move the Mustang II along at 105 miles per hour, however, and sent it down the quarter-mile in 17.9 seconds at 77 miles per hour.

With a regular 12-month model year, Ford saw production of the 1975 Mustang II taper off to 188,575 cars or 2.88 percent of the industry total. This was still an improvement over the last of the big Mustangs and helped keep sales trending in the right direction from the marque's lowest point.

*An ad for a 1976 Ghia "hardtop" declares "MUSTANG II: Our small, sporty personal car." Interestingly, a headline on the descriptive copy across from the photo calls the Mustang II, "America's best-selling small luxury car." (Ford)*

## 1976

There are signs that the Mustang II started its third model year with an identity crisis of sorts. In a factory sales catalog entitled *The 1976 Fords* (dated August 1975) a picture of a Ghia "hardtop" carries the message, "MUSTANG II: Our small, sporty personal car." Interestingly, a headline on the descriptive copy across from the photo calls the Mustang II, "America's best-selling small luxury car." A few months later, (October 1975), the company's 24-page *Free Wheelin'* sales booklet described the base models as "Mustang II MPGs." This "extension" on the model name indicated use of the base four-cylinder engine and reflected the growing importance of stressing good fuel economy in the first "oil embargo" era.

One thing that was for certain was that a new model came only in hatchback form—a car with the look, if not the performance, of a Shelby Mustang. "Cobra strikes again," said the *Free Wheelin'* catalog (which was a youth-oriented, 24-page color booklet and probably one of the sexiest pieces of factory literature Ford ever produced). "New Cobra II. Ford's Mustang II wrapped in an

*A new Silver Blue luxury option was available for the 1976 Mustang II Ghia. It had a half-vinyl top; body-side paint stripes; a hood ornament; interior with crushed velour seat inserts; and a full console. (Ford)*

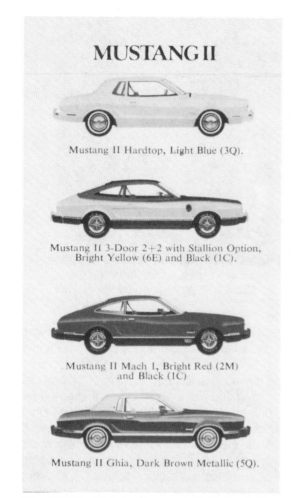

MUSTANG II

Mustang II Hardtop, Light Blue (3Q).

Mustang II 3-Door 2+2 with Stallion Option,
Bright Yellow (6E) and Black (1C).

Mustang II Mach 1, Bright Red (2M)
and Black (1C)

Mustang II Ghia, Dark Brown Metallic (5Q).

*The 1976 Ford Catalog shows a 2+2 with the Stallion option in Bright Yellow and Black. (Ford)*

appearance package that does justice to the Cobra name. So striking, it's already a sales success."

It was hard to believe from a piece of literature printed in October 1975, that the exciting-looking Cobra option had already sold many copies. However, such sales were possible, because the package was available on all 2+2s with any engine. The $325 option was definitely the model year's biggest Mustang news. Carroll Shelby even appeared in the sales catalog to promote the Cobra II.

As if to prove the new Cobra was primarily an appearance package, the car started with 1976 Mustang II MPG standard equipment like rack-and-pinion steering, front disc brakes, and the 2.3-liter four-cylinder, two-barrel engine (for added punch, the V-6 or V-8 could be added). Then the following special Cobra II equipment was added: bold racing stripes; a blacked-out grille; racing mirrors; rear quarter window louvers; a front air dam; a non-functional hood scoop; a rear deck lid spoiler; a brushed aluminum instrument panel and door panel appliqués; Cobra insignias on the front fenders; styled steel wheels; and BR70 steel-belted tires with raised white letters.

The 1976 Cobra II came in white with blue stripes, blue with white stripes, or black with gold stripes.

Another new-for-1976 offering was the Stallion model. It included the standard notchback or 2+2 ingredients, with the following changes: black grille and surround moldings; black moldings and wiper arms; bright lower bodyside moldings; Stallion decals; black-painted lower fenders, lower doors, lower quarter panels, lower front and rear bumpers, and rocker panels; and styled steel wheels.

The Stallion package (offered for Mustang MPGs, Pinto MPGs and Mavericks) was usually shown in black and silver and many books suggest this was the only choice of colors. However, The 1976 Ford catalog shows a 2+2 with the Stallion option in a Bright Yellow (6E) and Black (1C) two-tone combination. The *Free Wheelin'* booklet says Stallions came "with colorful paint masked by blackout body panels." It specifies colors of Silver Metallic, Bright Red, Bright Yellow, Polar White, and Silver Blue Glow (extra-cost) for the Maverick Stallion, suggesting that Mustang Stallions also came in these same five hues.

The base models, with the four-cylinder, were all called MPGs. They had the same standard equipment as before. The printed list looked longer, because body-color urethane bumpers, Ford Lifeguard Design safety features and bright window moldings were specifically mentioned. Ghia upgrades were basically the same, although the stand-up hood ornament was no longer standard. It was part of the Luxury Group option. The Mach 1 (the official name "Mustang II Mach 1 2+2 3-door" sounded almost algebraic) also had the same add-ons as before. Strangely, since the V-6 was standard, the Mach 1 did not come as an MPG, although the Cobra did.

Playing off Henry Ford's famous "any color as long as it's black" statement about the Model T Ford, the 1976 sales booklet put colorful promotional emphasis on an "all-black Mustang II with blackout grille, wipers and window moldings and styled steel wheels," a "classic black Mustang II MPG 2+2 with bright grille, window moldings, and wheel covers" and a "Red Mach 1." The three cars were photographed with eight young mechanics working on a street rod and a Mustang race car, with new Mustang IIs and a Cobra II parked nearby.

The smaller Mustang II engines were robbed of some power in 1976, with the four going from 97 to 92 hp and the V-6 dropping from 105 to 103 hp. However, the V-8 got a substantial boost from 122 to 139 hp.

Model year production for 1976 stayed at just about the same level at 187,567 units. That was 2.31 percent of the auto industry's total domestic output. The small Mustang still seemed to be struggling to find its real identity. In addition to everything else it was trying to be, the new Cobra II made it a muscle car "wannabe." As things turned out in the long run, adding some real muscle would be the key to success, but that would come after the Mustang II era.

### America's best-selling small luxury car.

You'll feel younger as soon as you see Mustang II's exciting choice of models and options. There are three glamorous Luxury Groups for your selection: Silver, Tan Glow or Silver Blue Glow.

Mustang II offers two body styles in four models: the fastback-styled 3-door 2+2 and Mach I with fold-down rear seat, or the formal roofline Hardtop and Ghia. The standard power is a thrifty 2.3 liter engine with 4-speed floor shift. You can get the optional 302 CID V-8 (with SelectShift Cruise-O-Matic) or 2.8 liter V-6 (with manual 4-speed). Or choose the exciting new Stallion Group exterior for the 2+2 and 2-Door Hardtop models. In small sporty cars, too, Ford means value.

**Mustang II Ghia Hardtop** (left) is shown in Creme (Code 6P) with Creme vinyl half roof. Exterior appointments include opera windows, wire design wheel covers, bright ornamentation and color-keyed urethane-covered bumper.

**Mustang II Ghia Interior** (right) is shown in Creme and Gold Westminster cloth (Code DV) □ Standard features include low-back bucket seats, shag carpeting, woodtone accents, deluxe door trim panels and choice of cloth or vinyl seats.

For more details and illustrations, see your Ford Dealer for a 1976 Mustang II Catalog.

### Notable Standard Features—Mustang II

FUNCTIONAL: 2.3 liter 4-cylinder engine with solid state ignition (2.8 liter V-6, Mach 1) □ Floor-mounted 4-speed trans. □ Rack and pinion steering □ Front disc brakes □ Fold-down rear seat and liftgate (2+2, Mach I) □ Tires: Bias-ply BSW on 2-Dr. HT and 2+2, steel-belted radials on Ghia (BSW) and Mach 1 (RWL) □ Tach, fuel, ammeter and temp gauges □ Ford Lifeguard Design Features.
APPEARANCE & COMFORT: Low-back vinyl bucket seats □ European-type armrests □ Woodtone instrument panel appliques □ Bright window, wheel lip moldings □ Carpeting □ Vinyl roof (Ghia) □ Color-keyed bumpers □ Wheel covers (Hardtop and 2+2), plus trim rings (Mach 1); wire design wheel covers (Ghia).

NOTE: Other items shown are optional.

*Specifications for early 1976 Mustang IIs first appeared in an August 1975 sales brochure that emphasized the Ghia hardtop model and the long list of standard features. (Ford)*

*The 1976 Mustang II Stallion had a sleek, racy appearance utilizing a two-tone paint and stripe treatment on fastback 2+2 and notchback models. Large stallion decals decorated the fenders. (Ford)*

The 1976 Stallion also had black paint and tape decorating its "green-house," lower body, hood, grille, rear deck lid, and lower back panel. Slotted mag wheels (shown) were also included in the package. (Ford)

Popular features included low-back buckets; disc brakes; sliding sun-roofs; and trunk racks. (Ford)

Contrary to its aggressive-sounding name, the new Cobra II started with 1976 Mustang II MPG standards like rack-and-pinion steering, front disc brakes, and the 2.3-liter four-cylinder, two-barrel engine. The more powerful 302-cid V-8 was optional. (Ford)

*Special 1976 Cobra II equipment included: bold racing stripes; racing mirrors; rear quarter window louvers; a rear deck lid spoiler; Cobra insignias on the front fenders; styled steel wheels; and BR70 steel-belted tires. (Ford)*

*Specifications for early 1976 Mustang IIs first appeared in an August 1975 sales brochure that emphasized the Ghia hardtop model and the long list of standard features. (Ford)*

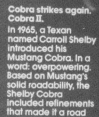

**Cobra strikes again. Cobra II.**

In 1965, a Texan named Carroll Shelby introduced his Mustang Cobra. In a word: overpowering. Based on Mustang's solid roadability, the Shelby Cobra included refinements that made it a road racing legend.

Now, Cobra II. Ford's Mustang II wrapped in an appearance package that does justice to the Cobra name. So striking it's already a sales success.

Cobra II starts with 1976 Mustang II MPG standards like rack and pinion steering, front disc brakes, 2.3 liter OHC 2V four-cylinder engine. For more punch, order 2.8 liter 2V V-6 or 302 CID 2V V-8.

Then the following special Cobra II equipment is added: bold racing stripes, blackout grille, racing mirrors, rear quarter window louvers, front air dam, rear decklid spoiler, brushed aluminum instrument panel and door appliques, Cobra insignia. On the road ...styled steel wheels with Cobra logo and trim rings, plus BR70 RWL steel-belted radials.

Cobra II. With the look of the legendary Cobra. Cobra strikes again.

1965 Shelby Cobra

*Ford's ad hinted that the exciting-looking 1976 Cobra option had sold many copies early in the model year. It's possible, since it was available on 2+2s with all three engines.*

*The $325 option was definitely the model year's biggest Mustang news. Inset photos show Cobra-creator Carroll Shelby with a 1965 GT-350. (Ford)*

"Any customer can have a car painted any color he wants so long as it is black."
—Henry Ford, 1912

Not much choice back then. Today, vehicles are in stripes, tones, shades and murals.

But black is strong as ever. Like the all-black Mustang II above with blackout grille, wipers and window moldings, styled steel wheels.

Or this classic black Mustang II MPG 2+2 with bright grille, window moldings, and wheel covers. Plus 2.3 liter OHC 2V 4-cylinder engine.

MPG Hardtop model also available shown on page 13.

Go colorful and bright, if you prefer. Like the Red Mach 1 shown. Or in almost any color you choose, with bright grille and moldings. Black lower bodysides, bumpers and back panel. Color-keyed dual remote control mirrors. Styled steel wheels and trim rings. RWL wide-oval steel-belted radials. 2.8 liter 2V V-6 engine. All are Mach I standard features.

Whether it's color, performance, wheels, whatever...you can make your own moving statement with Ford.

14

*Playing off Henry Ford's famous "any color as long as it's black" Model T comment, special promotional emphasis was placed on all-Black Mustang IIs and Red Mach 1s in 1976.*

*The three cars were depicted with eight young mechanics working on a street rod and a Mustang race car, with new Mustang IIs and a new Cobra II parked nearby. (Ford)*

## 1977

There were few significant changes in the Mustang II again in 1977. Updates included new colors and a revision in the wood-tone interior trim appliqués. They were changed from a burled walnut appearance to a simulated pecan woodgrain. New standard equipment for 2+2s included a Sport steering wheel; styled wheels; bias-belted raised white-letter tires; a blacked out grille; and brushed aluminum instrument panel applique's.

The four and the V-6 both lost more horsepower, as emission upgrades continued to choke off engine performance. The V-8 retained its 139 hp rating. A Sports Performance package consisted of the 5.0-liter two-barrel V-8; heavy-duty four-speed manual transmission; power steering; power brakes; and radial-ply tires.

New-for-1977 options included simulated wire wheel covers, painted cast-aluminum spoke wheels and a T-bar roof (adopted from a popular feature of a 1976 Mustang show car). California cars now had different carburetion setups and transmission choices.

Notchback, 2+2 hatchback, Ghia notchback, and Mach 1 hatchback models were offered again. The Cobra II option package climbed more than $220 in price, to $535. The 1977 Cobra again came in white with blue racing stripes, blue with white stripes, or black with gold stripes, plus a choice of two new color combinations: white with color-keyed red accent stripes and white with green stripes.

The Cobra II again included front and rear spoilers; louvered flip-out rear quarter windows; Cobra II emblems; a blacked-out grille; color-keyed dual sport mirrors; styled steel wheels with trim rings; raised white-letter tires; and brushed aluminum instrument panel; and door appliqués. Early-in-the-year Cobras had "C-O-B-R-A II" lettering low on the front doors. Later cars had much larger lettering that ran higher up on the doors.

Other desirable options were the Ghia Sports Group ($422) and the Rallye package. The latter was $88 on most cars, but only $43 for Mach 1s, Cobras, and cars with the Exterior Accent Group option. The Sports Group included black or tan paint with a black Odense grain or a Chamois Lugano grain vinyl roof. Other ingredients were bodyside moldings with matching vinyl inserts; a blacked out grille; a luggage rack with color-keyed leather hold-down straps and bright buckles; cast-aluminum wheels with chamois-painted spokes; and color-keyed interior appointments, plus a center console and a leather-wrapped steering wheel. Rallye equipment encompassed the extra-cooling package; heavy-duty springs; adjustable shocks; a rear stabilizer bar; and dual color-keyed door mirrors. The Stallion was gone.

Model year production was 153,173, an 18.3 percent decrease from 1976. It represented 1.68 percent of the total industry output. Dealer sales for the model year were counted at 161,313 units, down from 179,159 a year earlier. Both declines were due in part to a United Auto Workers strike at Ford. Just over 25 percent of all 1977 Mustang IIs were ordered with V-8s, versus 17.6 percent in 1976.

*The Cobra II returned in 1977 with more colors. New combinations were white with red paint stripes and white with green. Black with wide gold paint stripes, blue with white stripes and white with blue were retained. (Ford)*

While the Cobra II could be powered by any of the three engine choices for 1977, the "enthusiast" package dictated the 302-cid V-8 and four-speed manual transmission. (Brad Bowling)

The 1977 Cobra II's dash was attractively laid out, with a large, easy-to-read tachometer and speedometer. (Brad Bowling)

In 1977, this passed for a "full complement" of gauges. (Brad Bowling)

*The Mustang II's hatchback made a sporty little car more practical. (Brad Bowling)*

MUSTANG

*A thick, padded steering wheel gave a sporty feel to the cockpit. (Brad Bowling)*

*Louvers were standard on the Cobra II. (Brad Bowling)*

*Often maligned for its low power output, the Mustang II—in Cobra II V-8 trim—was one of the best bangs for the buck during the 1970s. (Brad Bowling)*

*The black with gold Cobra II was clearly supposed to remind Mustangers of the Shelby GT-350 Hertz models. (Ford)*

*This car toured the show circuit in 1976 to promote the new-for-1977 T-roof option. (Ford)*

*There were few significant changes for the Mustang II again in 1977. Updates included new colors and a revision in the wood-tone interior trim appliqués. They were changed from a burled walnut appearance to a simulated pecan woodgrain. (Ford)*

## 1978

Mustang II's sporty performance image and extensive model and option availability continued to make it the best-selling car in its class in 1978. The sub-compact appeared in basic notchback and 2+2 formats again. Separate rear seat cushions, plus new designs in door trim, seat trim and carpets were also added. Powered by a 2.3-liter four with four-speed transmission, the standard Mustang II featured an electronic ignition system, front disc brakes, rack-and-pinion steering, a tachometer and an ammeter, among its extensive list of standard equipment.

The Mustang's unique personality had special appeal to young buyers who liked cars loaded with extras. Many new options were offered on the Mustang II for 1978. A Rallye Appearance package featured gold and flat black accents combined with complementary cloth seat inserts to accentuate its sporty 2+2 appeal. For buyers who wanted the free, open-air feeling of a convertible, there was the new T-Roof, with twin removable glass panels. It was available for the 2+2 and the Mach 1.

For the third consecutive year, more power was robbed from the base four (now rated at 88 hp) and the optional V-6 (down to 90 hp). The V-8 was again credited with the same 139 hp. SelectShift Cruise-O-Matic transmission was $225 extra with V-8s or the King Cobra option and $263 in other models.

The Mach 1, a proven sales success, returned again. It included the 2.8-liter V-6, styled wheels and raised white-letter tires, plus black front and rear bumpers and lower bodyside paint. A brushed aluminum instrument panel appliqué and full instrumentation added to its youthful appeal.

Continuing as a fun-to-own, fun-to-drive car, the Cobra II had stylish exterior tape and paint treatments to stimulate enthusiast interest. Equipment encompassed black backlight trim, quarter window louvers, styled steel wheels with trim rings, raised white-letter tires, and the Rallye package. A new tri-color stripe treatment was seen.

The new "Boss of the Mustang stable" is how Ford described its King Cobra. It featured a far-out look with a wild Cobra decal on a distinctive scooped hood; a large front air dam; standard power assists; the Rallye package; King Cobra lettering on the doors and rear deck spoiler; dual color-keyed sport door mirrors; and an integrated rear deck lid spoiler. Responsive performance was provided by a 5.0-liter V-8 and four-speed manual transmission.

Another Mustang II variant was the Ghia hardtop, especially appealing when fitted with the Sports Group package. It had a luxurious, color-coordinated interior and complementary exterior accents. This year's edition came with the black and Chamois color choices, or Dark Blue exterior paint. Also included was a blacked-out grille; color-coordinated moldings; pin stripes; leather-wrapped steering wheel; floor console; and vinyl seat trim.

Model year production leaped to 192,410 units in the Mustang II's last season. That represented 2.15 percent of all domestic auto output. V-8 engines were optionally installed in 17.9 percent of all Mustang IIs. Dealer sales stood at 179,039 for the model year, up 11 percent (nearly 18,000 units) over 1977.

*For 1978 Mustang II buyers who wanted the free, open-air feeling of a convertible, there was the new T-Roof, with twin removable glass panels. It was available for the 2+2 and the Mach 1. (Ford)*

Mustang II with Rallye Appearance Package

Mustang II Mach I

Mustang II T-Roof Convertible

*Three popular 1978 Mustang II models were (top) 2+2 with Rallye Appearance package; (center) Mach 1 2+2; and (bottom) a 2+2 with what Ford described as the "T-Roof Convertible" option. (Ford)*

*Three of 1978's collectible Mustang IIs are (top) the King Cobra 2+2; (center) the Cobra II with a brand new paint stripe treatment (with the name along the center of the doors), and (bottom) the Ghia with Sports Group option. (Ford)*

*The 1978 King Cobra featured a Cobra decal on its scooped hood; a front air dam; power assists; Rallye package; King Cobra lettering; color-keyed sport mirrors; a rear deck lid spoiler; a 5.0-liter V-8 and a four-speed. (Ford)*

*The 1978 King Cobra was either the gaudiest or sportiest Mustang II ever, depending on personal opinion. It was Ford's attempt to out-Trans Am the Trans Am. (Ford)*

# CHAPTER 8

# MUSTANG

## A Turbocharged Future (1979-86)

*After five years of the Mustang II, 1979's all-new model looked positively futuristic. (Ford)*

*A hood scoop was a telltale sign of the turbocharged 2.3-liter four available for all regular Mustangs at extra cost. This 1979 two-door sedan also has the Sport Option, but without black window frames. (Ford)*

## 1979

The Mustang II years gave enthusiasts little to be excited about, and rumors that the Mustang name might be put out to pasture or relegated to an options package on a less-sporty Ford product made the rounds for the first time. (They would be repeated 10 years later when Ford threatened to produce a Mustang-badged, Mazda-designed front-drive economy car).

With the introduction of its all-new 1979 Mustang—more conservatively and proportionally styled in keeping with the original's mission—Ford announced to the world that America's first pony car was facing a bright and, literally, turbocharged future.

Just like the 1965 Falcon origins and the 1974 Pinto beginnings, the 1979 shared the same Ford gene pool as a more humble line of cars. The "Fox" unit-body platform was designed initially for a four- or five-passenger sedan/wagon (eventually the Ford Fairmont and Mercury Zephyr), but planners decided it could be shortened to provide the basis for the new Mustang.

"Aerodynamics" was the buzzword in Detroit in the late 1970s among designers. The Arab oil embargo that had spurred sales of the small Mustang II highlighted America's dependency on foreign oil as a national weakness, and the federal government put regulations into play to ensure it couldn't happen again. Corporate Average Fuel Economy (CAFE) rules encouraged the production of cars with higher gas mileage numbers than ever before.

Because engine technologies and computers were still relatively primitive, the best way to get good mileage from a car was to design a body that could cheat the wind and therefore reduce drag. Every planner, designer and marketing manager at every automaker sweated drag coefficient numbers and the all-important MPG—this was the corporate culture that gave birth to the 1979 Mustang.

The fifth-generation pony car turned out to be the most wind-friendly production car ever produced by Ford at a slippery 0.44 for the fastback and 0.46 for the notchback. (It's interesting to note how quickly these numbers were surpassed; the 1983 Thunderbird sliced through the wind with a 0.35 drag coefficient—a 20-percent increase in efficiency over the Mustang.)

Designers saved weight on the new Mustang through the use of advanced plastics, aluminum, high-strength/low-alloy steel, thinner but stronger glass, and slimmer passenger compartment components. The 1979 was, on average, about 200 pounds lighter than the II, despite being a larger, more comfortable car.

The Mustang now had a 100.4-inch wheelbase, an overall length of 179.1 inches, a body width of 69.1 inches and a 51.5-inch height. Both fastback and notchback registered in the 2,600-pound range.

Because the car's crisp, new styling was a major selling point, many customers didn't care that the powerplants were essentially carryovers from the Mustang II—the 88-hp 2.3-liter four-cylinder, 2.8-liter V-6 and 5.0-liter V-8. (A late-in-the-year supply problem forced Ford to substitute its ancient 200-cid inline six-cylinder engine for the V-6.)

Grabbing the enthusiasts' attention was an optional turbocharged version of the 2.3-liter four that was rated at 131 hp. While no threat to big-block V-8s of the past, the turbo engine had respectable performance, with one magazine clocking a four-speed turbo model at 12 seconds zero-to-60 mph. The heavier (and thirstier) 302 V-8 Mustang managed to reach the same speed in nine seconds.

1979 FORD
MUSTANG
A whole new breed.

*The new Mustang for 1979 was based on the Ford Fairmont's "Fox" platform and featured unit-body construction. (Ford)*

*A Sport Option package, extra on 1979 coupes, was standard on this hatchback. It featured black window frames and moldings. Forged aluminum wheels were extra. (Ford)*

*The notchback model with a trunk was called a coupe, a two-door sedan or simply a sedan. This 1979 coupe had 20 percent more interior space than 1978 models. (Ford)*

*In profile, it was easy to see the distinct shape of the 1979 sedan's rear quarter window glass. (Ford)*

*High-back bucket seats were standard, but these low-back buckets with Euro-style headrests were an extra-cost item. (Ford)*

The three-door was a hatchback. It had 16 more cubic feet of luggage space than the 1978 Mustang II 2+2, plus an estimated 32.4 cubic feet of cargo space with the back seat folded down. This 1979 example has the Turbo hood scoop. (Ford)

The 1979 Mustang two-door Ghia looked great in Black with the Chamois vinyl roof. It had a rear Ghia medallion; special interior; color-keyed louvers and window frames; rocker moldings; and standard turbine wheel covers. (Ford)

*The Ghia also came as a three-door. This 1979 has optional wire wheel covers. (Ford)*

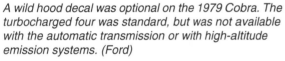

*Cars with the 302-cid small-block V-8 had 5.0 badges behind the front wheel opening. This 1979 two-door has the TRX package, which includes optional aluminum wheels and Michelin tires. (Ford)*

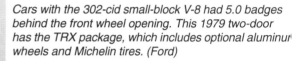

*A wild hood decal was optional on the 1979 Cobra. The turbocharged four was standard, but was not available with the automatic transmission or with high-altitude emission systems. (Ford)*

*(B) Cobra with hood graphics*

*Coiled beneath the sport 1979 Cobra appearance extras was a standard 2. liter turbocharged engine teamed with a fourspeed manual transmission. The special suspension was tuned for Michelin TRX tires and forged aluminum wheels. (Ford)*

Unlike the Mustang II era, performance packages actually contributed to the car's thrill-behind-the-wheel quotient. The TRX handling package, which included specially sized Michelin radials, higher spring rates, different shock valving and stiffer bushings, was a "Walter Mitty" dream on wheels when combined with the lightweight turbo 2.3-liter four. Two other levels of suspension equipment were available; "standard," which was tuned for bias-ply tires and "handling," developed for modern radial tires.

Ranging in base price from $4,494 to $5,216, the Mustang was "still sticker-priced to help you bring one home in two-door or three-door models," Ford advertised. A V-8-powered hatchback was selected to pace the 63rd annual Indianapolis 500 on May 27, 1979, and of course, there was a line of replicas made available to the public. The 1979 models were manufactured in two factories. The Dearborn plant produced 269,000 and a little more than 100,000 were turned out in a San Jose, California, factory.

Before the new Mustang was launched, Ford announced sales projections of 330,000 units or 16.5 percent of its 1979 plan. Considering the sluggishness in the auto market at the time, they did a great job breaking that goal with model year production of 369,936 units for a 4.02 percent industry share. Dealer sales stood at 302,309 Mustangs for the model year. Four-cylinders were ordered in 54.4 percent of 1979 Mustangs, while 31.3 percent had V-6s (or the late-year inline-sixes) and only 14.3 percent had V-8s.

One month after the new Mustang's press preview in 1978, Henry Ford II fired Lee Iacocca, perhaps out of fear that his powers as president were on the rise. Iacocca moved on to a troubled Chrysler, taking along some hand-picked executives to engineer his famous turnaround of the company. Phillip Caldwell became second in command under board chairman Henry Ford II, where he held titles of vice chairman and president.

*Dual tailpipe extensions, a special suspension with heavy-duty front/rear stabilizers and specially-valved shocks, semi-metallic front disc brakes, aluminum rear drums and a 3.45:1 axle were more 1979 Cobra extras. (Ford)*

*1979 Cobras also came standard with black window frames; black bodyside moldings; black lower perimeter finish; Cobra door decals; an 8,000-rpm tachometer; a black, engine-turned design appliqué; and Cobra insignia on the dash. (Ford)*

*Genuine leather with vinyl trim interior is shown here on top-of-the-line 1979 Ghia bucket seats. This option was also offered for Cobras or as part of Mustang's Interior Accent group. It came in six colors. (Ford)*

*1979 Mustang interior options were: (top left) check-cloth Interior Accent group; (top center) houndstooth cloth/vinyl; (right) Ghia cloth; (lower center) all-vinyl and (lower left) crinkle-vinyl Interior Accent group. (ford)*

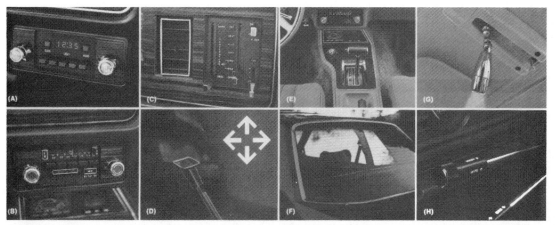

*Mustang options for 1979 included: A) AM digital clock radio; B) AM/FM stereo; C) SelectAire Conditioner; D) 4-Way manual seat; E) console; F) electric rear defroster; G) Light Group; and H) Interval windshield wipers. (Ford)*

*Other 1979 Mustang extras were: I) Fingertip speed control; J) rear window wiper/washer; K) Select-Shift automatic transmission; L) leather-wrapped Sport steering wheel and M) Power Lock group. (Ford)*

*A flip-open sunroof (A) and black-finished liftgate louvers (B) were popular options with many young buyers of 1979 Mustangs. (Ford)*

## Notable Standard Features

### MUSTANG 2-DOOR/3-DOOR
**FUNCTIONAL**
- 2.3 litre 2V overhead cam, 4-cylinder engine with DuraSpark Ignition
- 4-speed, fully synchronized, manual transmission with floor-mounted shifter
- Rack and pinion steering
- Front disc/rear drum brakes
- Strut front suspension/4-bar link rear suspension
- Front stabilizer bar
- 13-in. bias ply tires (BSW)
- Dual rectangular headlamps
- Wraparound taillamps
- Fluidic windshield washers
- Full instrumentation: tachometer, trip odometer, fuel/temperature/oil pressure/alternator gauges
- Steering column-mounted 2-lever system:
  1. Windshield wiper/washer
  2. Turn signal/horn/headlamp dimmer
- Anti-theft door lock plungers
- Hand-operated parking brake with warning light
- Inside hood release
- Glove box lock
- Day/night rearview mirror
- Passenger door courtesy light switch
- Cigarette lighter
- Continuous loop belts
- Unitized body construction
- Ford Motor Company Lifeguard Design Safety Features

**APPEARANCE AND COMFORT**
- High-back bucket seats with all-vinyl trim
- Deluxe cut-pile carpeting
- Full door trim with padded upper panel, bright moldings and carpeted lower panel
- Full-width woodtone instrument panel appliques
- Deluxe steering wheel (2-door), Sport steering wheel (3-door)
- Flat luggage floor, full mat, insulation package

- Fold-down rear seat/liftgate (3-door)
- Color-keyed louvers (2-door), Black (3-door)
- Color-keyed door and window frames with bright moldings (2-door)
- Black-painted door and window frames, belt and rocker panel moldings (3-door)
- Bright windshield, drip, side and rear window and headlamp moldings
- Black left-hand rearview styled mirror
- Black cowl molding, windshield wipers, grille and lower back panel
- Soft urethane-covered front and rear ends
- Color-keyed bumpers with Black rub strips (2-door), plus dual accent stripe inserts (3-door)
- Wide Black bodyside moldings with dual accent stripe inserts (3-door)
- Full wheel covers, 2-door (4)
- 13-in. Sport wheels, 3-door (4)

### MUSTANG GHIA
Most standard Mustang 2-Door features, plus these additions or variations:
- Low-back buckets with European-style headrests
- Color-keyed deluxe belts
- Luxury cut-pile carpeting
- Ghia door trim with badge, soft inserts, map pockets and carpeted lower panels
- Sport steering wheel
- Light Group (see page 16 for full details)
- Roof-mounted passenger-assist grab handle
- Right-hand visor vanity mirror
- Ghia sound package
- Carpeted luggage compartment (2-door)
- Ghia insignia on deck lid/third door
- Color-keyed window frames, louvers and dual remote control styled mirrors
- Bright belt and rocker panel moldings
- Pin stripes

- Wide Black bodyside moldings with dual color-coordinated accent stripe inserts
- Dual color-coordinated accent stripe inserts on bumpers
- Turbine wheel covers (4)
- 14-in. steel-belted (BSW) radial ply tires

### MUSTANG COBRA*
Most standard Mustang 3-Door features, plus these additions or variations:
- 2.3 litre Turbocharged engine**
- TURBO instrument panel lights, audible overboost and engine oil temperature warning system
- 8,000 rpm tachometer
- Black engine-turn design applique on instrument panel
- Cobra insignia on instrument panel and ribbed door trim insert
- Color-keyed side window louvers
- Front opening hood scoop (ornamental), bright TURBO nameplate
- Cobra door decal (hood graphics, optional)
- Black window frames, moldings and lower body
- Wide Black bodyside moldings with dual color-coordinated accent stripe inserts
- Bright dual tailpipe extension
- Michelin 190/65R 390 TRX (BSW) tires
- 390 mm-15.35-in. Forged metric aluminum wheels (4)
- Special suspension system with heavy-duty front and rear stabilizer bars, special shock valving
- Aluminum rear brake drums and semi-metallic front disc brake pads
- 3.45 axle ratio

*For content of optional packages, see pages 5, 6, 7, 10, 11. See options list on pages 16-19.
**Not available with automatic transmission or with High Altitude Emission System.

## Measurements

| | Wheelbase | Length | Height | Width | Tread Front/Rear | Trunk or Cargo Volume | Fuel Capacity | Curb Weight | Passenger Capacity |
|---|---|---|---|---|---|---|---|---|---|
| **2-DOOR** | 100.4" | 179.1" | 51.5" | 69.1" | 56.6"/57.0" | 10.0 cu. ft. | 11.5 gals.† | 2,516 lbs. | 4 |
| **3-DOOR** | 100.4" | 179.1" | 51.5" | 69.1" | 56.6"/57.0" | 32.4 cu. ft. | 11.5 gals.† | 2,550 lbs. | 4 |

†12.5 gal. on standard 2.3 litre Four with SelectAire Conditioner, 2.3 litre Turbo, 2.8 litre V-6; 16.0 gals. with 5.0 litre V-8.

## Notes

**CORROSION PROTECTION.** Ford takes steps to see that your new Mustang is engineered and built to high quality standards. And in order to keep your Mustang looking new we incorporate the use of precoated steels, such as galvanized steel and chrome/zinc-rich primer-coated steel, vinyl sealers aluminized wax in critical areas, and enamel as a finishing coat.

**REDUCED SCHEDULED MAINTENANCE.** As part of a continuing program to lower the cost of ownership, scheduled maintenance requirements on most new Fords have been reduced dramatically in recent years. For example, with the new 1979 Ford Mustang,

the recommended maintenance schedule is 10,000 miles (7,500 miles with V-8 engines), or 12 months (on V-6 engines and most I-4 engines), between scheduled oil changes and 30,000 miles between lubes. These are just two small parts of the comprehensive program, which, in total, can significantly lower the cost of scheduled maintenance for Mustang over 50,000 miles of driving.

**COLOR AND TRIM CODES.** Car colors and trims are coded, example: Tangerine (85). Your Ford Dealer will be pleased to show you color samples of paint and trim materials.

**OPTION AVAILABILITY.** Some features presented are optional at extra cost. Some options are required in combination with other options. Availability of some models and features described may be subject to a slight delay. Ask your Ford Dealer for the latest information on options, prices and availability.

**PRODUCT CHANGES.** Ford Division reserves the right to change specifications any time without incurring obligations.

**REPLACEMENT PARTS.** Be sure to specify genuine Ford-approved parts, Motorcraft Parts and Autolite Spark Plugs from your Ford Dealer.

*The standard equipment list for the all-new 1979 Mustangs was long and loaded with many items that were formerly extra-cost options. The basic series were called Mustang, Mustang Ghia, and Mustang Cobra. (Ford)*

*An extended service plan was available. Wheel options included: F) Turbine wheel covers; G) wire wheel covers; H) cast-aluminum wheels; I) forged metric aluminum wheels; and J) styled steel wheels and trim rings. (Ford)*

*John Cooper, president of Indianapolis Motor Speedway, tries out a 1979 Mustang Indy 500 Pace Car. Indy winner Rick Mears received a similar car. (IMSC)*

A V-8-powered 1979 Mustang three-door hatchback was selected to pace the 63rd annual Indianapolis 500 on May 27, 1979. This car had a T-roof and special Silver/Black finish with Red-Orange striping and graphics. (IMSC)

*This 1979 pace car replica was one of many such commemorative Mustangs that were stored for an anticipated rise in collector value. (Brad Bowling)*

## 1980

For 1980, the Mustang maintained just about the same portion of total automobile business, with a 4.01 percent market share, but the market had shrunk by two million units.

A 23 percent fuel economy improvement for the 88-hp base four was promoted as a selling point of the 1980 Mustang, and there were only minor improvements to the turbocharged version. The 200-cid straight six remained on the lineup after replacing the 2.8-liter V-6 at the end of 1979.

For the second time since it was introduced in 1968 (the first being the Mustang II's introductory year), the venerable 302-cid (5.0-liter) V-8 was dropped and replaced with a de-bored 255-cid (4.2-liter) version in an attempt to increase gas mileage. While it probably helped Ford reach its CAFE goals for the year, its 117 hp was 14 less than the lighter turbocharged four-cylinder.

New standard features included P-metric radial tires, halogen headlamps, and more accessible inside door handles. A new front and rear end treatment was created for the Cobra package. Base models shed a few pounds in the interest of fuel efficiency.

*Reclining Recaro seats were a new 1980 option in four color combos. (Ford)*

*This 1980 Mustang three-door has the turbocharged engine (note the scooped hood) and the Accent Tape Stripes option. The Turbo generated 131 hp and was the year's hottest motor. There was no 5.0-liter V-8 in 1980—only a downsized 4.2-liter V-8. (Ford)*

*The 1980 McLaren Mustang had a grille-less front end, spoilers, hood scoops, flared fenders, heavy-duty suspension, and 175 hp. (John Gunnell)*

During 1980, Ford renewed its interest in motorsports. The initials of the International Motor Sports Association were used on a concept car called the Mustang IMSA. It had the turbo four, fat Pirelli tires, and a lot of competition-like flares, spoilers, and air dams. Ford envisioned a return to the glory days of the 1960s, when its parts branch created a tidy profit center merchandising bolt-on performance hardware to enthusiasts.

Englishman Michael Kranefuss, Ford's European competition director, was brought to Dearborn to organize a Special Vehicle Operations (SVO) group. The purpose of the SVO team was threefold. First, they were to help interested race drivers build up competition versions of the new Mustang. Second, they were to create a series of specialty "image" cars to generate interest in GT sports car racing. Third, they were to help conceive/create kits of bolt-on

*Several 1980 Mustangs received a touch of elegance with the addition of an optional diamond-grained Carriage vinyl roof. This brand new roof option came in white, black, blue, or brown. It had a convertible look.(Ford)*

The three-door 1980 Cobra had a new grille with horizontal louvers. It also featured front/rear spoilers, dual fog lamps and a non-functional scoop. (Ford)

parts that could be purchased by average Mustang owners to modify their street cars for road-and-track use in IMSA or SCCA events.

Late in the year, a car named the McLaren Mustang was introduced with lots of fanfare, including a cover on *Motor Trend* and articles in many buff books. The $25,000 car looked like the IMSA Mustang concept vehicle, with many extensive body modifications and many special accessories like Euro-style BBS alloy wheels. The power plant was a version of the turbocharged four "tweaked" by McLaren Engines. It boasted 175 hp. Only 250 were made.

The 1980 Mustang Ghia again came in three-door (top) and two-door (bottom) models. Full wraparound bodyside moldings were included. (Ford)

Model year production of 1980 Mustangs peaked at 271,322 cars. Of that total, 67.6 percent had fours and 29.7 had six-cylinders. Increasing gas prices were partly responsible for the fact that only 2.7 percent of Mustang buyers specified the new 4.2-liter V-8. Dealer sales for the model year were counted at 246,008 cars.

### 1981

New for the Mustang in 1981 was an optional T-Roof featuring two removable tinted glass panels available on all two-door sedans and the three-door hatchbacks. The same limited array of powertrains continued to be available, with three optional engines and seven optional transmissions.

Production dropped off to 182,562 Mustangs, all produced in Dearborn. With dealer sales amounting to 173,329 units, the marque's 1981 share of industry also declined to 2.73 percent. The four-cylinders were most popular, with a 62 percent installation rate, while V-8 sales improved slightly to 3.3 percent.

### 1982

The most exciting news for Mustang buyers since the 1969 Boss 302 was the introduction of a 5.0-liter "high-output" engine for model year 1982. The 5.0-liter powerplant, when teamed with a two-barrel carburetor, low-restriction air cleaner, and four-speed transmission, is most often associated with the new GT model, although it could be installed in the entire Mustang line. It generated 157 hp and recorded the fastest zero-to-60 mph time of any American car at the time—some magazines reported times in the low seven-second range!

All other Mustang engines from 1981, including the unloved 4.2-liter V-8, remained on the option list; however, a turbocharger was no longer offered for the four. The 4.2-liter V-8 made 111 hp, 40 less than the new 5.0-liter. Strangely, the 4.2-liter was available in the GT as a $57 credit option.

Intermeccanica Conversion Corporation, an after-market vehicle converter, created this 1981 Mustang convertible. Notice the lack of rear windows for the backseat passengers. (Old Cars Weekly)

This Mustang soft top conversion of a 1981 Mustang featured small "Intermeccanica" badges behind the front wheel arches. (Old Cars Weekly)

A new T-Roof option was added to the Mustang option list for 1981. It was available on two-door and three-door models. Some sales literature promoted this type of Mustang as the "T-Roof Convertible." (Ford)

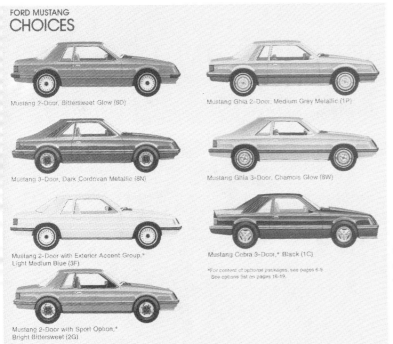

FORD MUSTANG
## CHOICES

Mustang 2-Door, Bittersweet Glow (8D)

Mustang Ghia 2-Door, Medium Grey Metallic (1P)

Mustang 3-Door, Dark Cordovan Metallic (8N)

Mustang Ghia 3-Door, Chamois Glow (8W)

Mustang 2-Door with Exterior Accent Group,*
Light Medium Blue (3F)

Mustang Cobra 3-Door,* Black (1C)

*For content of optional packages, see pages 6-9.
See options list on pages 16-19.

Mustang 2-Door with Sport Option,*
Bright Bittersweet (2G)

*One of the secrets of successfully marketing the Mustang was to give buyers lots of choices. Here are seven 1980 possibilities. (Ford)*

The $8,308 GT came in hatchback form only, sporting the top-grade TRX suspension, front and rear spoilers, foglamps, blackout treatment, console, luxury seat trim, and other bits of sportiness.

Fourteen-inch wheels were made standard on the 1982 Mustang, as well as a larger gas tank (up from 12.5 to 15.4 gallons).

When model year 1982 was over, Ford had produced only 119,314 Mustangs and dealers had sold only 116,804; however, an important swing in the market was taking place that would mean good news to the accountants at Ford. Due to lower gas prices, high-performance cars were becoming very marketable.

*1981 marked the last year that Ford would have to promote a "high-performance" Mustang without the 5.0-liter V-8. Still, the Cobra package, with TRX suspension and 255-cid V-8 made for a fun ride. (Ford)*

*"The Boss is Back," the advertisements declared. The first street machine to emerge from the SVO program was the 1982 Mustang GT "5.0-liter." It had an H.O. V-8 with 157 hp. (Ford)*

*Sporty car fans were especially happy to see a new four-barrel carburetor added to the 5.0-liter engine in 1983. It was standard in this GT three-door. (Old Cars Weekly)*

The Mustang 5.0-liter GT was well positioned to capitalize on this trend; in fact, in its first year, V-8 installations rose to 25.5 percent of all Mustangs. That was far above a goal of 20,000 to 25,000 V-8s that Ford had set at the start of the 1982 selling season.

The Mustang was mainly a carryover car in 1983, but it boasted improved aerodynamics (thanks to a smoother front cap), a re-tuned suspension system and a couple of very interesting options that included a new convertible and the return of the turbocharger.

(B) Mustang 2-Door with Sport Option, new Carriage Roof and Turbocharged Engine

(C) Mustang 2-Door with Sport Option

*Top: A 1980 Sport-optioned two-door with carriage roof and Turbo. (Ford)*
*Bottom: A Sport-optioned two door.*

(D) Mustang 2-Door with Exterior Accent Group

*A two-door with Exterior Accent group. (Ford)*

A limited-edition convertible was introduced midyear. Available only in the top-line GLX trim, it came complete with an electric convertible top, a real glass rear window and room for four. "It also comes complete with the wind in your hair and a pounding in your heart," said one advertisement. "And that makes it a Mustang." By the end of the year, 20,000 were sold at $13,560 (or more) each.

Cars & Concepts, of Brighton, Michigan, produced the convertibles outside the regular Ford assembly line. They could be ordered with any of the powertrains, except for the four-cylinder/automatic transmission combo.

Engine choices throughout the Mustang range were widened again. The base 2.3-liter four-cylinder (now with a more efficient one-barrel carburetor and long-reach sparkplugs) was supplemented with a 2.3-liter overhead cam turbocharged four with multi-port fuel injection, available only in the new Turbo GT package. The antique inline six-cylinder was replaced this year by a modern "Essex" 3.8-liter V-6 that cranked out 105 hp (versus the inline unit's 88) and 181 lb.-ft. of torque (versus 158) with a two-barrel carburetor.

The return of the turbocharged four-cylinder took many by surprise, considering it had been dropped for model year 1982. While the 1979-1981 iteration had been a simple mating of the stock 2.3-liter four to a high-tech device that produced more customer complaints than horsepower, the 1983 powerplant showed some real engineering savvy. Perhaps the greatest improvements were the elimination of the carburetor for Bosch port

*Dollar Rent-A-Car Systems rented 1980 Mustangs to many travelers. (Dollar)*

electronic fuel injection and the repositioning of the turbo so it sat upstream of the induction system instead of downstream. The four also benefited from forged-aluminum pistons, valves made from high-tech alloys, a lighter flywheel, and an oil cooler. With an 8.0:1 compression ratio the new fastback and convertible Turbo GTs produced 145 hp and 180 lb.-ft. of torque on premium unleaded gas.

Muscle car fans were happy to see more improvements made to the 5.0-liter H.O. V-8 in the form of a new four-barrel carburetor, aluminum intake, high-flow air cleaner, and valvetrain mods. The changes netted a 30 hp improvement to 175 hp.

Interestingly, the Turbo GT cost about $250 more than its 5.0 GT brother, yet couldn't be ordered in its first year with an automatic transmission or air conditioning. Measuring happiness with a stopwatch, the turbocharged car took just less than 10 seconds to reach 60 mph from a standstill, whereas the GT could rip off the same speed test in just over six seconds. Needless to say, some customers scratched their heads over that one before ordering the cheaper, faster V-8 GT—only 483 Turbo GTs were built in 1983. The turbo four sold in much higher numbers in the new Thunderbird Turbo Coupe, a larger car than the Mustang that, interestingly, had no V-8 option.

## FORD MUSTANG
## NOTABLE STANDARD FEATURES

### MUSTANG 2-DOOR/3-DOOR
FUNCTIONAL

- 2.3 liter 4-cylinder engine with DuraSpark Electronic Ignition
- Electronic voltage regulator
- Maintenance-free battery (heavy-duty in all states except California)*
- 4-speed fully synchronized manual transmission, floor-mounted shift
- Modified MacPherson strut front suspension with stabilizer bar; 4-bar link coil spring rear system
- Front disc brakes with lining wear indicators/rear drum brakes
- P-metric 13-in. BSW steel-belted radial ply tires; mini spare tire
- Rack and pinion steering
- Bumpers with black rub strips (2-door), dual argent stripe inserts (3-door)
- Dual rectangular halogen headlamps
- Fluidic windshield washer system
- Fold-down rear seat/liftgate (3-door)
- Column-mounted 2-lever system:
  1. Windshield wiper/washer
  2. Turn signal/horn/headlamp dimmer
- DirectAire ventilation
- Inside hood release
- Day/night inside mirror
- AM radio (may be deleted for credit or upgraded at extra cost)
- Full instrumentation: tachometer, trip odometer, fuel/temperature/oil pressure/alternator gauges
- Anti-theft door lock buttons
- Lockable glove box
- Passenger door courtesy light switch
- Cigarette lighter
- Ford's Limited Corrosion Perforation Warranty (see back cover)

APPEARANCE AND COMFORT

- High-back bucket seats in all-vinyl
- Color-keyed cut-pile carpeting
- Color-keyed carpeting on rear seat back and load floor (3-door)
- Full door trim with padded upper

panel, bright moldings and carpeted lower panel
- Full-width woodtone instrument panel appliques
- Deluxe steering wheel (2-door), sports steering wheel (3-door)
- Flat luggage floor, full mat (2-door)
- Rear pillar louvers, color-keyed (2-door), black (3-door)
- Color-keyed door and window frames with bright moldings (2-door)
- Black left-hand rearview styled mirror
- Black cowl molding, windshield wipers, grille and lower back panel
- Black-painted door and window frames, rocker panel moldings (3-door)
- Bright windshield, drip, side and rear window moldings
- Full wraparound wide black bodyside molding with dual argent stripe inserts (3-door)
- Bright headlamp doors (2-door), black (3-door)
- Wraparound taillamps
- Full wheel covers, 2-door (4)
- Sport wheels, 3-door (4)

### MUSTANG GHIA
Most standard Mustang 2-Door/3-Door features, plus these additions or variations:

- Low-back buckets with European-style headrests and inertia seat back releases
- Luxury color-keyed cut-pile carpeting
- Ghia door trim with badge, soft inserts, map pockets and carpeted lower panels
- Luxury rear seat trim panels
- Luxury 4-spoke steering wheel
- Light Group (see page 16)
- Roof-mounted RH assist handle
- Right-hand visor vanity mirror
- Color-keyed deluxe belts with tension eliminators
- Ghia Sound Insulation Package
- Carpeted luggage compartment (2-door)

- Color-keyed window frames, rear pillar louvers (3-Door)
- Dual remote-control styled mirrors
- Bright rocker panel moldings
- Pin stripes
- Ghia insignia on decklid/third door
- P-metric 14-in. BSW steel-belted radial ply tires
- Bright headlamp doors (3-door)
- Full wraparound wide black bodyside molding and bumpers with dual color-coordinated accent stripe inserts
- Turbine wheel covers (4)

### MUSTANG COBRA
Most standard Mustang 3-Door features, plus these additions or variations:

- 2.3 liter turbocharged engine†
- Sport-tuned exhaust with bright tailpipe extension
- Special suspension system with heavy-duty front and rear stabilizer bars, special shock valving
- Semi-metallic front disc brake pads
- Michelin 190/65R 390 TRX (BSW) tires
- Forged metric aluminum wheels (4), 390 mm (15.3-in.)
- 3.45 performance axle
- TURBO instrument panel lights, audible overboost and engine oil pressure warning system
- Black engine-turned design appliques on instrument panel
- Unique front end with integral spoiler and dual fog lamps; rear end spoiler
- Unique rear-opening hood scoop (non-functional)
- Dual black remote-control mirrors
- Black lower Tu-Tone paint treatment
- Unique bodyside and quarter window tape stripe treatment (see note page 9)
- Black window frames, door handles and locks
- Full wraparound black bodyside molding and bumpers with dual color-coordinated accent stripe inserts

*Conventional battery in early production models.
†Not available with High Altitude Emission System.
For options list see pages 16-19.

## Measurements

| | Wheelbase | Length | Height | Width | Tread Front/Rear | Trunk or Cargo Volume | Fuel Capacity | Curb Weight | Passenger Capacity |
|---|---|---|---|---|---|---|---|---|---|
| 2-DOOR | 100.4" | 179.1" | 51.4" | 67.4" | 56.6"/57.0" | 10.0 cu.ft. | 11.5 gal.* | 2,601 lb. | 4 |
| 3-DOOR | 100.4" | 179.1" | 51.4" | 67.4" | 56.6"/57.0" | 33.3 cu.ft. | 11.5 gal.* | 2,635 lb. | 4 |

*12.5 gal. on standard 2.3 liter Four with SelectAire Conditioner, 2.3 liter turbo with 4-speed manual, 3.3 liter (200 CID) "T" 6-cyl. and 4.2 liter (255 CID) V-8. 11.9 gal. on 2.3 liter turbo with SelectShift automatic.

*Standard features of the 1980 Mustangs varied according to trim level, model and body style. The basic model names were Mustang, Mustang Ghia, and Mustang Cobra. A 255-cid (4.2-liter) V-8 replaced the 302-cid (5.0-liter) engine. (Ford)*

*Left: A 5.0-liter, four-barrel H.O. V-8 was used in the 1983 Mustang GT. (Old Cars Weekly)*
*Right: Bucket seats were standard in the 1983 Mustang. This is the GT trim. (Old Cars Weekly)*

*Left: T-Roof panels were securely stored in this 1983 hatchback's luggage bay. (Old Cars Weekly)*
*Right: Cast metric aluminum wheels and TRX tires were 1983 GT options. (Old Cars Weekly)*

*Left: A functional air dam was standard on the 1983 Mustang GT. (Old Cars Weekly)*
*Right: Integral rear spoiler and chrome-tipped Sport exhaust are 1983 GT hints. (Old Cars Weekly)*

*A GLX nameplate was on the left side of the trunk lip, next to the Mustang name on 1983 GLX convertibles. Unlike some other convertibles appearing around this time, the Mustang version had glass all around. (Ford)*

*"It also comes complete with the wind in your hair and a pounding in your heart," said one convertible ad. "And that makes it a Mustang." The V-6 was standard in 1983 GLX soft tops with no engine call-out fender badges. (Ford)*

At midyear 1983, a limited edition Mustang convertible was introduced. It came complete with an electric convertible top, a real glass rear window and room for four. This one has badges indicating the optional 5.0-liter V-8. (Ford)

Optional cast aluminum wheels looked great on the sporty 1983 Mustang GLX convertible. The interior provided room and comfort for four people plus luggage. Convertibles with V-6 power also had SelectShift automatic transmission. (Ford)

By the end of the year, 23,438 Mustang convertibles had been sold. The GLX convertible listed for $12,467 and the GT version carried a $13,560 base price. This is the GLX with optional 5.0-liter V-8. (Ford)1984

Many have speculated on Ford's insistence at pushing the turbo on a reluctant public, although the mostviable theory is that management was hoping to develop powerful but efficient engines that would be in the production line should another fuel shortage or economic downturn develop.

Model year production for 1983 came to 108,438 Mustangs. Only 25.7 percent had a four-cylinder engine, as the V-8 zoomed to 30.3 percent popularity. The rest had a V-6. Automatic transmissions were installed in 56 percent, while 24.2 percent had four-speeds and 19.8 had five-speeds. Model year sales were counted at 116,120 cars.

## 1984

For 1984, the base model was the Mustang L, offering a high level of equipment at a relatively low cost, including the 2.3-liter overhead cam four with a four-speed manual transmission, an upshift indicator light to help motorists save fuel and a starter interlock that prevented drivers with manual transmissions from engaging the car's starter without depressing the clutch pedal.

Mustang buyers could now get the base L in hatchback form as well as notchback. Convertible lovers could enjoy droptops in LX form (where the V-6 was now standard), as V-8 GTs or Turbo GTs.

Throttle-body electronic fuel injection was added to the 3.8-liter V-6, which increased the horsepower to 120 and lb.-ft. of torque to 205. Only the SelectShift automatic transmission could be mated to the 1984 V-6.

The 1984 GT came standard with the increased power of the 175-hp 5.0-liter H.O. V-8 with its four-barrel carburetor and a standard five-speed manual transmission. In addition to a striped hood and GT decals, the GT sported a functional front air dam. Integral fog lamps were added to cars produced in early 1984 and thereafter. Automatic overdrive transmission was a new option.

A new, less powerful, version of the 302-cid V-8 joined the lineup in 1984, producing 165 hp with throttle-body injection. It was for non-GT Mustangs ordered with either the three-speed automatic or four-speed automatic unit with overdrive.

Once again, the Turbo GT model combined the efficiency of a 2.3-liter, overhead cam four-cylinder engine with the response of electronic fuel-injection and the on-demand power of turbocharging. By the end of the 1984 model year, only 3,000 Turbo GT hatchbacks and 600 convertibles had been sold for the entire 1983-1984 run, leaving Ford no choice but to cancel the unusual model.

For 1984, the Mustang line offered (top-to-bottom) the high-tech SVO; the GT and Turbo GT; the one-step-up Mustang LX; and the new base Mustang L. (Ford)

Left: The new-for-1984 front cap was designed so airflow worked to reduce lift. (Ford)

Right: All-cloth seats with reclining backs were standard in 1984 Mustangs. (Ford)

The 1984 Mustang GT came with the increased power of a 5.0-liter H.O. V-8 with four-barrel carburetor and a fivespeed transmission. It had a striped hood, GT decals and front air dam. Integral fog lamps were added at midyear. (Ford)

SelectShift automatic transmission was standard in 1984 LX convertibles, which also had four-place seating, a powered retractable top, roll-down quarter windows, and a glass rear window. (Ford)

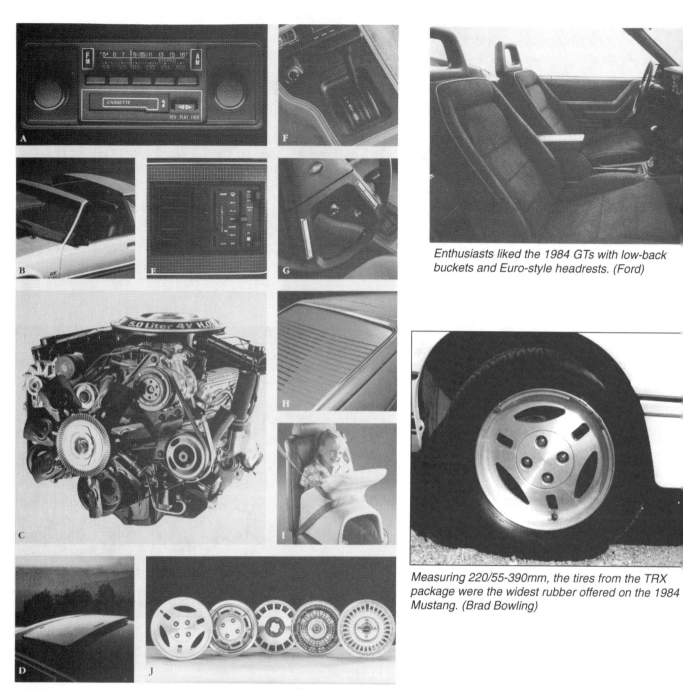

Enthusiasts liked the 1984 GTs with low-back buckets and Euro-style headrests. (Ford)

Measuring 220/55-390mm, the tires from the TRX package were the widest rubber offered on the 1984 Mustang. (Brad Bowling)

1984 extras: A) AM/FM; B) T-Roof; C) 5.0L H.O. V-8; D) sunroof; E) air; F) automatic; G) cruise; H) rear defroster; I) tot seat, and J) wheels. (Ford)

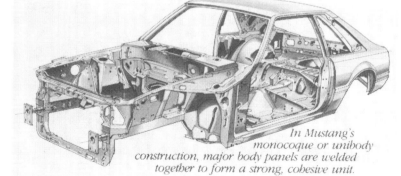

In the 1984 Mustang's monocoque construction, major body panels were welded together to form a strong, cohesive unit. (Ford)

*In Mustang's monocoque or unibody construction, major body panels are welded together to form a strong, cohesive unit.*

## SVO MUSTANG

The SVO Mustang gained a little more acceptance from performance enthusiasts. Targeted toward more affluent, car-conscious consumers, it included such special features as multi-adjustable, articulated bucket seats, a performance suspension with adjustable Koni gas shock absorbers, and a 2.3-liter port-fuel-injected 175 hp turbocharged four-cylinder engine. At $15,596, it cost $8,124 more than a standard Mustang, which sold for $7,472 and $6,018 more than the faster $9,578 V-8 GT.

This exceptionally well-balanced performance machine was a direct result of Ford's involvement in motorsports, and its standard equipment list read like a speed freak's dream. The turbo system included a variable, computer-controlled, electronic turbo boost system and an air-to-air intercooler. Boost could be restricted to 10 psi, to protect the motor during normal driving, while high rpm boost up to 14 psi (the highest of any production engine at the time) was possible.

The SVO engine was linked to a five-speed manual transmission with overdrive fifth gear and a Hurst shifter. It had a Traction-Lok rear axle with a 3.45:1 final drive ratio. Large disc brakes, measuring 10.92 inches in front and 11.25 inches in rear, were fitted at all four corners, and Goodyear NCT 225/60-16 steel-belted radial racing tires (later Goodyear Eagle GTVR "gatorbacks") were mounted on 16x7-inch cast-aluminum wheels.

Only the three-door hatchback body was delivered as an SVO. Identification features included unique dual rectangular halogen headlamps; a front air dam with integral foglamps; a functional hood scoop; rear wheel opening "spats;" a dual-wing rear spoiler; a full wraparound bodyside protection molding system; and dual remote-control mirrors. Inside, the optional leather bucket seats were trimmed with unique all-cloth seat material and the steering wheel, emergency brake handle, shift boot, and shift knob were leather-wrapped. A console with integral armrest and glove box and a premium AM/FM sound system were other attractions.

The SVO got rave reviews in the automotive press. "This may be the best all-around car for the enthusiast driver ever produced by the U.S. industry," said *Road & Track*. "The appeal of the car is in its balance, which transcends even the outstanding individual characteristics." *Car and Driver* said, "This is an important vehicle, a harbinger of things to come . . . a Mustang with a mission." *Motor Trend* called it, "Bold in concept and intelligent in execution."

*In mid-1985, the SVO received flush-mounted, aerodynamic headlamps and turbo improvements that boosted horsepower to 205. Motor Trend called the SVO, "the best street machine the factory has ever produced." (Ford)*

This dual-wing spoiler was standard on the 1984 SVO, but not available on other Mustangs. (Ford)

The 1984 Mustang SVO boasted a sophisticated turbocharged 2.3-liter 175-hp intercooled four coupled to a five-speed transmission. (Ford)

The 1984 SVO came with Sport Performance bucket seats, leather-wrapped wheel and gear shift lever. (Ford)

The 1984 SVO dash with full instrumentation. (Ford)

The SVO's Goodyear NCT steel-belted VR radials had aggressive tread and a low profile for wide footprint and great traction on wet or dry pavement. (Ford)

It was considered to be ahead of its time in 1984. The SVO Mustang suffered because it excelled in a way that no one asked for. (Ford)

*Race driver Jackie Stewart promoted "New Turbo Math" in a 1985 SVO advertisement. Price of the high-tech sports car dropped to $14,521. Sales fell to 1,954. (Ford)*

*In mid-1985, the Mustang SVO Turbo received flush-mounted aero headlamps and turbo improvements that boosted horsepower to 205. (Ford)*

*Here is the first of 5,260 limited edition 1984 20th Anniversary Mustangs made at Dearborn. Plant manager Jim Korwin (tie) shows the Turbo GT three-door to Frances Jones and Don Johnson, who were Ford employees when the first Mustang bowed. (Ford)*

A 20-year legend GT-350 was officially recognized when the first of 5,260 limited-edition Ford Mustangs rolled off the assembly line at Ford's Dearborn, Michigan, plant in 1984. Any GT could be ordered in 20th Anniversary trim, meaning there were V-8 and turbo four versions with hatchback and convertible bodies. Records show that all but 500 were ordered with the V-8 engine.

Anniversary models featured white exteriors and red interiors; unique front fascias; unique bodyside moldings; GT-350 tape stripes; pony badges on the fenders that matched those used on 1965 Mustangs; and a 20th Anniversary instrument panel appliqué. Buyers of the cars received a personalized plate with the vehicle's serial number.

*Ford posed a 20th Anniversary Turbo GT convertible with the first production Mustang made. Features of the 1984 included white paint, red interior, unique front fascia and side moldings, tape stripes, horse ornament, and dash plaque. (Ford)*

*Here are both body styles (with the turbocharged four-cylinder powerplants) of the 20th Anniversary GT-350. (Brad Bowling)*

Ford's use of the GT-350 designation was planned without an okay from Carroll Shelby, who had once been promised that Ford would not use the name without his permission. This led to a legal battle over copyright infringement. Though not high-volume cars, the 1984 SVO and the 20th Anniversary Mustang added to a good year for the marque in general.

For the model year, the Dearborn factory turned out a grand total of 141,480 Mustangs, for a 1.74 industry share. Dealer sales for the same period were counted at 131,762 cars. That was a 13 percent gain for the Mustang among all of the various Ford products. The total included 4,508 SVOs and more than 17,600 Mustang convertibles.

Things were going quite well for the company. In addition to great sales, quality audits for 1984 revealed that Ford was second in quality among all domestic automakers (and its Lincoln-Mercury division was first).

*The Limited Edition 20th Anniversary Mustang GT came out late in 1984. "A Legend Turns 20" said an advertisement for the GT-350 convertible. (Ford)*

*Standard on 1985 LXs, like this convertible, were power steering, power brakes, interval wipers, luxury sound system and right-hand remote-controlled mirror.*

## 1985

The Mustang was now available in LX (base) and GT trim for 1985 alongside the specialty SVO model. Standard equipment on LX models now included power steering, power brakes, interval windshield wipers, a luxury sound system and a right-hand, remote-controlled mirror.

The GT's 5.0-liter H.O. V-8 enjoyed a power boost to 210 hp through the use of low-friction roller tappets and a high-performance camshaft, and the fuel-injected version (still only available with automatic transmission) jumped to 180 hp. 1985 marked the last year a four-barrel carburetor would appear on the 5.0-liter H.O. powerplant before Ford followed the industry trend to fuel-injection.

In the middle of the 1985 model year, the SVO received flush-mounted, aerodynamic headlamps and turbo improvements that boosted horsepower to 205. *Motor Trend* called the SVO, "the best street machine the factory has ever produced" and said it could outrun a Datsun 280-ZX and outhandle a Ferrari 308 or Porsche 944.

Race driver Jackie Stewart, a Ford consultant, promoted "The New Turbo Math" in an advertisement for the SVO. He said "Proven in race cars, the intercooled turbo is now in the Mustang SVO, the only American production car to have this kind of turbo. Ford is in the forefront of this new turbo technology." The price of the all-out sports car dropped slightly to $15,272, but sales also fell to 1,954 units.

*1985 was the final year for a four-barrel carburetor on the 5.0-liter V-8. (Brad Bowling)*

*A 1985 Mustang advertisement drove the car's revived performance image home with the symbol of a trooper in his 1984 "police pursuit" Mustang. (Ford)*

As a final sign that the public was just not ready to pay a premium for a turbocharged four-cylinder when a perfectly good V-8 put out more power, it is interesting to note that Ford made one more attempt to sell the Turbo GT model in 1985 before retiring the idea permanently.

Robert L. Rewey took over as vice president and general manager of Ford Division in 1985. He enjoyed a great first year at the helm, as the company's sales increased the third year in a row. At the start of the model run, Ford made a forecast of 128,000 Mustang sales. In reality, dealer sales leaped to 159,741 units and model year production went to 156,514 cars, an even two percent of total industry output. Records showed that 31.7 percent of all 1985 Mustangs were V-8s and that 7.4 percent of those were fuel-injected. Fours were used in 55.5 percent, with 1.3 percent of those having turbochargers. Another 12.7 percent had the throttle-body-injected V-6.

## 1986

Since 1986 was the last model year before a major face-lift, there were not many equipment or cosmetic changes. Ford boosted its anti-corrosion warranty, added sound-deadening material, and adopted a single-key lock system.

Gone was the four-barrel 5.0-liter H.O.; taking its place was the sequential port fuel-injected 5.0-liter H.O. rated at 200 hp and 285 lb.-ft. of torque. The new V-8 was standard in the GT and an option for the LX.

Model choices began with the sporty and spirited LX coupe or hatchback powered by the standard 88-hp four-cylinder and trimmed with full bodyside striping. Inside were extras like interval wipers, the Luxury Sound package and an AM/FM stereo radio that could be deleted for a credit. A four-speed manual transmission, power brakes and power steering were base equipment. The throttle-body-injected 120-hp V-6 was standard in LX convertibles and optional in other models.

Standard GT equipment was oriented toward the performance-car buyer, with such things as a five-speed manual overdrive transmission; special suspension; Goodyear Eagle VR tires; quick-ratio power steering; and articulated front sports seats.

In 1986, the SVO, still equipped with its 205-hp turbo four, continued with a higher-again $15,272 price tag. It sold a slightly higher total of 3,382 units (bringing its three-year total to 9,844), but 1986 would be its last year of production.

Overall Mustang production was up, too. Way up! For the model year, 244,410 were made. This was a 2.84 percent market share, up almost a full percent! United States dealers moved 175,598 cars for the model year. Apparently, a lot were sold overseas or as 1986 carryovers.

## Ford Woos the Mustang Clubs

"April 17, 1984, marks the 20th anniversary of Mustang," said a letter that Ford's general marketing manager, T.J. Wagner, sent to several car magazines in 1984. " And these 20 years have been spent improving the breed. Today's Mustang offers performance characteristics for all tastes—from the straight-line acceleration of the 205-hp V-8 Mustang GT, available for June production {**Editor's note**: The 205-hp GT never made it to production, and a 210-hp version was introduced in 1985}, to the European-inspired sophisticated technology of the Mustang SVO. One of America's true automotive classics, Mustang has captured the hearts of many and continues to do so in 1984."

Wagner said that dealers would commemorate the Mustang's anniversary across the country with a "Spring Celebration" offering special values on Mustangs, as well as other Ford cars and trucks. "We invite you to stop by your local Ford dealer to review the Ford line and to preview that latest genre of Mustang—the Mustang SVO. As stated in our advertising, 'This Machine Speaks For Itself' when it comes to performance and handling," he added.

This letter was also circulated to Mustang Club of America members to try to spark enthusiasts' interest in the upcoming SVO. Accompanying the correspodence was an 11x5-inch, eight-page booklet titled *The Mustang Story*. It showed a white 1964 hardtop and a black SVO hatchback on the cover and traced the marque's history inside. The undated piece of literature did not mention a 20th anniversary car; however, such a model was released later on.

The 1986 three-door in the foreground has the hood and rear panel GT emblems as well as the 5.0 engine badge. The convertible in the background is also a 1986 Mustang GT. The heart of the GT was a 200-hp multi-port-injected small-block V-8. (Ford)

Enthusiasts loved the lightness of the coupe body with a 5.0-liter hidden underneath; so did the cops. (Ford)

Pictured above
from (left to right)
Donald E. Petersen
Philip Caldwell
Harold A. Poling

*These men steered Ford and the Mustang back to success in the 1980s: (left to right) Donald E. Peterson, Philip Caldwell, and Harold A. Poling. (Ford)*

*1982 Ford Mustang GT (Ford)*

# CHAPTER 9

MUSTANG

## The Mazda Mustang? (1987-93)

*A 1987 revamp of the Mustang LX included new front/rear fascias, aero headlamps, and a lower feature line accented with heavy moldings. Inside was a redesigned instrument panel, pod-mounted headlamp switches, and a center console. (Ford)*

*How could Ford consider replacing this with . . . (Brad Bowling)*

## 1987

Perhaps the most important aspect of the 1987 Mustang is not that it retained the pony car's position as one of the fastest American performance cars available, but that Ford was considering replacing it with a Japanese-designed front-driver.

Five years earlier, corporate planners had considered development of a project codenamed SN-8 (Ford-speak for sporty, North American project no. 8) that would replace the Mustang's rear-drive Fox platform with a small, high-tech, European-style chassis. Fortunately for the happiness of Mustangers everywhere, this scheme was not approved but another plan was soon hatched to have Japanese partner Mazda develop a similar platform that would be shared between the two companies and built in a plant in Flat Rock, Michigan.

It might seem unusual for a company to try to kill off a successful, legendary product that's selling in high numbers, but remember that automakers must think anywhere from three to eight years down the road and consider all economic, political and market possibilities. Clearly, Ford was concerned about getting caught in the middle of another fuel crisis with showrooms full of thirsty V-8 performance cars; otherwise, it would not have spent so many development and marketing dollars on the 1979-86 turbocharged models. Chrysler had earned its financial salvation by selling millions of bog-slow four-cylinder K-cars in the early 1980s, whereas Ford went from red ink to billions of dollars in cash reserves by creating an exciting, but balanced, product line anchored by its top-selling Taurus.

Ford saw in Mazda a way to get a "next-generation Mustang" without committing hundreds of millions of dollars. Mazda stood to benefit from the deal by further aligning itself with an American corporate giant and perhaps escape the brunt of threatened import taxes and tariffs.

Traditionalists were opposed to the idea of killing everything the all-American, rear-drive, V-8 Mustang stood for. Only after publishing pictures of a sleek-looking, front-drive prototype wearing the Mustang name was Ford made aware of the public outrage over its decision. Car magazines rallied, and the resulting letter-writing campaign convinced executives that buyer loyalty was nothing to tamper with.

The "Mazda Mustang" made its appearance in Ford showrooms for model year 1989 as the Probe. It is interesting to note that Ford never reported losing Mustang sales to the Probe or vice versa—apparently, there weren't a lot customers who saw the choices as similar. Mazda's version of the shared platform was the MX-6.

Although the 1987 Mustang was not an all-new car, the year did bring styling changes that were significant enough to mark a new era in the nameplate's history and performance numbers that brought new Mustang buyers to the showroom. The attractive revamp included new

*. . . this? (Brad Bowling)*

front and rear body fascias, aero headlamps, and a prominent lower feature line accented with heavy moldings. It was the first major face-lift since the Fox-based Mustang debuted in 1979.

Not only was the new car pleasant to the eye, but the wind tunnel as well. In base hatchback form the slick little pony registered a 0.36 drag coefficient (compared to the 1979 model's 0.44), with the bulky GT three-door turning out a 0.38. Other changes inside the Mustang were a redesigned instrument panel that created a roomier passenger compartment, pod-mounted headlamp switches, and a center console.

The new Mustang retained a 100.5-inch wheelbase and 179.3-inch overall length. It was again 69.1-inches wide and about 52-inches high (depending on body style) with a track of 56.6 inches in the front and a slightly narrower 57 inches in the rear. Weights for various models ranged from 2,862 pounds (base coupe) to 3,214 pounds (GT convertible)—roughly a 100-pound increase model-for-model over 1986 specs.

The standard engine in the base LX model notchbacks, hatchbacks, and convertibles was the ubiquitous 2.3-liter four, improved for 1987 with a new multiport fuel-injection system. Its output was up slightly to 90 hp and 130 lb.-ft. of torque. Optional in LX models and standard in GTs was a 225-hp 5.0-liter V-8—its 25-hp gain being the result of a return to a pre-1986 cylinder head design. The V-6 and turbocharged four from 1986 were no longer offered. The SVO was gone, but the LX coupe with the 5.0-liter H.O. V-8 seemed nearly as exciting to speed freaks on a budget, and at far less money.

Both 1987 Mustang engines came with either a five-speed manual transmission or an optional automatic overdrive transmission. Other technical features

included vented disc brakes in front, rear drum brakes, and a modified MacPherson strut front suspension with coil springs. The rear suspension featured a live axle with links and coil springs.

The lengthy standard equipment list for the LX model also included a maintenance-free battery; a coolant recovery system; electronic ignition and engine controls; a three-speed heater/defroster; an inside hood release; a dual-note horn; a high-mount rear brake lamp; a 6,000-rpm tachometer; P105/75R14 black sidewall tires; two-speed electric windshield wipers; blacked-out radio antenna, door handles, door lock bezels, and front and rear bumper strips; body-color front lower fender extensions; dual halogen headlamps; dual remote-control mirrors; a body-color rear spoiler; full, single pinstripes; full wheel covers; color-keyed carpeting; a cigarette lighter; a center console; inside door trim panels; a trip odometer, voltmeter, temperature gauge, fuel gauge, and oil pressure gauge; a day/night rearview mirror; twin visor mirrors; an electronic AM/FM stereo radio with four speakers and an integral digital clock; color-keyed seatbelts; cloth seat trim; a two-spoke steering wheel; and dual sun visors.

In addition to, or instead of, these features, three-door hatchbacks had tinted glass; a cargo area cover; and a lockable glove box. Convertibles also had tinted glass; a retractable power cloth top; power vent windows; roll-down rear quarter windows; a rear luggage rack; and a top dust cover.

Mustang GTs added alert lights; a Traction-Lok axle; a sport-tuned exhaust system with dual outlets; a remote-control fuel-filler door; nitrogen gas shocks; a luxury sound package; front and rear stabilizer bars; power steering; a tilt steering wheel; a Quadra-Shock rear suspension; a 7,000-rpm tachometer; P225/60VR15

The 1987 GT suspension was really a piece of high-tech work. (Ford)

The Mustang 5.0-liter (302-cid) H.O. V-8 had electronic fuel injection. (Ford)

black sidewall tires; a body-color front lower fascia with air scoop fender extensions; cast-aluminum wheels; a driver's footrest; a front air dam; a scooped hood; body skirting; and wider, louver-slotted tail lamps.

Getting lots of attention was the convertible, priced at under $13,000, in LX form, or under $16,000, with GT equipment. About one out of every eight 1987 Mustangs built (a total of 20,328 cars) were reported to be droptops.

Total model year production was 159,145 units for 1987. Dealer sales for the model year hit 163,392. Both numbers were noticeably down from 1986, and industry analysts were ready to write off the Mustang as an "old" rear-drive car that had had its day. Mustang sales were only beginning to take off again, which would disprove the predictions of an early demise. Since the Mustang's major development and tooling costs had already been absorbed, it wound up generating extremely good profits. Ford maintained it, without any really major alterations, all the way through the end of model year 1993.

## 1988

After its extensive 1987 makeover, the 1988 Mustang was virtually unchanged. LX models got a battery with more "juice" and that was about the extent of improvements. Three basic body styles were again offered in LX trim, with a pair of GTs also available. Prices jumped around $700 per closed model and around $1,100 for convertibles. The cars ranged from $8,700 up to $16,700.

Engine choices remained the basic 2.3-liter four-cylinder or the pavement-pounding 5.0-liter H.O. V-8. The latter was often compared to 1988's flock of "high-tech" powerplants and regarded as an old-fashioned, but still exciting engine. As *Motor Trend* writer Tony Swan said, "Ironically, the best all-out performer

*Three basic body styles were again offered in 1988 in LX trim, with a pair of GTs also available. Prices jumped around $700 per closed model and around $1,100 for convertibles. This is the 5.0-liter GT convertible. (Ford)*

The 1989 GT hatchback sold for $13,272. It included such standard equipment as aero body upgrades, the 225-hp 5.0-liter H.O. V-8 and a five-speed manual transmission. (Ford)

The 1989 Mustang LX two-door came standard with the 2.3-liter four-cylinder engine. (Ford)

In 1989, the Mustang LX 5.0-L Sport was offered for the first time in all three body styles. It combined GT's performance attributes with the smoother body of the LX series. (Ford)

*The LX with 5.0-liter V-8 once again provided bang for the buck. (Ford)*

in the Ford power ladder is another yestertech 5.0-liter pushrod V-8, the one that's almost as venerable as those employed by GM."

This was the year of a boom for the Mustang, as model year output zoomed to 211,225 cars (of which 33,344 were convertibles). Dealer sales for the same period were 170,601 units.

## 1989

1989 was a milestone year in which the six-millionth Mustang was assembled. Prices climbed again and each model gained a small amount of weight, but the engine and technical features stayed about the same. "Mustang is the remedy for dull, boring driving," said one sales brochure. "If you don't believe that, you haven't driven one lately."

The base Mustang LX was fun to drive with its responsive 2.3-liter four-cylinder engine; a five-speed manual transmission; power front disc brakes; modified MacPherson strut suspension; 20.0:1-ratio rack-and-pinion power steering; styled road wheels and P195/75R14 black sidewall steel-belted radial tires. Comfortable interiors, with cloth reclining seats, were standard. The three-model line had list prices from $9,050 to $14,140, and with the optional Special Value Group buyers got power locks, dual electric mirrors, an electronic AM/FM stereo with a cassette tape player and, more.

The GT hatchback ($13,272) and convertible ($17,512) added such niceties as aero body upgrades; the 225 hp 5.0-liter H.O. V-8; a five-speed manual transmission with overdrive fifth gear; 14.7:1 ratio power rack-and-pinion steering; a taut handling suspension system; and P225/60VR15 Unidirectional Goodyear Eagle tires on 15-inch diameter, 16-spoke, cast-aluminum wheels.

The GT suspension was really a piece of high-tech work, with gas-pressurized hydraulic struts, variable-rate coil springs and a stabilizer bar up front. The rear also featured variable-rate coils, plus a Quadra-shock setup with vertically-mounted, gas-pressurized shock absorbers; horizontally-mounted, freon-filled axle dampers; and a fat stabilizer bar.

A new LX 5.0-L Sport series combined the entry-level model, 5.0-liter V-8 and the GT's multi-adjustable seats. Prices started at $11,410 for the coupe and reached $17,001 for the convertible.

From the time production started on Aug. 31, 1988, to when it ended on September 5, 1989 (later than usual), the factory at Dearborn cranked out 46 of the new Mustangs every hour. Model year output fell just slightly, to 209,769 cars and dealer sales were 161,148 units. A most revealing statistic was that 51.4 percent of all Mustangs built carried V-8 engines. The extreme popularity of the 5.0-liter H.O. Mustang had obviously given the marque a new lease on life, primarily based on its reputation and appeal as a high-performance car.

*Identifying Mustangs was a lot easier in the late1980s than it had been in the1960s. This1989 is clearly an LX with four-cylinder engine because there is no 5.0-liter badge. (Ford)*

### 1990

For 1990, Ford gave the Mustang a driver's side air bag and standard rear shoulder belts. Map pockets were added to the door panels, while tilt steering and an armrest on the console disappeared. As the company promised, the Mustang tradition was recognized in sales literature. It included passages such as, "Mustang, the first pony car, brought affordable sporty car performance and styling to every street and highway in America. And what it did best 25 years ago, it still does the best today."

Sedans, hatchbacks, and convertibles again came in LX and LX 5.0-liter series, with the hatchback and convertible available as GTs. The LX 5.0-liter models had the same beefy suspension and tires as the GT, while the GT package added spoilers and an air dam.

The base three-model line had list prices from $9,456 to $15,141. Standard equipment included the 2.3-liter four with electronic fuel injection; power front disc brakes; five-speed manual overdrive transmission; P195/75R14 black sidewall tires; sport bucket seats; and a tachometer, plus all the other regular Mustang features. This year, the LX had the 14.7:1 steering of last year's GT and new 14x5-inch stamped steel wheels with turbine wheel covers.

*Buyers of 1990 LX 5.0-liter convertibles got the same no-extra-cost "Special Value Package" as hatchback buyers, but it was only a $328 "value" for them, as some of the option's ingredients were already standard on convertibles. (Ford)*

*All Mustangs, starting with the 1987 model, were available with standard five-speed manual transmissions or optional four-speed automatics (shown is a 1990 model GT). (Ford)*

The LX 2.3-liter also continued its tradition of affordability, by offering Special Value Packages all its own, which included power locks; dual electric remote-controlled mirrors; power side windows; a premium sound system; and speed control (worth $835) for no extra charge. Convertible buyers got the same package free, but it was only a $328 "value" for them, as some of these ingredients were standard on convertibles. The LX 5.0-liter models offered three body styles, with prices starting at $12,164 for the coupe and reaching $18,949 for the convertible. The GT hatchback ($13,986) and convertible ($18,805) again added aero body upgrades and a long list of additional goodies. The LX 5.0-liter Sport GT option rose in price to $1,259. The factory built 128,189 of the 1990 Mustangs, making it the fifth most popular compact car sold in America.

*All 1990 Mustangs received driver-side air bags as standard equipment. (Brad Bowling)*

*The five-spoke wheel seen on this 1991 convertible was one of three designs offered on the GT during the1987-1993 run. (Ford)*

## 1991

The 1991 Mustang models had 2.9 to 3.3 percent price increases. That put even the lowest-priced Mustang over the $10,000 barrier for the first time. Sedans, hatchbacks and convertibles again came in LX and LX 5.0-liter series, with the hatchback and convertible available as GTs.

The base three-model line had list prices from $10,157 to $16,222. Standard equipment included the overhead cam 2.3-liter four with electronic multi-port fuel injection, power front disc brakes (rear drums), five-speed manual overdrive transmission, and P195/75R14 black sidewall all-season LX tires.

EPA mileage figures for the 1991 models varied by engine/transmission combination. The four-cylinder received a 21/28 (city/highway miles per gallon) rating with the five-speed and 22/30 with automatic. For the multi-port fuel-injected V-8, the figures were 18/25 with a five-speed and 17/24 with the automatic. These figures reflect the standard rear axle ratios.

The base LX 5.0-liter models offered three body styles, with prices starting at $13,270 and climbing to $19,242. The GT hatchback ($15,034) and convertible ($19,864) had the aero body upgrades.

*1991's GT hatchback was little changed from previous models. (Ford)*

```
POWERTRAIN

Engine and Transaxle                         Drive ratios

2.3-liter EFI I-4; Manual five-speed overdrive   3.45
2.3-liter EFI I-4; Automatic overdrive  3.73
5.0-liter EFI HO V-8; Manual five-speed overdrive 2.73 (a)
            (3.08 Traction-Lok axle optional)
5.0-liter EFI HO V-8; Automatic overdrive        2.73 (a)
            (3.27 Traction-Lok axle optional)
(a) Includes Traction-Lok as standard
```

| DIMENSIONS AND CAPACITIES* | SEDAN/HATCHBACK | CONVERTIBLE |
|---|---|---|
| Wheelbase | 100.5 | 100.5 |
| Overall Length | 179.6 | 179.6 |
| Overall height | 52.1 | 52.1 |
| Overall width | 68.3 | 68.3 |
| Tread, front | 56.6 | 56.6 |
| Tread, rear | 57.0 | 57.0 |
| Curb weight (lbs.) | 2,761/2,827 | 2,975 |

FRONT

| | SEDAN/HATCHBACK | CONVERTIBLE |
|---|---|---|
| Head room | 37.0 | 37.6 |
| Shoulder room | 55.5 | 55.5 |
| Hip room | 56.1 | 56.1 |
| Leg room (max.) | 41.7 | 41.7 |

REAR

| | SEDAN/HATCHBACK | CONVERTIBLE |
|---|---|---|
| Head room | 35.9/35.7 | 37.0 |
| Shoulder room | 54.3 | 48.9 |
| Hip room | 47.1 | 38.5 |
| Leg room (min.) | 30.7 | 30.7 |

| | SEDAN/HATCHBACK | CONVERTIBLE |
|---|---|---|
| Luggage compartment(cu. ft.) | 10.0/12.2 | 6.4 |
| EPA Volume Index (cu. ft.) | 83.5/83.3 | 80.7 |
| Fuel tank capacity (gals.) | 15.4 | 15.4 |

```
CHASSIS
Type of construction                 Unitized body
Front suspension
        Type                         Modified MacPherson strut
                                     with separate spring on
                                     lower arm; both strut and
                                     arm rubber bushed at
                                     attachment points
        Springs                      LX (four-cyl.) -- Helical
                                     coil GT, 5.0-liter LX --
                                     Helical coil, variable rate,
                                     rubber insulated
        Shock absorbers              LX (four-cyl.) -- Integral
                                     with strut, Nitrogen gas-
                                     pressurized hydraulic
        Stabilizer bar diameter      LX (four-cyl. -- .94 in.
                                     GT, 5.0-liter LX -- 1.3 in.
```

*The basic specifications of 1990 Mustangs varied according to powertrain and body style selections, although all models shared the same type of suspension system.*

225 horsepower at 4200 rpm. 300 ft. lbs. of torque at 3200 rpm. Gas-pressurized struts up front. Quadra-Shock system in the rear. And four patches of extra fat rubber on the pavement. Mustang GT. Grab onto the five-speed and make your move. It's a kick in the tranny.

**Best-built American cars.**
The best-built American cars are built by Ford. This is based on an average of consumer-reported problems in a series of surveys of all Ford and competitive '81-'89 models designed and built in North America. At Ford, "Quality is Job 1."

**All 1990 Mustangs are equipped with a driver air bag supplemental restraint system.**

# Ford Mustang GT

## 225 horses are bound to kick something.

Buckle up—together we can save lives.

Have you driven a Ford...lately?

*"225 horses are bound to kick something," said this catchy ad for the 1990 Mustang GT. All of the 1990 models were equipped with a driver-side air bag supplemental restraint system. (Ford)*

*The 1992 Mustang got several new color choices and an optional six-way power driver's seat. The LX convertible seen here has 5.0-liter V-8 fender call-outs. (Ford)*

## 1992

Mustang production for model year 1991 totaled 98,737 units, a 1.7-percent share of the overall market (down from 2.1 percent the previous season). Domestic dealers marketed 80,247 Mustangs for the calendar year. For 1991, 63 percent of all Mustangs, a total of 62,204 cars, had V-8s below their hoods and 36,533 had four-cylinder powerplants.

There were few changes to report in 1992, when the Mustang again came in LX and LX 5.0-liter series, with the hatchback and convertible available as GTs. This year's GT convertible had the dubious honor of being the first Mustang with a suggested retail price over $20,000.

The base three-model line had list prices from $10,215 to $16,899. Standard equipment included the overhead

*The 1992 LX 5.0-liter convertible was base-priced at $20,293. Standard extras for this series included the 5.0-liter H.O. V-8 with electronic fuel-injection, Traction-Lok and dual sport-tuned exhaust system. (Ford)*

*The monochrome look was popular in the early 1990s. This 1992 LX convertible with 5.0-liter V-8 was a tastefully done example. (Ford)*

cam 2.3-liter four with electronic fuel-injection, power front disc brakes (rear drums), five-speed manual overdrive transmission, and P195/75R14 black sidewall all-season tires. The base LX 5.0-liter models offered three body styles, with prices starting at $13,422 to $19,644. The GT hatchback ($15,243) and convertible ($20,199) had the aero body upgrades.

When all was said and done, the 1992 Mustang had a 79,280-unit model year, making it the fifth most popular compact car in the United States. Production was split almost evenly between four-cylinder models (36,307 made) and V-8s (36,893 built). Domestic dealers reported sales of 86,036.

# MUSTANG

*The lower perimeter skirting on the sides and rear of the GT 1992 model announced the car's name. (Ford)*

## 1993

In this, the last year for what was essentially a 1979 design, the 14-year-old Fox-platform Mustang (one of the longest runs in American automaking history) came in LX, LX 5.0-liter, and GT series. The LX models were $10,719 for the sedan, $11,224 for the hatchback, and $17,548 for the convertible.

Standard Mustang LX equipment included a driver's side air bag; a heavy-duty 75-ampere alternator; a heavy-duty 58-ampere battery; power brakes with front discs and rear drums; color-keyed front and rear bumper rub stripes; full carpeting; a digital clock; a center console with armrest; the 2.3-liter four-cylinder engine; a fuel cap tether; tinted glass; a color-keyed cloth headliner; dual horns; luxury sound insulation; dome, cargo area, under-hood, ashtray and glove box lamps; dual, manual remote-controlled rearview mirrors; dual covered visor mirrors; color-keyed bodyside moldings; an AM/FM radio with electronic tuning and four speakers; reclining low-back bucket seats; a front stabilizer bar; power steering; bodyside paint stripes; a tachometer; a five-speed manual transmission; a trip odometer; cloth upholstery; a headlight warning chime; finned wheel covers; intermittent windshield wipers; and P195/75R14 steel-belted radial all-season black sidewall tires.

Hatchbacks also had a carpeted cargo area; a pivoting map lamp; a split-back, fold-down rear seat; and a rear spoiler. Convertibles also came with a power top; a top cover; a glass back window; power side windows; dual-powered, outside rearview mirrors; a trunk luggage rack; and a Lock Group including power door locks, a deck lid release, and a fuel filler door release.

LX 5.0-liter models were priced at $13,926 for the sedan, $14,710 for the hatchback, and $20,293 for the convertible. Standard extras for cars in this series (plus or instead of the basic equipment listing) included the 5.0-liter H.O. V-8 with electronic fuel-injection; Traction-Lok differential; a dual, sport-tuned exhaust system; articulated Sport seats with power lumbar support; constant-ratio power steering; a leather-wrapped steering wheel; a sport-type suspension package; cloth/vinyl upholstery; diagnostic warning lights; cast-aluminum wheels; and P225/55ZR16 black sidewall all-season steel-belted radial tires.

The GT hatchback ($15,747) and convertible ($20,848) also had a front air dam; fog lights; color-keyed, flared rocker panel moldings; no bodyside paint stripes; and performance tires of the same size as LX 5.0-liter models.

Mustang production amounted to 101,095 units for model year 1993, an increase due in part, to the fact that the figures included examples of the all-new 1994 model, which entered production in the fall of 1993 and gained immediate popularity.

## What Anniversary Model?

Because 1989 marked the 25th anniversary, Mustang collectors anticipated a really spectacular model and celebration. None came, at least not in 1989. There were whispers of a Jack Roush-built birthday GT with a 351-cid V-8, twin turbochargers and 400 hp, but no one at Ford would confirm its existence and it never came to pass.

In April of 1989, West Coast tuner Steve Saleen announced his Anaheim, California-based company would produce a limited run of 250 SSC Mustangs available only as white hatchbacks. With 300-plus hp on tap from the modified (but 50-states certified) 5.0-liter V-8 and a slew of high-tech suspension, stereo and body-stiffening components, the SSC was the public's "unofficial" choice for a 25th anniversary model.

In response to anniversary car questions, Ford clumsily sidestepped the issue by claiming that the first Mustang was a 1965 model, making 1990 the "proper" year for a 25th anniversary celebration. Technically, Ford was correct, but that doesn't explain why the company issued "anniversary" models for 1984!

The truth of the matter is probably two-fold. Considering that the 1984 GT-350 birthday model kept Ford lawyers in trademark court against Carroll Shelby, the legal department was understandably skittish about any more commemorative packages. Also, the Mazda Mustang question led to some corporate confusion about just how much support Ford wanted to lend fans of the Fox-platform cars.

In 1990, the company released 3,800 Emerald Green 5.0-liter LX convertibles with special anniversary badges, but the timing of the offering put off fans.

*After a year of waiting, this Emerald Green 5.0-liter convertible with white interior was released as the 25th anniversary model. (Ford)*

*The 1992 LX 5.0-liter convertible was base-priced at $20,293. Standard extras for this series included the 5.0-liter H.O. V-8 with electronic fuel-injection, Traction-Lok, and dual sport-tuned exhaust system. (Ford)*

*The last of the brick-shaped LXs was in 1993. (Ford)*

# CHAPTER 10

# MUSTANG

## A New Mustang for a New Millennium (1994-2001)

With a 5.0-liter sequential electronic fuel-injected H.O. V-8, stainless steel dual exhaust system, and suspension with variable-rate coils, gas struts and shocks, and Quadra-shock rear suspension, the 1994 GT was spirited. (Ford)

A substantially restyled 1994 Mustang was introduced Oct. 15, 1993. It remained a front-engine/rear-drive machine with a muscle car flavor. In reality, its improvements were evolutionary, rather than revolutionary. (Ford)

## 1994

The substantially restyled 1994 Mustang, a front-engine/rear-drive machine with a muscle car flavor, was introduced Oct. 15, 1993. In reality, its improvements were evolutionary, rather than revolutionary — just what the fans of the first Mustangs wanted.

"Team Mustang," a group of Ford employees dedicated to the new car's concept and design, set up camp in an old Montgomery Ward warehouse south of Dearborn late in 1990. They were on a tight budget and even tighter schedule to meet aggressive goals for ride, handling, steering, powertrain performance, brakes, climate control, comfort, and noise/vibration/harshness (NVH).

The team's surveys of Mustang owners and collectors turned up a desire for a car that was not a clone of European or Japanese vehicles. At a time when cars from Germany and Japan were considered the standard-bearers for sophistication and quality, Ford was happy to continue producing a traditional American-designed-engineered-built package.

Ford considered the 1994 to be an all-new Mustang, although it was technically a giant evolutionary step for the Fox platform introduced in 1979. While under development, the 1994 was referred to as "SN-95," which translates to sporty, North American concept no. 95, but the updated platform itself was known as the Fox-4. The SN-95 contained 1,850 parts, 1,330 of them new. Ford's visual aid for this point was a stripped chassis on a rotisserie that displayed areas in white (carryovers—mostly simple floorpans and non-structural bracketry), red (all new components), green (GT-specific—such as upper strut tower brace) and yellow (convertible-only pieces—such as the anti-resonant mass vibration damper and underbody X-brace).

Engineering goals for stiffness and chassis rigidity that far exceeded the first Fox-derived cars were met. The new convertible improved by 80 percent in the area of chassis torsion and 40 percent in bending, while the coupe saw upgrades of 44 percent in torsion and 56 percent in bending.

Coupe stiffness was achieved through a variety of clever techniques, such as bonding the windshield and backlight to their frames with a rigid urethane adhesive and by enlarging certain box sections as the rocker panels and roof rails. The GT structure was further stiffened by the addition of a bolt-in brace that tied together the front strut towers and the cowl/firewall, a trick Mustang modifiers had been performing since the mid-1980s. The desire for a tight, noise-free body is one factor that led to dropping the fastback model from the Mustang family, as opening a large hatch lid on a car is equivalent to taking off the top of a shoebox.

The convertible benefited from a thicker gauge of metal in the rocker panels (from 0.8 to 2.3 mm) as well as other stress-bearing panels. To ensure a quiet top-less ride, a 25-pound tuned mass damper was installed inside the right front fender well. Looking ahead, Ford's engineers designed the 1994 around upcoming side-impact specifications that involved ramming the side of the car with a 3,000-pound test sled traveling at 33 mph.

If the 1993 Mustang was shaped like a bar of soap, then the 1994 was that same bar after sitting in the shower for a few days. From the front, the new pony had a distinct family resemblance to several models from the past, without really copying any of them directly. The aerodynamic headlights sat on either side of a curved grille cavity that, when combined with the smooth bumper cover and integrated air dam, provided a pleasant, smiling face. The long-hood/short-deck theme was somewhat re-interpreted for the 1994 as the sloping, air-cheating hood no longer gave the impression of hiding an extremely large engine. Whereas the 1965 fastback body had married a gently radiused roof to an otherwise slab-sided and angular body, the 1994's roofline seemed to perfectly complement the curvy body. Three-element taillights (lying horizontally on the 1994, unlike the 1965's vertical units) recalled some of the Mustang's early heritage and contributed to the impression of great body width when viewed from directly behind. A twin-cockpit theme ran throughout the new interior.

At 181.5 inches, the 1994 was 2.4 inches longer bumper-to-bumper than the 1979 it was essentially replacing. The wheelbase increased between the two models by 0.9 inches to a total of 101.3. The most striking change was in the dimension of width, wherein the 1994 was a muscular 78.1 inches compared to the slab-sided 1979's 69.1 inches. The 1994 Mustang's roofline was 1.4-inches higher than the 1979 at 52.9 inches.

In addition to being more modern in appearance, the 1994 Mustang received some power upgrades. A torquey 3.8-liter 145-hp V-6 replaced the four-cylinder powerplant as the base engine, representing a horsepower increase of 38%. It was the same unit already doing duty for happy Taurus, Thunderbird, and Lincoln Continental customers. The 5.0-liter H.O. V-8 was rated 215-hp at 4,200 rpm for 1994, courtesy of a low-profile intake manifold (to fit under the more steeply raked hood) and pistons cast in hypereutectic aluminum alloy. Both engines were available with standard five-speed manual or optional four-speed automatic transmissions.

The base model wore 15-inch steel wheels with plastic covers and 205/65-15 all-season black sidewall Goodyear Eagle GA tires. As an option, those same tires could be mounted on three-spoke, 15-inch alloy wheels.

## PAINT AND TRIM COLORS

| Exterior Paint Colors | Interior Trim Colors | | | | |
|---|---|---|---|---|---|
| | Bright Red | Saddle | Opal Grey | Black | White* |
| Canary Yellow Clearcoat** | | | ■ | ■ | ■ |
| Vibrant Red Clearcoat** | | | ■ | ■ | ■ |
| Rio Red Tinted Clearcoat | ■ | ■ | ■ | ■ | ■ |
| Laser Red Tinted Clearcoat Metallic | | ■ | ■ | ■ | ■ |
| Iris Clearcoat Metallic | | | ■ | ■ | ■ |
| Bright Blue Clearcoat Metallic | | | ■ | ■ | ■ |
| Deep Forest Green Clearcoat Metallic | | ■ | ■ | | ■ |
| Teal Clearcoat Metallic | | | ■ | ■ | ■ |
| Black Clearcoat | ■ | ■ | ■ | ■ | ■ |
| Opal Frost Clearcoat Metallic | ■ | | ■ | ■ | ■ |
| Crystal White | ■ | ■ | ■ | ■ | |

*Convertible model only. **Exclusive Mustang GT color. Note: the convertible roof is available in White, Black, and Saddle.

## PREFERRED EQUIPMENT PACKAGES AND OPTIONS

| P = Package feature (content subject to change) <br> O = Optional feature  S = Standard feature | Mustang | | GT |
|---|---|---|---|
| | 241A | 243A | 261A |
| Group 1: power side windows, door locks and decklid release (standard in convertible and GT) | – | P | S |
| Group 2: speed control; dual illuminated visor mirrors (standard in convertible and GT); electronic AM/FM stereo radio with cassette player and premium sound system; 15" cast aluminum wheels (16" wheels standard on GT) | – | P | P |
| Group 3: remote keyless/illuminated entry system and cargo net | – | P | O |
| CFC-free manual-control air conditioning | P | P | P |
| Electronic AM/FM stereo sound system with cassette player | P | – | – |
| Anti-lock brake system | O | O | P |
| Anti-theft system | – | O | O |
| Removable hardtop roof* | – | O | O |
| Rear window defroster | O | O | O |
| Bodyside moldings | – | O | O |
| Front floor mats | – | O | O |
| Electronic 4-speed automatic overdrive transmission | O | O | O |
| Engine block immersion heater | O | O | O |
| Optional axle ratio | – | – | O |
| 15" cast aluminum wheels | O | P | – |
| 17" cast aluminum wheels with 245/45ZR17 BSW performance tires | – | – | O |
| Mach 460 electronic AM/FM stereo sound system with cassette player | – | O | O |
| Compact disc player** | – | O | O |
| Leather seating surfaces | – | – | O |
| Leather seating surfaces (White upholstery only in convertible) | – | O | – |
| Power driver's seat credit (deletes standard power driver's seat) | – | O | O |

*Must be factory-ordered. See your dealer for date of availability and selection of colors. **Requires electronic AM/FM stereo/cassette premium sound system or the Mach 460 sound system.

*Paint and trim colors for the 1994 Mustangs appear in the top part of this chart. The bottom shows Preferred Equipment and Options. (Ford)*

Ford's surveys showed Mustangers wanted a car that was not a clone of European or Japanese cars. This resulted in an all-American design (1994 shown). (Ford)

Standard equipment on the 1994 included reclining cloth bucket seats with cloth head restraints and a four-way power driver's seat. (Ford)

The 1994 GT convertible listed for $21,790. It had 16x7.5-inch five-spoke cast-aluminum wheels, a 150-mph speedometer, GT bucket seats with cloth trim, cloth head restraints, and a leather-wrapped steering wheel. (Ford)

The $17,280 1994 GT coupe had front and rear fascias with GT nomenclature and black finish on the lower rear end, Mustang GT fender badges, fog lamps, and a single-wing rear spoiler. (Ford)

*Before it appeared in showrooms, the new-ford 1994 Mustang was a hit on the show circuit. (John Gunnell)*

Standard GT wheels were five-spoke, 16-inch rims wearing 225/55-16 Firestone Firehawk rubber. An optional upgrade for the GT was a set of three-spoke, 17-inchers shod with 245/45-17 Goodyear Eagle GTs. Base and GT cars came standard with four-wheel disc brakes—an improvement long awaited by Mustang fans everywhere—although ABS was an extra-cost option.

The car's 30-year heritage was evident in the styling, performance and advertising. "It is what it was," said the slogan used to advertise the car. The body sides were even scooped out to resemble the "coves" of the original pony car. "This car will appeal to younger and older buyers alike," Ford Division general manager Ross H. Roberts said, adding, "There was no 'typical' Mustang buyer back in 1964 when the original came out (and) we're counting on rekindling that fervor."

The 1994 Mustang offered two models in each of two car lines: The base coupe was priced at $13,365 and its convertible counterpart retailed for $20,160. Standard equipment included front and rear body-colored fascias

*The 1994 Mustang offered two models in each of two car lines. The base coupe was priced at $13,365 and the convertible counterpart at $20,160. Shown is the base convertible. (Ford)*

with Mustang nomenclature; Mustang emblem fender badges; aerodynamic halogen headlamps; wraparound tail lamps featuring three horizontal elements; dual, electric, remote-control mirrors (convex mirror on right-hand side); color-keyed rocker panel moldings; driver and passenger air bags; a front ashtray; three-point "active" seat belts; sixteen-ounce carpeting; a cigarette lighter; a digital quartz clock; a stand-alone console with armrest, storage bin, cup-holder and CD/cassette storage; a driver's side foot rest; a glove box; full-instrumentation (including tachometer and low-fluid lamp); an extensive Light Group assortment; dual visor mirrors with covers; reclining cloth bucket seats with cloth head restraints and four-way power driver's seat; split-back fold-down rear seat (not in convertibles); leather-wrapped shift knob and parking brake lever with automatic transmission; stalk-mounted controls; tilt steering with center horn-blow; soft, flow-through vinyl door trim panels with full armrests and cloth or vinyl inserts; a color-keyed headliner (including convertibles); color-keyed cloth sun visors; heavy-duty electrical components; power, side window de-misters; electronic engine control (EEC-V) system; stainless steel exhaust system; 15.4-gallon fuel tank with tethered cap; full tinted glass; Power Vent ventilation system; dual-note horn; a Power Lock Group option; a tunnel-mounted parking brake; an ETR stereo sound system with four 24-watt speakers; constant-ratio, power rack-and-pinion steering; modified MacPherson front suspension with stabilizer bar, links and coil springs; gas-pressurized front struts and rear shock absorbers; a mini-spare; and interval-type windshield wipers.

Convertibles also had a power retractable soft top with a hard convertible top boot; illuminated visor mirrors; power deck lid release; power door locks; and power side windows. The 1994 was Ford's first post-1973 Mustang convertible to be built as a topless car on the factory assembly line—earlier convertibles started life as coupes and had their roofs removed. A glass backlight was standard, with a built-in defroster costing extra. Convertible tops came in black, white, or saddle.

The automotive trend toward bright, vibrant colors was not lost on Ford's planners. The 1994 Mustang could be ordered in one of 11 eye-catching hues, including Canary Yellow (GT only), Vibrant Red (GT only), Rio Red, Laser Red, Iris, Bright Blue, Deep Forest Green, Teal, Black, Opal Frost, and Crystal White.

Interiors were available in five colors: Bright Red, Saddle, Opal Grey, Black, and White (convertible only).

To show that the new Mustang was truly a notch above the competition, there were some exciting options offered. In addition to (or in place of) standard equipment, the GT coupe ($17,280) and convertible ($21,970) had front and rear fascias with GT nomenclature and black finish on the

lower rear end; Mustang GT fender badges; fog lamps; a single-wing rear spoiler; 16x7.5-inch wide five-spoke cast-aluminum wheels with locks; a 150-mph speedometer; GT bucket seats with cloth trim, cloth head restraints, adjustable cushions, power lumbar support, and a four-way power driver's seat; a leather-wrapped steering wheel; a Traction-Lok rear axle; handling brace to stiffen the engine compartment ("similar to those utilized by Ford NASCAR teams," said the brochure); stainless steel dual exhaust system; GT suspension package with variable-rate coil springs, unique-calibrated gas struts and shocks, and Quadra-shock rear suspension with strut lever brace; and illuminated visor mirrors with hard covers.

Moving into territory once reserved for Mercedes SL owners, Ford introduced a removable hardtop for the convertible, but supplier problems and the high cost of the option ($1,825) killed the company's enthusiasm and only 499 were delivered as 1995 models. The 1994 Mustang was also the first Ford to offer a dealer-installed, mini-disc sound system, as well as a new Mach 460 system that used eight speakers to put out 460 peak watts of sound. The all-new Mustang readily won *Motor Trend* magazine's "Car of the Year" award, and it became the Indianapolis 500 pace car for the third time since 1964.

When the model year closed, sales of the new Mustang were respectable, with a total run of 123,198 units. That number included 42,883 base coupes (listing at $13,365 each), 18,333 base convertibles ($20,160), 30,592 GT coupes ($17,280), 25,381 GT convertibles ($21,790), 5,009 Cobra coupes ($21,300), and 10,000 Cobra convertibles ($25,605).

## 1995

With such a successful first-year launch of the new design, there were precious few changes for 1995.

The legendary 5.0-liter V-8 that had served the Mustang well since its introduction in 1968 (with interruptions in 1974, 1980 and 1981) would be discontinued at the end of the 1995 model year. Mustang purists were cautiously awaiting its replacement—a 4.6-liter, overhead cam version of Ford's new "modular" family—as the "Five Oh" was the only powerplant many of them had ever known.

A GTS model was offered in 1995 that was a slightly stripped GT (missing the sports seats, rear spoiler and foglamps). A power driver's seat moved from the standard equipment list to the options list. The only change in color choices was the departure of Iris and the introduction of Sapphire Blue. Interior and convertible top colors remained unchanged. The removable hardtop option that Ford touted at every opportunity during early promotion of

*The Mustang GT returned in 1995 with practically no changes. It would mark the last year for the legendary 5.0-liter V-8. (Brad Bowling)*

*The removable hardtop option was no longer offered for convertibles. (Ford)*

*Some of the beautiful details of the 1994 Mustang recalled the original car. (Ford)*

the 1994 Mustang was quietly dropped from all sales literature by the time the 1995 models were introduced.

Prices across the board were only increased slightly in 1995. The base coupe listed for $14,530; the base convertible, $20,995; the GTS coupe, $16,910; the GT coupe, $18,105.

Sales were up in the second year of the new design, with a total of 185,986 units sold. That number included 137,722 coupes and 48,264 convertibles.

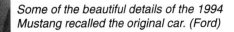

*The optional high-performance Mach 460 electronic AM/FM stereo system, introduced on the 1994 Mustang, was worth the money if you had a discerning ear. (Ford)*

## 1996

From the outside, the Mustang did not change much for 1996. Ford stuck a screen in the grille; vertical, three-element taillights returned (the 1996 Mustang had the first tail lamps sold on an American car with clear lenses and complex reflectors) and a new, five-spoke, 17-inch wheel was offered as an upgrade on the GT model. The only other external difference was on the GT, was a mysterious fender badge announcing to the world the birth of a new Mustang powerplant.

For many reasons pertaining to its customer base, Federal regulations and corporate culture, Ford dropped the legendary 5.0-liter V-8 with the 1995 model and debuted the 4.6-liter, single-overhead cam (SOHC) "modular" engine in 1996. Although it displaced a full 21-cubic inches less than the 5.0 (281 vs. 302), the 4.6 maintained the same horsepower and torque ratings from the previous year (215 hp and 285 lb.-ft. of torque). Because of its overhead cam and other efficient components, the 4.6-liter won fans over right away with its ability to produce power right up to 6,000 rpms, besting the old 5.0's useable revs by 1,200-1,500.

The Mustang's 4.6-liter V-8 was part of a family of modular engines Ford developed from a common platform. By this system, certain components are interchangeable across a line of powerplants, despite differences in displacement and number of cylinders.

The sales catalog showed a hardtop option for the convertible, but quality control problems limited availability to a few months in 1994 and 1995. (Ford)

The 1994 Mustang came equipped with four-wheel power disc brakes as standard equipment, with a computer-controlled ABS system optional. (Ford)

The first modular Ford appeared in the 1991 Lincoln Town Car, then became standard in the 1992 Crown Victoria/Mercury Marquis twins.

The largest improvement in operating efficiency for the 4.6-liter was in the elimination of pushrods; the Mustang's two valves per cylinder were now actuated directly by the overhead camshaft. Less reciprocal weight means greater power transfer. Reliability was also improved with the new design. A unique cylinder head bolt design and spacing meant that cylinder and block distortion under stress were no longer factors in a high-performance application. Another interesting aspect of the 4.6 engines is Ford's patented oil cooling system, which has no external oil or coolant lines but uses returning water from the radiator.

High-technology was brought to bear on the new Mustang's engine, with lightweight pistons and connecting rods and a composite (plastic) intake manifold that increased runner length without taking up as much room as previous alloy versions. The alternator, air-conditioning compressor, and power steering pump were all directly mounted to the block, reducing underhood clutter.

Platinum-tipped spark plugs and the accessory drive belt were rated for 100,000 miles before replacement.

More refinements for 1996 included a new distributorless electronic ignition and a second-generation onboard diagnostic program (OBD II) that signals the driver and technicians about specific engine management problems in need of attention.

Some changes had to be made underhood because of the 4.6-liter's taller height. The brake booster was redesigned into a much smaller package; it built its boost through the power steering pump. The crossmember that supports both engine and front suspension components had to be reconfigured to accommodate the different engine shape. Steering gear and suspension arms were lowered.

Even the base V-6 came in for some improvements, most notably in the form of a stiffer block (from the Thunderbird Super Coupe) and an increase to 150 hp. Gone were the perennial T-5 five-speed manual transmission and old-style four-speed automatic; in their places were a beefier T-45 and more computer-dependent 4R70W—the first performance application of an automatic transmission from Ford in many years. The GT received larger stabilizer bars, along with retuned shocks, progressive rate springs, and different bushings.

Additional standard equipment on the base model included: AM/FM ETR stereo radio (four speakers); four-wheel power disc brakes; cloth reclining bucket and split folding rear seats; carpeting; console; dual remote

*The optional high-performance Mach 460 electronic AM/FM stereo system, introduced on the 1994 Mustang, was worth the money if you had a discerning ear. (Ford)*

*The cigarette lighter was thoughtfully placed to double as a 12-volt auxiliary outlet for small accessories. (Ford)*

mirrors; dual air bags; side glass defoggers; tinted glass; power steering; tilt wheel; oil press, tach, temp, and volt gauges; digital clock; trip odometer; front and rear stabilizer bars; front MacPherson struts; visor mirrors; "headlights on" warning tone; intermittent wipers; rocker panel moldings; and courtesy lights.

Four new colors were available on the Mustang for 1996: Moonlight Blue, Deep Violet, Pacific Green, and Bright Tangerine (GT application only). In an effort to keep Mustangs in the hands of the people who paid for them, Ford applied its Passive Anti-Theft System (PATS) to all 1996 GT and Cobra models. PATS-equipped cars cannot be hot-wired due to a specially coded ignition key and switch.

In 1996, a base coupe cost $15,180 (61,187 units were produced), with the onvertible coming in at $ 21,060 (15,246 made). The sporty GT ran $17,610 (31,624 made) with standard equipment and $23,495 (17,917 made) as a droptop.

*The center console included an armrest storage bin and cup holder. (Ford)*

## Mustangs to Japan

In an interesting twist of events, during early February 1994, Ford announced that it had begun building the redesigned Mustang for export to Japan and that it planned to ship 3,000 Mustangs to the Asian nation. That figure was twice the total number of cars that Ford sent to Japan in 1993.

Ford said the Japanese Mustangs would have left-hand steering, despite the fact that people in Japan drive on the left side of the road and usually operate right-hand drive cars.

During the Chicago Automobile Show, Ford general manager Ross Roberts said the company had received orders from its domestic dealers for 76,000 new Mustangs since it started building the cars in October. "It's obvious that the Mustang has struck a nerve, not only among Americans, but also the Japanese," he noted.

*Standard GT wheels ('96 model shown) were these five-spoke 16-inchers. (Ford)*

*This 1997 convertible shows the vertical, three-element taillights that returned to the Mustang in 1996. (Ford)*

## SPECIFICATIONS

**Mustang Engine**

| | |
|---|---|
| Type | V-6 |
| Valves | 12, OHV |
| Displacement | 3.8L (232 cu. in.) |
| Bore x Stroke (in.) | 3.81 x 3.40 |
| Compression Ratio | 9.0:1 |
| Horsepower (SAE net) | 145 @ 4,000 rpm |
| Torque (SAE net lbs./ft.) | 215 @ 2,500 rpm |
| Fuel system | Sequential multi-port electronic fuel injection |
| Exhaust system | Single, stainless steel |

**Mustang GT Engine**

| | |
|---|---|
| Type | V-8 |
| Valves | 16, OHV |
| Displacement | 5.0L High-Output (302 cu. in.) |
| Bore x Stroke (in.) | 4.0 x 3.0 |
| Compression Ratio | 9.0:1 |
| Horsepower (SAE net) | 215 @ 4,200 rpm |
| Torque (SAE net lbs./ft.) | 285 @ 3,400 rpm |
| Fuel system | Sequential multi-port electronic fuel injection |
| Exhaust system | Dual, stainless steel |

**Transmissions**

| | |
|---|---|
| Type | 5-speed manual overdrive (std.) |
| | Electronic 4-speed automatic overdrive (opt.) |

**Body/Chassis**

| | |
|---|---|
| Drivetrain type | Rear-wheel drive |
| Body type | Unitized |
| Front suspension | Modified MacPherson strut-type, tubular stabilizer bar, nitrogen gas-pressurized hydraulic shocks (higher-rate handling components in GT) |

**Body/Chassis, cont'd**

| | |
|---|---|
| Rear suspension | 4-bar link coil spring system, tubular stabilizer bar, nitrogen gas-pressurized hydraulic shocks (higher-rate handling components plus horizontally mounted axle dampers in GT) |
| Steering | Power rack-and-pinion, 14.7:1 on-center constant ratio |
| Brakes | Power 4-wheel disc (std.) Anti-lock brake system (opt.) |
| Tires | Std. P205/65R15 92T BSW all-season (Mustang) Std. P225/55ZR16 BSW all-season (GT) Opt. 245/45ZR17 BSW (GT) |
| Fuel capacity | 15.4 gallons |

**Dimensions**

| | Coupe | Convertible |
|---|---|---|
| Wheelbase | 101.3" | 101.3" |
| Length | 181.5" | 181.5" |
| Height | 52.9" | 52.8" |
| Width | 78.1" | 78.1" |
| Front tread* | 60.6" | 60.6" |
| Rear tread** | 59.1" | 59.1" |
| Front head room | 38.2" | 38.1" |
| Rear head room | 35.9" | 35.4" |
| Front leg room | 42.6" | 42.6" |
| Rear leg room | 30.3" | 30.3" |
| Front shoulder room | 53.6" | 53.6" |
| Rear shoulder room | 52.1" | 41.2" |
| Trunk volume (cu. ft.)† | 10.8 | 8.5 |
| Passenger capacity | 4 | 4 |

*60.1 with GT. **58.7 with GT. †Rear seat backs up.

*Specifications for the 1994 Mustang V-6 and Mustang GT V-8 are listed here, along with information about transmissions, the body/chassis, and dimensions. (Ford)*

## Down with Diversity

From a historical standpoint, it is interesting to note that the 1994 Mustang ties with model year 1974 for the lowest possible number of powertrain and body style combinations ever offered.

The 1965 Mustang, advertised as having been "Designed to be Designed by You," had three body styles and four engines (depending on what period of 1965 we survey). In 1969 Mustang buyers had three body styles and 10 engines—not to mention the various Grandé, Boss, Shelby, GT, and Mach I configurations. The 1975-1978 Mustang II and 1979-1982 Mustangs got by with only hatchback and notchback bodies before the convertible returned in 1983—each of which could be combined a minimum of three powerplants. Only the 1974 Mustang II, with a four-cylinder and V-6 to offer in two body styles, had as few combinations to choose from.

How do fans of the legendary pony car feel about the dearth of choices? No one has complained yet, probably owing to the clever design of the 1994-and-up coupe and the powerful engines available.

In a way, the new design is a hybrid package in that it has a curved roofline and pronounced rear glass like a fastback, a flat trunklid like a notchback and fold-down back seats that allow storage of long or oddly shaped items. In other words, one design accomplishes several goals and appeals to many different tastes.

Dropping the four-cylinder engine from the 1994 lineup was a good idea from a marketing standpoint. With the base 3.8-liter V-6 output raised to 145-hp and the 5.0-liter V-8 putting out 215-hp, the performance bar was raised for the Mustang—no longer would the low-end pony suffer the indignity of being compared to four-cylinder front-drivers as Toyota's Celica and Mazda's MX-6 by potential buyers or the buff books.

Despite the rhetoric of the early car's advertisements suggesting that every buyer's personality could be matched up to a Mustang model through manipulation of the options list, all a Mustanger ever wanted was enough power to chirp the tires in a body stylish enough to make the neighbors jealous.

*1999 brought a new, squarer styling to the Mustang, reminding many of its muscle car heritage. (Ford)*

*A new front fascia for the 1999 model included tucked-away driving lights on the GT. (Ford)*

1965 Ford Mustang hardtop (Marcella Knight)

1965 Ford Mustang hardtop (Sarah Calvillo)

1965 Ford Mustang GT convertible (Old Cars Weekly)

1966 Ford Mustang Shelby GT350H (Steve Mason)

1966 Ford Mustang GT 2+2 Fastback (Tom Cannizzaro)

1966 Ford Mustang convertible (Brad Bowling)

1967 Ford Mustang Fastback (Richard Seiverling)

1967 Ford Mustang Fastback (Mark K. Spaude)

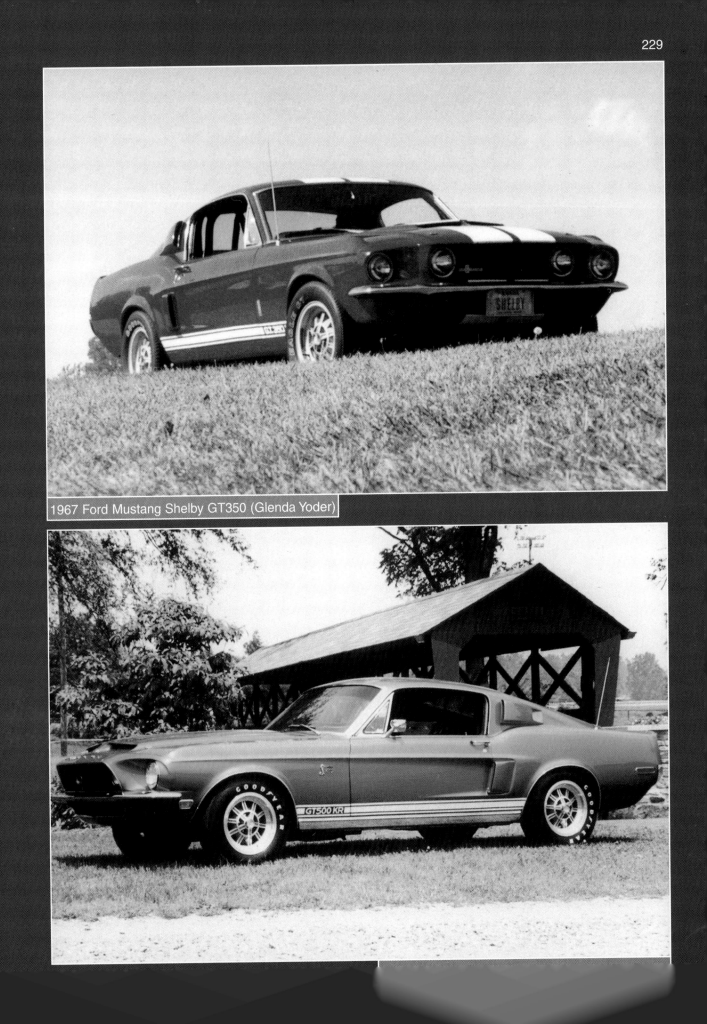

1967 Ford Mustang Shelby GT350 (Glenda Yoder)

1968 Ford Mustang Shelby GT350 (Mark K. Spaude)

1968 Shelby Mustang GT350 convertible (Brad Bowling)

1969 Ford Mustang Shelby GT500 convertible (Steve Mason)

1969 Ford Mustang Mach 1 Fastback (Jim Dombrowski)

1969 Ford Mustang convertible (Jack and Ardeen Gasser)

1969 Ford Mustang Mach 1 (Brad Bowling)

1970 Ford Mustang Shelby GT500 Fastback (Larry B. Scott)

1970 Ford Mustang Mach 1 Fastback (Colin B. Bruce, III)

1971 Ford Mustang Boss 351 Fastback (Old Cars Weekly)

1971 Ford Mustang hardtop (Richard Fuchs) This unrestored driver now boasts over 440,000 miles and is only driven between May and October.

1973 Ford Mustang convertible (William M. Dilick)

1976 Ford Mustang Cobra II (Ford)

1977 Ford Mustang Cobra II (Ford)

1978 Ford Mustang King Cobra (Old Cars Weekly)

1979 Ford Mustang Indianapolis 500 Pace Car (Richard Pollard)

1982 Ford Mustang GT hatchback (Old Cars Weekly)

1983 Ford Mustang 5.0 Liter convertible (Old Cars Weekly)

1984 Ford Mustang SVO (Ford Motor Company)

1987 Ford Mustang GT (Ford Motor Company)

1988 Ford Mustang Saleen coupe (Brad Bowling)

1994 Ford Mustang GT convertible (Jay Gasser)

1994 Ford Mustang Cobra (Old Cars Weekly)

1995 Ford Mustang Cobra (Norm and Karen Demers)

Brad Bowling's 1995 Ford Mustang GT convertible

1997 Ford Mustang convertible (Old Cars Weekly)

1999 Ford Mustang GT convertible

2000 Ford Mustang Cobra R (Ford Motor Company)

2000 Ford Mustang Saleen (Morrison Motor Co.)

2001 Ford Mustang GT convertible (Richard and Julie Canter)

## 1997

After making such a risky marketing change the year before (dropping the 5.0-liter V-8 for a new SOHC 4.6-liter V-8), Ford used 1997 to maintain a steady course and continue developing the cosmetic upgrades the car would receive for 1999.

Base model standard equipment included: five-speed manual transmission; PATS anti-theft system; AM/FM ETR stereo radio (four speakers); power front and rear disc brakes; cloth reclining bucket and split folding rear seats; cloth and vinyl door trim panels; carpeting; console w/armrest; dual power remote mirrors; dual air bags; side glass defoggers; tinted glass; power steering; tilt wheel; tachometer, oil pressure, temperature and volt gauges; digital clock; trip odometer; front stabilizer bar; front MacPherson struts; 15-inch steel wheels with covers and P205/65R15 BSW tires; dual visor vanity mirrors; "headlights-on" warning tone; intermittent wipers; rocker panel moldings; courtesy lights; and trunk light.

New 17-inch rims with dark gray metallic centers became optional on the GT. The PATS anti-theft system became standard equipment across the Mustang board in 1997. A slight change in the upper grille opening allowed more air to the new cooling system.

After a peak in 1995, the new Mustang design had its second straight year of decreased sales at 108,344. For 1997, Ford produced 56,812 base coupes (at a price of $15,880), 11,606 base convertibles ($21,280), 18,464 GT coupes ($18,525), 11,413 GT convertibles ($24,510), 6,961

## 1998

Why mess with a good thing? The Mustang had a strong following among sporty car buyers, so the only change worth advertising on the 1998 car was an additional 10 horsepower out of the GT's standard 4.6-liter V-8.

The instrument panel-mounted clock pod was removed, with the clock function now falling to the radio display.

Two new option packages were introduced to this carryover model: a GT Sport Group that included the 17-inch aluminum wheels; hood and wraparound fender stripes; leather-wrapped shift knob, and engine oil cooler; and the V-6 Sport Appearance Group that gave the buyer 16-inch cast aluminum wheels, rear spoiler, leather-wrapped steering wheel, and a lower bodyside accent stripe.

1998 produced a big spike in production, with 175,522 Mustangs going to new homes. The total included 99,801 base coupes (at $16,150 list price), 21,254 base convertibles ($20,650), 28,789 GT coupes ($20,150), and 17,024 GT convertibles ($24,150).

## 1999

The Mustang turned 35 years old in 1999; it was a birthday that Ford celebrated with zeal. Perhaps remembering the bad press it received 10 years earlier when the 25th anniversary came and went with minimal corporate fanfare, Ford created a 1-2-3 punch that made Mustangers happy.

The first gift came in the form of jewelry, sort of. All 1999 Mustangs wore beautiful wreath-design emblems on their front fenders featuring the running horse and tri-color bar enclosed by a solid ring.

The second gift was a much-needed face-lift. What had seemed fresh in 1994 had grown commonplace and done-to-death by 1998. Ford designers must have longed for the muscular blockiness of the 1967-1968 pony cars, because they pumped up the 1999 body to the point that it looked like the Mustang's older brother. Smoothly rounded fenders and body lines gave way to strong creases and straight lines. The sides of the car took on a more vertical angle, and the tallest scoop ever to grace a Mustang was installed just behind the door. The GT hood grew a simulated recessed scoop that recalled the air-grabber the 1968 sported when it received its first big-block V-8. GT exhaust tips were enlarged slightly, from 2.75 inches to 3 inches.

Up front, the Mustang's headlights took on a sinister appearance that seemed to ask, "You talkin' to me?" The taillights received the same treatment as the rest of the car, going from soft and rounded to hard and harsh. Weight was reduced through the use of a new trunk lid made from a sheet-molded compound.

Refinements took place in areas that couldn't be seen by the casual observer, such as the revised floorpan sealing and foam-packed rocker panels — both of which reduced road noise. Sub-frame connectors on the convertible reduced a "mid-car shake," according to Ford. Engineers gained a tiny bit of rear suspension travel by raising the drive tunnel 1.5 inches.

New technology came to the Mustang in the form of an optional all-speed Traction Control System (TCS), a $230 option that worked in harmony with the also-optional (on base models) ABS to reduce tire spin in slippery conditions. The driver's seat track gained an inch of travel for the comfort of taller drivers.

Along with the muscular body came more power for the engines. The 3.8-liter V-6 increased to 190 hp and the 4.6-liter V-8 won over quite a few more fans when its rating jumped to 260 hp. New intake manifold and cylinder head improvements were responsible for the V-6 increase; a higher-lift camshaft, coil-on-plug ignition, bigger valves, and a revised intake manifold massaged the extra ponies from the V-8.

*The floating corral and galloping Mustang for 1999 were definitely intended to remind owners of the first cars. (Ford)*

MUSTANG

*Blockier bodies made the 1999 Mustangs look more muscular. (Ford)*

*The 1999's rear taillights displayed a stylized version of the original's three-element vertical units. (Ford)*

*Even the aerodynamic halogen headlights of the 1999 Mustang looked menacing. (Ford)*

*1999 brought the largest fake scoop ever put on the side of a Mustang. (Ford)*

*The '99 Mustang's non-functional hood scoop was a real throwback to '60s styling. (Ford)*

*The base V-6 gained 40 hp in 1999 due to improved breathing—the result of split-port induction. It was rated at 190 hp. (Ford)*

*All '99s, regardless of powerplant or body style, wore the commemorative badge. (Ford)*

*While all 1999 Mustangs wore special 35th Anniversary badges, there was a separate run of Limited Edition cars decked out in what would become the scoops and vents of the 2001 model. (Ford)*

*The Limited Edition was available in four colors and both body styles. (Ford)*

*The Limited Edition was introduced to a receptive crowd at Charlotte Motor Speedway during the Mustang Club of America's 35th anniversary show. The SVT Cobra R (on right), with its race-car styling and screaming red paint, managed to draw attention as well. (Ford)*

*Body styles for 2000 again included the convertible (base model seen in front) and coupe (GT shown). (Ford)*

*All Fox-4 Mustang convertibles, such as this 2000 GT, came standard with a glass rear window. (Ford)*

*The 2000 Mustang convertible featured the 3.8-liter V-6 as the standard powerplant. (Ford)*

*The 2000 GT had the same aggressive stance that made the first Mustang so popular with driving enthusiasts. (Ford)*

*Everything fell readily to hand the 2000 cockpit. (Ford)*

# MUSTANG

The third birthday gift to the Mustang came in the form of the 35th Anniversary Limited Edition model, available in either convertible or coupe. For a mere $2,695 above the cost of a GT, Mustang buyers could drive home in one of 5,000 cars featuring a special, raised hood scoop (at the end of a wide black stripe); rear deck wing; stand-out side scoops, black honeycomb deck lid appliqué; body-color rocker moldings; Midnight Black GT leather interior with silver leather inserts; special floor mats with 35th anniversary script and special aluminum shift knob (five-speeds only). Exterior colors were limited to Black, Silver, Crystal White, and Performance Red. The Limited Edition incorporated many of the radical scoops and coloring that would be introduced with the 2001 model.

The heavily face-lifted 1999 model, despite positive reviews from the motor press, saw a decline in sales from the previous year, at 133,637 total cars. The base coupe sold 73,180 units (at $16,470 apiece); the base convertible, 19,299 ($21,070); the GT coupe, 19,634 ($20,870); and the GT convertible, 13,699 ($24,870).

## 2000

A carryover year for the new, bulked-up Mustang brought little in the form of change.

Child seat tether anchor brackets were added to the rear seating areas of all Mustangs. Another new safety item, introduced after a rash of incidents where people were locked in their own trunks, was an interior deck lid release with glow-in-the-dark illumination.

Three new colors—Sunburst Gold, Performance Red, and Amazon Gold—replaced Chrome Yellow, Rio Red, and Dark Green Satin.

The base coupe listed for $16,520; the base convertible, $21,370; the GT coupe, $21,015; the GT convertible, $25,270.

## 2001

If the 1999 Mustang design was a throwback to the square-jawed 1967-68 styling, then the 2001 model was a Boss 302 reincarnated!

To the already tough-looking body was added a tall (though non-functional) hood scoop, side scoops, a revised spoiler and black-out trim around the headlights.

Aluminum, 17-inch wheels became standard on the GT model, with the optional 17-inchers bearing a strong resemblance to the American Racing Torq-Thrust rims of the 1960s. To reduce the number of order combinations from the previous year's 2,600 to approximately 50 for 2001, Ford combined option packages into Standard, Deluxe, and Premium Equipment Groups.

The Standard Equipment Group for the Mustang coupe included: 15-inch painted alloy wheels; P205/65R15 all-season tires; electronic ignition; multi-port fuel injection; four-wheel disc brakes; stereo CD/radio/cassette; air conditioning; driver and passenger air bag; split fold-down rear seat; and SecuriLock Passive anti-theft system.

The Deluxe Equipment Group for the base or GT model included: a rear spoiler; power driver's seat; leather-wrapped steering wheel (GT only); cloth front sport bucket seats (GT coupe/convertible); speed control; and 17-inch painted aluminum wheels (GT only). These options could be added to the Deluxe package: automatic transmission; anti-lock brake system with Traction Control (requires automatic on coupe; standard on GT); Sport Appearance Group (V-6 only); Mach 460 in-dash six-disc CD changer and AM/FM radio; leather-trimmed front bucket seats (V-6 convertible only); and leather-trimmed front Sport bucket seats (GT convertible only).

The Premium Equipment Group included: automatic transmission (optional on convertibles); 16-inch bright alloy wheels; P225/55R16 all-season tires; Mach 460 in-dash six-disc CD changer and AM/FM radio; leather-wrapped steering wheel; anti-lock brake system with Traction Control; leather-trimmed front sport bucket seats (GT only); and 17-inch five-spoke premium alloy wheels (GT only). Leather-trimmed front buckets seats could also be added optionally (standard on convertibles).

The rear window defroster became standard for all models, while the "smoker's package" and block heater moved from the options list to become dealer-installed accessories. A new six-disc CD changer became optional with the Mach 460 sound system.

The base coupe for 2001 listed for $15,644; the base convertible, $20,518; the GT coupe, $20,716; and the GT convertible, $24,546.

*Whereas the 1994 from which it sprang was curvy and pointy, the new-for-2001 design is more muscular and brick-like. (Ford)*

*With an ever-escalating number of scoops, vents and openings, the 2001 Mustang recalled the heady days of muscle car heaven when Boss 302s and Shelbys roamed the roads. (Ford)*

*A revised interior for 2001 continued the dual-cockpit theme that returned to the Mustang with the 1994 models. (Ford)*

*Enthusiasts cheered at the return of a classic rim to the 2001 Mustang line. This five-spoke, 17-inch alloy wheel recalls the popular American Racing Torq-Thrust D that was often seen on Shelbys and race cars of the 1960s. (Ford)*

*Even in the base V-6 coupe, driving a 2001 Mustang looked like you paid for—and got—an expensive high-performance car. (Ford)*

*The base 2001 Mustang had its share of scoops and vents—there was even a rear spoiler. (Ford)*

*Mustang enthusiasts got a glimpse at the future of high performance when the FR 500 was unveiled at the SEMA show in 1999. (Ford)*

# MUSTANG

## *You Can't Spell Future without "FR"*
## *What is the future of the Mustang?*

Such crystal ball gazing is always helped by a peek at what's going on behind closed doors at Ford Motor Company, where cars are being designed and studied years before they reach showrooms. The FR 500 is perhaps the compass needle with the strongest reading right now about the direction the high-performance pony car might head in the early years of the 21st century.

Ford Racing Technology unleashed this rolling advertisement for its high-tech parts catalog at the 1999 Specialty Equipment Market Association (SEMA) show in Las Vegas to the collective applause of the Mustang world. The FR 500, whose name means simply "Ford Racing 5.0-liter," is a production Mustang Cobra platform that's been modified into a world-class supercar by the addition of more than 100 of the company's catalog parts.

The most eye-catching change is probably the five-inch wheelbase extension, a feat managed entirely without welding or cutting of the subframe. The stock Cobra front MacPherson strut suspension was replaced with upper and lower A-arms. The uppers were sourced from the rear of a Lincoln LS sedan; the rears built from steel. Coil-over shocks replace the Cobra's front struts, which bolt to the shock towers. Front brakes are 14-inch, cross-drilled Brembo units.

What wasn't so easy about the five-inch stretch was designing a crossmember that could clear the V-8's oil pan—the solution eventually involved the creation of a unique eight-quart pan. The hard work was worth the trouble as the FR 500 has a perfect 50/50 front-to-rear weight distribution.

Changes to the rear include stiffer shocks and springs and a Torsen differential cooled by a small radiator. Rear brakes are 13-inch discs pulled from the front of the Cobra. Yards of carbon fiber were baked to create the longer hood, front fenders, bumper cover and various other smaller bits of hardware on the car.

As with any Mustang, it's what's under the hood that gets the enthusiast's heart beating. An entirely new twin-cam, 32-valve V-8 was created for the FR 500, starting with an aluminum block bored out to 5.0 liters of displacement. The engine uses a stock Cobra crankshaft and rods. Ford Racing cylinder heads feature more radical cams and larger ports and valves than the Cobra. A magnesium intake manifold hooks to two 70 mm throttle body injection units pirated from Ford's 5.4-liter truck engine.

A six-speed Tremec T56 manual transmission (a Dodge Viper piece) corrals the 415 horses from the engine to the 4.10:1 rear gears. Top speed for this pony is in excess of 168 miles an hour, and it rockets to 60 miles an hour from a standing start in 4.5 seconds. That's Ferrari territory without the Ferrari price.

Throwing $26,000 worth of Ford Racing catalog parts onto a $28,155 Cobra (plus labor costs) means that reproducing the FR 500 is a wildly expensive proposition—but one well worth it for the ultra high-performance enthusiast. If Ford ever puts it into production, list price estimates are in the mid-$50,000 range.

Will the FR 500 ever see Ford showrooms around the country? Probably not in the form you see on these pages, but Ford will no doubt introduce some of its forward-thinking components to the Mustang line in years to come.

*Its five extra inches of wheelbase—compared to the stock Mustang Cobra from which it is derived—gives the FR 500 a perfect 50/50 front-to-rear weight distribution. (Ford)*

*The FR 500 showed its stuff on the track at Road Atlanta, in Georgia. (Ford)*

*The FR 500's rear panels don't look so different from the stock Mustang. (Ford)*

Dan Davis, director of Ford Racing Technology, and NASCAR Winston Cup driver Rusty Wallace pose with the FR 500 at Road Atlanta. (Ford)

NASCAR Winston Cup driver Rusty Wallace evaluated the FR 500's suspension settings on the racetrack. (Ford)

*Of the two initial FR 500s built, the grey car was kept nice for shows; the white car was thrashed on the track for evaluation. (Ford)*

*Zero-to-60 mph in 4.5 seconds; a top speed in excess of 168 mph—what's not to love? (Ford)*

# CHAPTER 11

## Cobra—A Pony that Bites! (1993-2001)

*The street version of the 1993 Cobra was more subtle in style that the GT. (Jerry Heasley)*

*The 1993 R model was lighter than the street model by some 50 pounds. (Jerry Heasley)*

*The first SVT Cobra was available only in Red, Teal, and Black. (Ford)*

## 1993

The birth of the SVT Cobra Mustang in 1993 was a blessed—if a little confusing—event.

Is SVT the same thing as SVO? And who are these SVE people we keep reading about? Is this just a remake of the 1984-86 SVO Mustang?

Ford's attempt in the 1980s to bring a limited-edition, high-profile, high-tech Mustang to market was run through the corporate enthusiasts at Special Vehicle Operations (SVO). The story of the turbocharged SVO Mustang is discussed in Chapter Eight of this book, so we'll fast-forward to 1991.

The Special Vehicle Team (SVT) and Special Vehicle Engineering (SVE) groups were formed late in 1991 to make a more studied attempt at bringing some upscale, high-performance Ford products to market. SVT's role was to handle the marketing, training and customer relations chores; SVE was the arm devoted to developing and building the final product. In February of 1992, it was announced that the first two SVT vehicles would be introduced as 1993 models—a fast turnaround for any car company!

Increasing popularity of pickups convinced SVT that a short-wheelbase F-150 with a 351-cid 240-hp V-8 would help Ford establish itself as the leader in the performance truck market.

More conventionally, SVT's other product was a hopped-up version of the Mustang to be built using many of the go-fast parts already sold through Ford's existing dealer network.

SVT's choice of the "Cobra" name for the Mustang made enthusiasts suspicious that the promised Camaro-killer might just turn out to be another tape-and-stripe job. After all, the coiled snake emblem had meant nothing since Carroll Shelby stopped using it on his line of Ford-powered aluminum-bodied roadsters in 1967. The 1976-78 Mustang II Cobra II, 1978 King Cobra and anemic Cobra models of the early 1980s had pretty much turned the hooded serpent into a defanged garter snake.

When the 1993 Cobra hit showrooms in mid-year, fans declared it to be a true successor to the revered nameplate. The hatchback-only model sported a 235-hp 280-lb.-ft. version of Ford's forever-young 5.0-liter V-8. Power was added to the 302 by a new upper and lower intake manifold; revised "GT40" heads with larger intake and exhaust ports; larger valves; and revised rocker arms. Throttle body and mass air sensor size were increased to 70mm and 65mm, respectively, for better flow and a different cam spec was used. Smaller crank and underdrive pulleys—a hot rod trick long used by late-model Mustang modifiers—were fitted to the Cobra.

The Borg-Warner T-5 transmission was similar to the stock Mustang component, but with phosphate-coated gears and stronger bearings. A short-throw shifter made for more positive gear changes, and the rear axle was fitted with 3.08:1 cogs.

Keeping a rein on all that new power were big disc brakes on all four corners—a setup not seen on a factory Mustang since the SVO's demise in 1986. Goodyear 245/45-17 Eagle uni-directional tires were mounted on Cobra-unique 17-inch seven-blade alloy rims. The suspension, surprisingly, was set up to ride softer than Ford's stock GT as part of SVT's "controlled compliance" philosophy. The low-profile tires and lower body ride height gave the Cobra its great handling ability.

Despite its higher price tag and high-tech speed parts, the car's body was a fairly conservative package, free of the contrasting stripes and "look-at-me" badges that had adorned the 1980s Cobra Mustangs. The GT's lower grille and bumper were used, but with a slight grille opening sporting a galloping pony. Side-mounted ground effects were smooth from one end to the other, in marked contrast to the GT's boy-racer design. In back was a one-piece fascia with dual exhaust pipes poking out beneath and a square-shouldered wing mated to the hatch lid. Modified SVO Mustang taillights gave the new car a link to its legendary past. If not standing close enough to see the small coiled-snake emblem on the front fender or subtle "SVT" initials just below the rear wing, the average car enthusiast would be hard-pressed to identify the Cobra.

Interiors drew mostly from the GT standard equipment list, differing only in the white-faced instruments that have since been used on all successive Cobras.

Cobra drivers could watch the white-faced speedometer reach 60 mph in less than six seconds and a quarter mile in 14.5 seconds, while keeping the tachometer needle hovering in the stratospheric 6,000-rpm neighborhood.

Very few options were offered as a way to keep the limited production running smoothly. Available only in red, teal, or black, the 1993 SVT Cobra was clearly the pinnacle of the Fox-bodied Mustang platform.

Since it was common knowledge by mid-1993 that the Mustang was due for a major redesign within months, writers for the car magazines were curious as to why SVT would put out so much effort for a one-year-only model. Even though no official explanation was forthcoming, the consensus is that Ford wanted to draw attention away from General Motors' new-for-1993 275-hp Camaros and Firebirds.

*The SVT Cobra had a model-specific rear spoiler. (Jerry Heasley)*

*Modified SVO taillights were applied to SVT's Cobra in 1993. (Jerry Heasley)*

## 1993 COBRA R

Rather than rest on the immediate success of the Cobra, SVT decided to send the Fox platform to its final resting place in style with a competition model. The Cobra "R" was released in the summer of 1993 to improve Ford's status in the International Motor Sport Association (IMSA) Firestone Grand Sport Series and Sports Car Club of America (SCCA) World Challenge Class B Series.

Race-ready Koni shock absorbers, an engine cooling kit, upgraded brakes and five-lug wheels were added to the package, while non-necessities such as air conditioning, the back seat, power windows, sound deadening, and auxiliary lights were removed to save weight. Special wheels with three twin-spoke arms were installed.

SVT's goal of selling 5,000 Cobras was all but met by the end of the model year, with 4,993 of the $18,505 hatchbacks going to new owners. An additional 107 "R" models were sold for $25,692 apiece.

## 1994

Although it was wrapped in an all-new Mustang body for 1994, the SVT Cobra powertrain and suspension formula were remarkably unchanged. The heart of the beast, the 5.0-liter V-8, enjoyed some computer tinkering that boosted it to 240-hp. While the GT used a lower-profile intake manifold to fit under the steeply sloped hood, SVT decided to retain the taller 1993 piece. In order to fit everything under the hood, the strut tower-to-cowl brace was removed.

Cobra springs were still softer than the production GT setup, aided by a smaller diameter sway bar in front (25mm vs. 30-mm) and larger unit in the rear (27mm vs. 24mm). Four-wheel disc brakes with a five-lug pattern became the standard Mustang setup for 1994; the Cobra went one better with larger ABS-equipped discs assigned to handle the extra horsepower. Larger Goodyears were

used than on the 1993 Cobra—255/45-17 uni-directional Eagle GS-Cs mounted on 17x8-inch alloy rims.

In order to look different from the lower-priced GT, the Cobra received a new bumper fascia that incorporated round auxiliary lights. European-style reflector headlamps gave the Cobra the edge for nighttime driving. The Cobra's pedestal-mounted rear spoiler had an LED brake light built in. There was no hatchback body style available for Mustangs after 1993; instead, the Cobra emulated the GT by being available in both coupe and convertible.

When Ford arranged to have the new 1994 Mustang pace that year's Indy 500, it was only natural the Cobra was tapped for that duty. Three convertibles were modified for heavy-duty "real" pace car chores, while SVT turned out 1,000 Rio Red replicas with Saddle leather interiors and Saddle tops. As with most pace car knockoffs, decals were shipped to the dealers inside the cars (not on them) and left to the buyer's discretion to install.

The three race-day duty pace cars were modified by Roush Racing in Allen Park, Michigan, with specially "tweaked" four-speed automatic transmissions, 15-gallon racing fuel cells, heavier rear springs (to accommodate the weight of television camera equipment), a Halon fire-extinguisher system, a roll bar with 50,000-watt strobe lights built in, and special lights in the rear spoiler.

Regular Cobra standard equipment included dual air-bags; articulated sport seats (with four-way power driver's seat); premium stereo; Power Equipment Group; rear window defroster, speed control, Cobra floor mats, and dual illuminated visor mirrors. Options for 1994 included leather interior, remote keyless entry system, and the Mach 460/CD equipment. The pace car replica included all of these options as standard.

Colors for the 1994 Cobra included Rio Red, Crystal White, and Black. Interior options were cloth or leather in Black or Saddle. SVT turned out 5,009 copies of its high-performance Cobra coupe at $20,765 apiece and 1,000 convertibles (all Indy Pace Car replicas) at $26,845 each.

*The 5.0-liter V-8 in the 1994 Ford Mustang Cobra produced 240 hp at 4,800 rpm. (Ford)*

*Based on an all-new 1994 Mustang, the Cobra featured a unique front fascia, 17-inch wheels, Goodyear Eagle GS-C tires and Cobra fender badges. (Ford)*

*In midyear of 1993, Ford announced that an all-new Mustang Cobra had been created by its Special Vehicle Team. A Cobra production run limited to 1,000 convertibles and 5,000 coupes started at the Dearborn plant in early March 1994. (Ford)*

Modifications to the Cobra's sequentially fuel-injected V-8 included the addition of GT-40 cylinder heads, Ford/Crane roller rockers, stronger valve springs, and a tuned-length, cast-aluminum upper intake manifold. (Ford)

Jack Roush prepared three 1994 Cobra convertibles to pace that year's Indy 500 race, marking the third time in its history Mustang was chosen to lead the field. (Ford)

## 1995

The 1995 Cobra was practically identical to the 1994 model. A convertible was permanently added to the lineup; for 1995 it was only available in Black, with a Black leather interior and black top. Coupe colors were restricted to Rio Red, Crystal White, and Black.

An interesting collectible in the form of a removable hardtop was available briefly during 1995 for the convertible. Considering the high-dollar clientele of the Cobra line, it probably wasn't the option's $1,825 price tag that killed it; instead, Ford's problems with the supplier and concerns about quality were more likely the culprits. Only 499 of the special tops were made, supposedly Cobras account for the majority of models so equipped—if not all models so equipped.

## 1995 COBRA R

The late-model Mustang reached a new peak of high-performance in 1995 with the introduction of the Cobra's second-generation R model. With 351 cubic inches of small-block V-8 under the slightly enlarged hood, the R contained the largest factory Mustang powerplant in 22 years.

Demand for the 1993 R had easily exceeded the 100-car run, so SVT increased the availability to 250 units for 1995. Realizing that many of the first Rs had gone straight to collectors' garages (bypassing the racetracks they were built to compete on), Ford insisted that sales of the 1995 would be made only to licensed, active competitors in the SCCA and IMSA series.

Because the 351-cid V-8 that SVT shoehorned into the R is in the same "family" as the 5.0-liter 302-cid V-8 in the standard Cobra, emissions certification was easier than if a different powerplant had been chosen. A Ford marine block formed the basis for the super V-8, with a special camshaft; aluminum alloy pistons; forged steel connecting rods; GT40 heads; and lower intake and specially designed upper intake manifold making up most of the performance gains. Visually topping off the package was a "5.8 Liter Cobra" plate on the intake manifold. The greater displacement produced 300 hp and 365 lb.-ft. of torque.

Dropping the usual Borg-Warner T-5 for a beefier Tremec five-speed gave Ford's warranty department peace of mind concerning broken gears, while the 3.27:1 rear axle ratio ensured that the R would accelerate like a rocket. Like any good race car built from a production model, the R was stripped of unnecessary weight. Gone

*These 17-inch five-spoke alloy wheels became standard Cobra equipment with the 1994 model.*

were the air-conditioning system, power windows, radio, rear seat, some soundproofing materials, and fog lamps.

The suspension was tuned for ultimate handling with Eibach springs; Koni adjustable shocks; firmer bushings; five-spoke wheels measuring 17x9 inches; and 255/45-17 BFGoodrich Comp T/As. Other race-oriented pieces included a fiberglass hood, 20-gallon fuel cell, and radiators for engine oil and power steering fluid. All 250 cars were painted Crystal White and fitted with the saddle cloth interiors.

Despite the addition of a hot-selling R model, overall Cobra sales were down in 1995. The $21,300 coupe saw 4,005 sales; the $25,605 convertible rang up 1,003 new customers, and the $35,499 (plus $2,100 gas guzzler tax) R quickly pre-sold all 250 copies.

## 1996

For its fourth year of production, the SVT Cobra made a giant leap forward in technology and horsepower. The stock Mustang GT line switched over to Ford's newest "modular" motor, a 4.6-liter, single-overhead cam V-8 that cranked out a peppy 215 hp and 285 lb.-ft. of torque. (See Chapter 10 of this book for more on the modular Mustang motor.)

Since the SVT crew had been assembled to create a new level of performance for the Mustang, it was decided to install a motor in the 1996 Cobra that would really separate the snake from the pony. What they developed was a double-overhead cam, four-valve-per-cylinder, aluminum-block 4.6-liter V-8 that produced 305 hp at 5,800 rpm and 300 lb.-ft. of torque at 4,800 rpm. The aluminum block was specially cast by the Teksid company in Italy and shipped to Ford's Romeo, Michigan, engine assembly plant where it was fitted with four-valve heads and twin 57mm throttle bodies. Twelve two-person teams assembled all 10,000-plus 1996 Cobra motors on the special "Niche Line," then personally autographed a metallic plate on the passenger-side cam cover.

Cobras received the same new Borg-Warner T-45 five-speed transmissions as standard 1996 GTs—these units were more than capable of handling the stump-pulling torque of the DOHC 4.6-liter.

Exterior colors offered were Laser Red, Crystal White, Black and an unusual "Mystic" paint scheme. Developed by GAF, Mystic was a combination of colors that show themselves from different angles—the green, purple, blue and black hues reacted in different ways to the light and created a love-it-or-hate-it $815 option for 1996

*The most technologically advanced engine ever installed in a Mustang was the 4.6-liter DOHC V-8 shown here. It was introduced as the standard powerplant in the 1996 Cobra, where it produced 305 hp. (Ford)*

*The domed hood was introduced in 1996 in order to clear the slightly taller 4.6-liter DOHC V-8. (Ford)*

Cobra coupes only. Controversial though it was, 1,999 customers happily drove home Mystic-painted coupes.

A slight dome was built into the Cobra hood starting in 1996 to clear the taller 4.6-liter engine. Other appearance changes included "COBRA" lettering stamped into the rear valance panel and a new rear spoiler (the spoiler became a "customer delete" option this year). Three-inch dual exhaust tips were fitted to the Cobra—an upgrade from the previous model 's 2.75-inch units.

Enthusiasm for the new DOHC 4.6-liter engine may have been a factor in the year's sales results—the biggest in SVT history! Customers drove home 10,006 of the high-

*The rear spoiler became a $215 option in 1996. (Ford)*

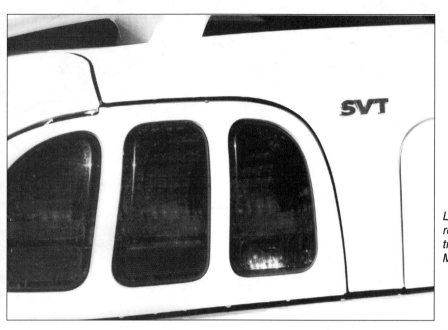

*Like the base Mustang and GT, the Cobra received the vertical three-element taillight treatment starting in 1996. (Morrison Motors)*

## 1997

performance Mustang Cobras. Coupes were the most abundant, with 7,496 selling for $24,810; convertibles had strong sales, with 2,510 produced for a list price of $27,580.

It was business as usual for SVT in 1997. The only noticeable change in the Cobra was a slightly larger grille opening, which was shared by the entire Mustang lineup due to a wider and taller radiator design across the board.

For 1997, Pacific Green shared the Cobra paint chip chart with Rio Red, Black, and Crystal White.

*This picture of a 1997 Cobra convertible shows the raised hood area that was introduced the previous year to accommodate the taller 4.6-liter V-8. (Morrison Motors)*

*From 1994 to 1995, the only clue from behind that you were following a Cobra was the small "SVT" logo on the left side of the deck lid. Starting in 1996, the Cobra name was stamped into the rear valance (1997 model shown). (Morrison Motors)*

*Black, Saddle, and White tops were offered in 1996 and 1997 on Cobra convertibles. (Morrison Motors)*

*The 1998 Cobra's aggressive stance appealed to old-time Mustangers who longed for the muscle cars of the 1960s. (Morrison Motors)*

SVT established another sales record for its Cobra in 1997 by an additional 43 units. Of the 10,049 Cobras produced, 6,961 were $25,335 coupes and 3,088 were $28,135 convertibles.

## 1998

The only change of note on the 1998 Cobra was a switch to five-spoke wheels similar to what SVT put on the 1995 R models.

Interior changes reflected the stock GT Mustang: the console was re-designed; the clock pod was removed from the instrument panel leaving the radio in charge of telling time, and a CD player became standard with the premium sound system.

Body color choices were the most numerous to date in 1998, including perennial favorites Laser Red, Crystal White, and Black with the addition of Atlantic Blue and Canary Yellow.

*A new 17-inch five-spoke wheel was used on the 1998 Cobras. It was a slightly narrower version of the rim fitted to the 1995 R model. (Morrison Motors)*

The new wheels really showed off the massive brake discs at each corner of the car. (Morrison Motors)

The scoops and slight bulge to the hood let everyone know that this is not a run-of-the-mill Mustang. (Morrison Motors)

A coiled snake emblem on the fender was a very subtle difference between the GT and the Cobra. (Morrison Motors)

The 1998 Cobra's rear spoiler was a $195 option. (Morrison Motors)

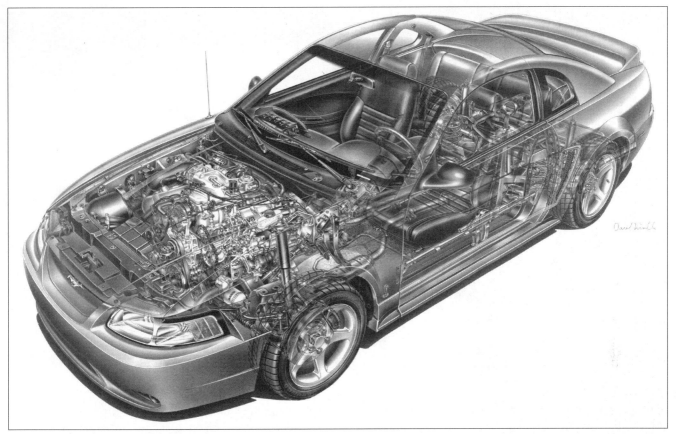

*The Cobra wasn't all-new for 1999, but it sure looked like it. (Ford)*

*An upgrade in combustion raised the 4.6-liter's output to 320 hp for 1999. (Ford)*

*The 1999 Cobra front looked rounder than the stock Mustang for that year, thanks to a few details changed by SVT. (Ford)*

The 1998 carryover model sold in respectable numbers, with 8,654 overall sales for SVT. Coupe production measured 5,174 units (listing for $25,710 apiece) and convertibles sold 3,480 models ($28,510 each).

## 1999

For the Mustang's 35th anniversary year, Ford went all out with a new body design and several chassis and engine improvements on the base and GT models. (For details, see Chapter 10 of this book.)

SVT, once again, went many steps beyond the stock Mustang upgrades and turned out one of the best muscle cars of the 20th century.

The 4.6-liter DOHC engine received a different combustion chamber design and reconfigured intake port geometry that created a more efficient "tumble" of the air/fuel mixture. Improved combustion raised the Cobra V-8 to 320 hp and 317-lb.-ft. ratings. A coil-on-plug ignition system and new type of knock sensor contributed to the Cobra's reliability and smooth power delivery.

Handling all that power was the Borg-Warner-designed T-45 five-speed introduced on the 1998 Mustang and Cobra models, but for 1999 the Cobra unit was built by Tremec. The rear axle's differential case was made of aluminum, although the same gears as before were installed.

For 1999, SVT's gift to the Mustang world was a long-awaited independent rear suspension (IRS) using short and long arms mounted on a tubular subframe. With an eye toward the thousands of Mustangers who would want the same IRS system on their cars, SVT designed it to mount to the four very same points as the stock GT's solid rear axle. Although the IRS weighed 80 pounds more than the previous setup, it reduced the all-important *unsprung* weight by 125 pounds, resulting in sharper handling and a better ride. SVT applied much stiffer rear springs and a thicker sway bar than ever before.

The Mustang's optional all-speed Traction Control System (TCS) was standard on the Cobra, providing a great safety benefit as it worked in concert with the car's ABS to limit wheel spin in slippery conditions.

SVT changed the Cobra's body to reflect the standard Mustang's new design, but left out the running horse's chrome surround and installed the traditional coiled serpent emblem in place of the stock car's 35th Anniversary logo. Even though the 1999 Mustang was quite blocky, the Cobra managed to have rounder features thanks to an SVT-designed front bumper cover and hood without scoops.

A new 17-inch five-spoke wheel debuted on the 1999 Cobra, again offering a nearly unobstructed view of the large disc brakes at each corner. Four exterior colors were offered: Ultra White, Ebony, Rio Red, and Electric Green. New upholstery patterns and colors were available, although only in leather—there were no cloth options for seats in 1999.

The Cobra's reputation for high performance continued to grow in its seventh year of production, but with

*The 1999 Cobra's rear valance was a stock Mustang piece. (Ford)*

one glitch. Car magazines, while testing the supposedly more powerful 1999 4.6-liter, reported that their test cars seemed slower than the previous model. Consideration was given to the extra weight of the IRS system, but in the end dynamometer tests revealed the new Cobra was not reaching its advertised output. In a move that is extremely rare in the car business, Ford ceased the sale of unsold Cobras at dealerships on Aug. 6, 1999, and recalled those models already in private hands. SVT replaced the intake manifold, engine management computer, and entire exhaust system from the catalytic converter back on every single 1999 produced. Their efforts impressed the media as well as their customers.

An unusual balance was reached for 1999, with coupe and convertible sales nearly equal. Of the 8,095 total cars sold, 4,040 were the $27,470 coupe and 4,055 were the $31,470 convertible.

## 2000

There was no SVT Cobra Mustang built for model year 2000.

The truth of the matter is the company sat out the year to evaluate its gaff over the 1999 Cobra's power deficit and to fix all of the recalled cars. This statement on the SVT Web site gave the official explanation:

*The reason for the cancellation is simply that our top priority has been our 1999 Cobra owners. Our focus and resources—and those of our SVT dealers—have been directed to the 1999 Cobra owner notification program. Rather than rushing to produce a limited number of 2000 models—and risking production/manufacturing issues by hurrying—we're choosing to focus our efforts on the timely production of the 2001 SVT Mustang Cobra.*

### 2000 COBRA R

With even more technology and manufacturing prowess at its disposal since the birth of the R model in 1993, SVT charged ahead with the third-generation of its homegrown supercar.

Not wanting to repeat themselves, the engineers at SVT developed an all-new powerplant for the 2000 R. Digging into the modular family parts bin, they settled on a 5.4-liter DOHC, 32-valve V-8 and tweaked until it turned out an awe-inspiring 385 hp and 385 lb.-ft. of torque. A lot of four-valve head work went into the creation of all that power and peak airflow was increased by 25 percent over standard Cobra components.

To appreciate the R's tremendous power (without benefit of a test drive), realize that the 5.4-liter generates 71.3 horsepower per liter, compared with 51.7 for the 1995 Cobra R, and 69.5 for the 1999 4.6-liter Cobra. Compared

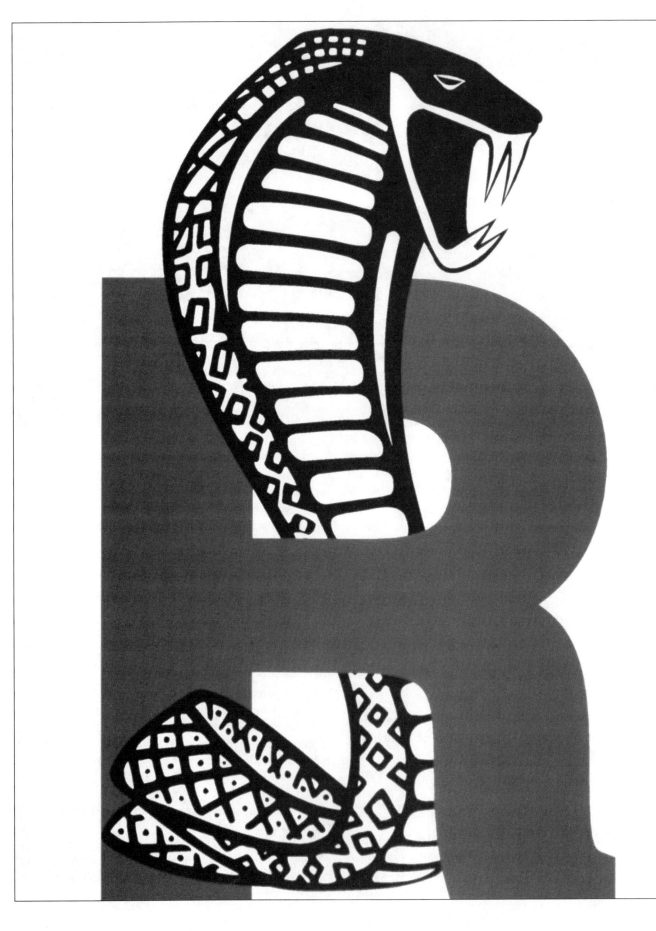

*Is the 2000 SVT Cobra R the fastest factory-produced Mustang ever? Yes. (Ford)*

MUSTANG

*Even with its super-wide 265/40-18 tires, the R's powerful engine can break traction without trying. (Ford)*

*Here's the source of the 2000 Cobra R's motive force—a 385-hp 5.4-liter V-8. (Ford)*

*Dzus fasteners are used to remove and install the R's wind splitter. (Ford)*

*Only 300 Cobra Rs (and no standard Cobras) were made in 2000. (Ford)*

*The Cobra R has an unusual side-exit exhaust system owing to a clearance problem with the 21-gallon fuel cell in the car's rear. (Ford)*

to its competition, the 8.0-liter V-10 Dodge Viper produces 56.3 horsepower per liter.

The R's unique dual exhaust system exits just in front of the rear tire on each side so as to allow maximum ground clearance for the 21-gallon fuel cell that sits just behind the rear axle.

A Tremec six-speed manual transmission—the first six-speed ever installed in a factory-built Mustang—was specified to handle the 5.4-liter's tremendous torque. Final drive ratio was a short 3.55:1 for increased acceleration.

Suspension tweaks included Eibach coil springs that lowered the car 1.5 inches in front and 1.0 inches at the rear and made the chassis 30 to 40 percent stiffer than the 1999 Cobra. Brembo four-wheel disc brakes were activated through four-piston aluminum calipers. Air inlets designed into the Cobra fog light openings were used to provide extra cooling for the R's front brakes, with air ducts shipped and installed by SVT dealers if requested by the customer.

Eighteen-inch five-spoke wheels were fitted with 265/40-18 BFGoodrich tires, which contributed somewhat to the R's astounding 1.0g of lateral acceleration. The Cobra R's rear deck and fascia were from the base V-6 Mustang, as rear-exit dual exhaust cutouts were unnecessary with the R's side-exit setup.

The front of the R included a specially designed front air splitter that, in concert with the large rear wing, reduced front lift and increased rear downforce. Because it also reduced ground clearance to a few inches, the splitter was shipped with the cars and installed at the customer's request by the dealer.

Racing Recaro seats, a thickly padded steering wheel and a B&M Ripper shifter were the R driver's only points of contact during this Mustang's wild ride. Many stock Cobra pieces were left off of the R to reduce weight, including some soundproofing material, trunk trim, spare tire cover, rear seat, air conditioning, power windows, power locks, and power seats.

How does all of this power and suspension engineering work in the real world? Quite well, it seems. The 3,590-pound R could zip to 60 mph in less than five seconds, with a top speed of more than 170 mph.

*Recaro seats keep driver and passenger in place when the R is sticking to corners at 1.0g. (Ford)*

*The huge rear wing works with the front wind splitter to reduce lift. Notice the stock V-6 Mustang rear valance panel. (Ford)*

*It's a rare opportunity to see all three generations (1993 at rear, 1995, 2000) of Cobra Rs together. (Ford)*

*How fast will it go? More than 170 miles an hour. (Ford)*

*The massaged suspension is about 40 percent stiffer than the standard Cobra. (Ford)*

Even with its short gearing, second gear is enough to earn its driver a speeding ticket in most parts of the country. At $54,995, the SVT Mustang Cobra R models sold all 300 examples before the first cars hit dealer showrooms.

## 2001

As of this printing, the 2001 SVT Cobra has been previewed by the press but is not available yet for testing and evaluation.

According to the company's releases, the 2001 model will reflect basic changes in the Mustang line and will continue to offer the 320-hp 4.6-liter introduced in 1999.

Color availability is the broadest ever in the Cobra's history, with eight tones for the choosing: Zinc Yellow, Laser Red, Performance Red, True Blue, Mineral Grey, Black, Silver, and Oxford White.

Leather is again the only seat material, available in either Dark Charcoal or Medium Parchment.

The coupe lists for $29,235 and the convertible is priced at $33,235.

*Eighteen-inch five-spoke wheels allow plenty of air to cool those huge Brembo disc brakes. (Ford)*

# CHAPTER 12

# MUSTANG

## Shelby's Amazing Mustangs (1965-70)

*The 1965 GT-350's interior was Spartan, even by standards of the day. Notice the stock Mustang's base speedometer. (Brad Bowling)*

*The GT-350's tachometer was installed in a dash-mounted gauge pod. (Brad Bowling)*

*This 1965 Shelby American GT-350R model was campaigned by Trans-Am racing series driver Jerry Titus. (Jerry Heasley)*

*Carroll Shelby used his Cobra-building recipe on the new Mustang in 1965.*

Shelby Mustangs are more sought after and valuable today than in the 1965-70 period, when the tiny Shelby American company worked its magic at 6501 West Imperial Highway, behind Los Angeles International Airport. Why the cars should be more in demand now makes an interesting story, one outdone only by the highlights of the cars themselves.

In an all-too-short period of time, Carroll Shelby won the 1959 24 Hours of LeMans race, was forced to retire from racing due to an ailing heart, and began looking for a way to make his mark in the international arena of racing without getting in the driver's seat.

In 1962, Shelby's luck was turned on full when he talked Ford Motor Company into making a high-performance production car by combining the 260-cid V-8 with a superlight British roadster chassis and body. Henry Ford II's eagerness to create a stable of world class race cars and stand on the same European podiums as Ferrari made the company an easy sell for the smooth-talking Texan.

There was as much luck on the part of Ford as Shelby; he had also been courting Chevrolet.

"When I was trying to get off the ground, I had a lot of support at Chevrolet," Shelby later revealed in an interview. "In fact, I nearly had the deal pulled off and then a couple of guys in the Corvette program naturally didn't want to see it happen. So, they kind of killed it. But, Ford wanted something to combat the Corvette. Ford was willing to spend a little money, and I was there with an idea."

Shelby introduced the first roadster prototype at the 1962 New York Auto Show billed as the "260" Cobra (the snake part of the name having appeared to Shelby in a dream, legend has it). Subsequent versions were the fast "289" and the fantastically fast "427" types. Although only about 1,000 Cobras were built up through the mid-1960s, they were so startling that even now, nearly 40 years later, the Cobra name universally translates as "ultimate, unparalleled performance!"

Shelby's Cobras dominated every series they were eligible to compete in and came within six points of catching Ferrari for the 1964 World GT Championship, so it was not surprising that the California-based modifier was tapped to breathe some life into Ford's new Mustang.

What Shelby put together was a pony that could strike like a snake!

*Although the over-the-roof LeMans stripes are quite popular with today's GT-350 owners, not all of Shelby's Mustangs had them when new. (Brad Bowling)*

*In the SCCA's Trans-Am Series, the Mustang won the annual Manufacturer's Trophy three times in six years with help from Shelby American.*
*(John Gunnell)*

*The 1965 GT-350 R-model was a pure competition machine that produced between 325 and 350 hp. Other modifications included the larger front opening seen here. (Wally Wyss)*

*The Cobra Caravan made many stops at race tracks and car shows to promote the Shelby American products. (Shelby American)*

The "Monte Carlo" bar ran across the engine bay of the GT-350's 289-cid 306-hp V-8. (Brad Bowling)

Workmen altered the 1965 Mustang fastbacks to conform to Shelby's specifications. The result was a brutal street racer with no frills. The GT-350 on the left is a competition-prepared R-model; on the right is a stock Shelby. (Shelby American)

*Racing stripes on production cars were not common in 1965, when they appeared on the Shelby GT-350. (Applegate & Applegate)*

## 1965 GT-350

Production of the GT-350 (a nonsense name created when Shelby asked how many feet were between the main assembly line and the engine room) started in October of 1964. Shelby's arrangement with Ford for 1965 gave him an allotment of Wimbledon White fastbacks directly from the San Jose, California factory with black interiors and the 289-cid 271-hp K-code V-8.

The decision to run the first year's production all in white was made more for practicality than a sense of style. Economy of scale dictated that Ford and Shelby stick to one color so the two assembly lines could be better coordinated; white was the obvious color choice since it was assumed that many GT-350s would find their way to racetracks and be painted to suit the owner's taste.

Shelby was aware that the Sports Car Club of America (SCCA) required he build a minimum of 100 cars for public purchase before it would allow his GT-350s to compete in the production car series. With the Jan. 1, 1965 deadline fast approaching, he ordered that many stock white 2+2s from the San Jose plant and parked them in his ready-to-ship lot when the sanctioning body inspectors visited. Homologation was never so easy.

The GT-350 formula was a simple one: remove anything from the car that didn't directly make it faster. This meant that many stock Mustang parts were either deleted at the Ford factory or pulled at Shelby American including hoods, rear seats, exhaust systems, and the decorative grille bars.

While Shelby American was run with the precision and resourcefulness of a race team, many factors—including budget considerations, supplier issues and time constraints—made for "running changes" throughout the Shelby Mustang's life. For example, the 16-inch wood-rimmed, three-spoke steering wheel on early Shelbys was found to rub against some drivers' thighs and was replaced by a 15-inch unit. Once that change was in place, Shelby's English supplier for the steering wheel (the same craftsmen who produced similar pieces for the Cobra) began randomly changing little style elements from batch to batch. Such running changes were almost never recorded and mattered little to the crew on the production line.

The suspension modifications included thicker front sway bars, longer idler and Pitman arms, lowered upper control arms, over-ride traction bars, stiffer springs and

Koni adjustable shock absorbers. Heavy-duty brake components such as the Kelsey-Hayes ventilated front disc rotors were installed.

The most important aspect of the GT-350's performance, the V-8 engine, was modified with a new camshaft; a "Cobra" aluminum high-rise intake manifold; 715-cfm Holley four-barrel carburetor; "Cobra" cast aluminum finned valve covers; a "Cobra" cast aluminum finned 6.5-quart oil pan; steel tubing "Tri-Y" exhaust headers; low-restriction mufflers; and dual side-exit exhaust pipes. Shelby advertised that his modifications resulted in 306 hp.

With such a brutal powerplant sitting between the fenders, it was necessary to shore up the engine compartment and firewall with a "Monte Carlo" bar. This device was simply a strong piece of steel that ran between the two shock towers to prevent torque twisting of the chassis under hard acceleration or cornering. Another change to the engine compartment on some GT-350s was the relocation of the battery to the trunk for better weight distribution. Other mechanical hard parts included a heavy-duty shortened Galaxie rearend with a Detroit Automotive no-spin gear unit and an aluminum-cased Borg-Warner T-10 four-speed transmission.

Stock wheels were stamped steel 15x5-1/2-inch production pieces from Ford's big station wagons, painted silver and minus any type of hubcap. Cragar and American Racing produced optional rims to Shelby's specifications. High-performance Goodyear Blue Dot tires were mounted to give the GT-350 the best street rubber available (it was probably no coincidence that Shelby was a Goodyear distributor).

All GT-350s got fiberglass hoods, although several different versions were produced during the 1965-66 run as attempts were made to solve a problem with cracking. Initial hoods were made entirely of fiberglass; later versions had metal framing. The hood latch mechanism was deleted and NASCAR-style pins were installed to lock everything down. A low-profile, but functional, scoop drew outside air into the air cleaner.

A fiberglass shelf sat where the stock Mustang rear seat would be, with the spare tire taking up the bulk of the useable room.

Each GT-350 received a tri-bar Guardsman Blue paint stripe along the rocker panel and door bottom. The stripes broke only for a "G.T. 350" logo rendered in 3M tape. Twin, 10-inch-wide blue racing "LeMans" stripes were a popular option that ran from front to rear over the top of the car.

According to accounts from 1965, the GT-350 was the most brutal car ever built for the general public. Like a race car, it was beastly fast and required a heavy foot and strong arms to drive it to its potential. Unlike a race car, it could be purchased at Ford dealerships and came with a full warranty.

In all, only 525 GT-350s were sold in 1965 for an advertised base price of $4,547. Approximately 36 of those cars were a special competition-only package known as the R-model. The stripped GT-350R, which sold for $5,950, produced between 325 and 350 hp.

## 1966 GT-350 AND GT-350H

A quirk of mass production created several running changes for the GT-350 at the beginning of its second

The 1966 Shelby Mustang GT-350 was quite a package that came for an amazingly low $4,428 factory price. The easiest way to distinguish the 1966 from the 1965 at a glance is by the clear plexiglass triangular rear window replacing the stock Mustang vents. (Old Cars Weekly)

*Some took Hertz ads literally. There were stories of renting a Shelby Mustang for a quarter-mile Sunday afternoon drive. (John Gunnell)*

*Only 2,380 Shelby Mustang GT-350s were produced in 1966 and 936 of them went to Hertz Rent-A-Car Company. They carried a "GT-350H" call-out in their rocker panel stripe. Initially equipped with four-speed manual transmissions, Hertz quickly decreed Shelby install automatics on the later cars. (Old Cars Weekly)*

*Shelby Mustangs came closest of all to achieving the so-called ideal combination of Saturday racer/Sunday go-to-church sedan. This 1966 edition gets attention from its Sunday-racer owner at Elkhart Lake. (Ron Kowalke)*

year of life. Ford Motor Company shut down every July for the annual new model changeover but Shelby American built cars year round based on the San Jose plant's output. The ever-resourceful Carroll Shelby worked around this problem by taking delivery of 252 1965 fastbacks—before the temporary shutdown—to be converted into 1966-model GT-350s.

Work began immediately on the mechanical conversions and new-for-1966 body pieces such as a plexiglass insert in place of the Mustang's rear air vents and a functional rear brake air scoop mounted just rearward of the door. Once the new Mustang grille (the only change Shelby would make to the stock 1966 package) arrived, the cars could be sold as 1966 models.

Coinciding with the modification of the "carryover" cars was a visit to Shelby American from some Ford execs and efficiency experts looking to lower the operation's per-unit cost. Some costly and time-consuming procedures performed on the 1965 GT-350 had been the subject of customer and dealer complaints, such as the expensive, but clunky, Detroit Locker rear axle and the super-stiff competition suspension.

Dealers wanted sporty, but comfortable, cars that could seat four people and be serviced by a regular Ford technician. In other words, they wanted a Mustang that was just a little bit faster than the factory's own GT option. They wanted more colors, an automatic trans-

mission and a back seat, for starters. Shelby had already anticipated some of the requests in his plans for the 1966 GT-350. For example, the noisy Detroit Locker was already listed as an option in 1966 literature.

The carryover cars were already in the process of having their A-arms lowered, but all GT-350s afterwards would retain stock factory geometry. Those race-ready traction over-ride bars were replaced by cheaper units that were easier to install. The Koni adjustable shocks became optional equipment, as did the fiberglass shelf that had replaced the back seat on 1965 Shelbys. The expensive imported real-wood steering wheels were replaced with stock Mustang GT units wearing special GT-350 logos and the previous year's Guardsman Blue side stripes were now entirely a 3M tape product.

All of the cost-savings produced a more comfortable, "user-friendly" car that, at a retail price of $4,428, was cheaper than the 1965 GT-350. Other amenities offered to attract customers included new colors: Candy Apple Red, Guardsman Blue, Ivy Green, and Raven Black. An automatic transmission option was an easy decision to make as Ford already had its excellent C-4 in many high-performance applications (a 595-cfm carburetor was specified when the automatic was ordered). An AM radio became a factory-installed option halfway through the year.

Perhaps the greatest option for the GT-350 came toward the end of the model year when Shelby offered a Paxton supercharger for $670, including factory installation. Shelby American claimed the option would produce up to 46% more horsepower from the 289-cid V-8. Apparently, Shelby wasn't too sure how much abuse the blowers could take from his customers because the warranty was only for 90 days or 4,000 miles. It is estimated that only 150 GT-350s were ordered with this high-performance option.

Total GT-350 production for 1966 was 2,380 cars—quite an increase over the previous year's sales numbers. Nearly 40% went to the Hertz car rental fleet as part of the company's Hertz Sports Car Club. A special run of 936 GT-350H fastbacks were put into service as rental cars, initially in black-with-gold paint schemes, but later in all 1966 Shelby colors. The first H-models were built as part of the 1965 carryover line and included all of the heavy-duty suspension mods. Eventually, Hertz asked that all its GT-350s come with automatic transmissions and a power booster for the stiff competition-style brakes.

In hindsight, receiving the high-profile Hertz order (Shelbys were featured in their national advertising) was probably the pivotal point in Shelby production. Guaran-

teeing nearly 1,000 cars—the original pitch to Hertz executives was for 25-50 units—put Shelby American in a better position to bargain with its suppliers. The sale also meant that the average traveler could be exposed to the GT-350, a point that no doubt increased non-Hertz sales for 1966 and later.

## 1967 GT-350 and GT-500

1967 marked another step away from the hard-core enthusiast product the first GT-350 had been.

*Though super-valuable, many Shelby Mustangs such as this 1967 model, still compete in vintage racing.*

*Shelby designed his 1967 GT-350 around the fatter, more indulgent Mustang of the same year. The result was a smooth, clean look, though a bit "pregnant" in places, particularly as seen at this angle of the fastback. (Applegate & Applegate)*

*This 1967 has its grille-mounted lights close together, suggesting that it was produced early in the year. Some states' vehicle laws dictated a minimum distance between headlights, forcing Shelby to reconfigure the grille. (Old Cars Weekly)*

From the standpoint of appearance, the GT-350 became its own car in 1967, separating itself cosmetically from the stock Mustang while becoming more similar mechanically. Ford dealers were happy with this change in direction because it created a visually exciting product to sell that had as much creature comfort as a basic Mustang, but without the need for specialized maintenance equipment and training.

Because the base Mustang had been given a redesign for 1967, the Shelby cars followed suit. Shelby cleverly made his fastbacks look longer and lower than the stock Mustangs by the tasteful use of more fiberglass than in previous years.

The fiberglass twin-scooped hood (complete with racing-style lock-down hood pins) jutted forward further than the Mustang's all-steel piece and gave the grille the appearance of a dark, menacing mouth. Two round auxiliary lights were placed side-by-side in the middle of that grille (although some states' department of motor vehicles would cause later cars to have the lights pushed out to the edges). A stock chrome Mustang bumper, minus the vertical bumperettes, stood guard at the front of the Shelby. A fiberglass, forward-facing scoop sat just in front of the rear wheel well on each side of the car to channel air into the rear brakes (depending on the Shelby factory's ducting supplies, some cars' scoops were not functional). The stock Mustang's rear vents were covered with a rear-facing scoop that helped draw air out of the passenger compartment. (Early 1967 cars had a red running light installed in this scoop, but the accessory was dropped later due to wiring concerns.) A three-piece spoiler was applied to the rear of all 1967 Shelby Mustangs and accented by the extra-wide taillights mounted in a flat panel.

*1967 changed Shelby American. Its emphasis and product line were redirected for broader appeal. Production was increased and more Ford dealers handled the now-prestige line because so many mechanical parts were stock Mustang. The big-block GT-500 model was new for 1967. (Applegate & Applegate)*

*GT-500 was Shelby's designation for the Shelby Mustang with a big 428-cid V-8. Some enthusiasts winced at the placement of such a heavy motor in what started as a light, agile car. (Applegate & Applegate)*

*This couple has two ways to enjoy horsepower, on the hoof or through their GT-500. (Applegate & Applegate)*

The luxurious 1967 was built only with the Mustang's Deluxe Interior package available in black or parchment (some examples in white have been documented), and a sporty, entirely functional roll bar was installed into every car.

Shelbys came standard that year with power steering and power-assisted brakes. Suspension enhancements were largely stock Mustang, including the special handling package, front disc brakes, thicker front stabilizer bar, export brace, and adjustable Gabriel shock absorbers. Stock wheels were 15-inch stamped steel units with hubcaps; various sporty rims from Kelsey-Hayes and American Racing were optional.

Power for the GT-350 was, once again, the Ford 289-cid V-8 with various Shelby modifications. Although the factory continued to claim an output of 306 hp, it is noteworthy that Shelby dropped the tubular exhaust headers in 1967, preferring the lower cost of Ford's high-performance cast-iron manifold. Paxton's powerful supercharger remained on the option list, as did SelectAire air conditioning and the high-performance C-4 automatic transmission.

Happy Ford dealers sold 1,175 1967 GT-350s for $3,995 apiece. This marked the second straight year in which GT-350 prices had decreased.

The big news for the GT-350 for 1967 was that it gained a big brother in the form of the GT-500. Shelby managed to one-up Ford by installing the 428-cid big-block V-8 in his top-line offering—the massive power-plant produced at least 50 more horsepower than the stock Mustang's big 390-cid V-8. Fed through a pair of 600-cfm four-barrel Holley carburetors and boasting a special high-rev hydraulic valvetrain, the 428 was rated at a conservative 355 hp; realistically, it probably registered around 400 hp. Ford's four-speed "toploader" transmission was standard with the GT-500, with the stout "police spec" C-6 doing automatic shifting duties.

Shelby's new big-block supercar retailed for $4,195 and sold 2,050 units.

## 1968 GT-350, GT-500 AND GT-500KR

The decision had been made mid-year in 1967 to relocate GT-350 and GT-500 production closer to Ford's home in Michigan. Shelby American was about to lose the lease on its airport buildings and needed a new location suitable for the construction of nearly 5,000 high-performance Mustangs.

All 1968 and later GT-350s and GT-500s were assembled by the A.O. Smith Company in Ionia, Michigan, from stock Mustangs produced at the Metuchen, New Jersey, plant. A.O. Smith manufactured fiberglass panels, among other things, and was in a perfect position to tighten the supply chain between the Ford factory and the dealership network.

*The 1968 styling looked more like a Thunderbird than a Cobra. (Brad Bowling)*

*Borrowing from the Ford parts bin, Shelby put 1965 Thunderbird sequential taillights on the back of his 1968 GT-350 (pictured) and GT-500. (Brad Bowling)*

*In 1968, production of the GT-350/500 Shelby Mustang was relocated to the A.O. Smith Company in Ionia, Michigan. There, the Shelby shocks, high-performance tires, locking rear end, and fiberglass body pieces were installed. (Brad Bowling)*

*For some reason, women found themselves attracted to the 1968 Shelby Mustang GT-500 fastback. (Old Cars Weekly)*

*SelectShift automatic transmission became a $50 option in the GT-350 and an obvious shot at attracting a new type of buyer to increase sales. (Brad Bowling)*

*The comfort level of Shelby Mustangs had increased quite a bit since 1965. Notice the second switch in the doorjamb of this 1968 GT-350 convertible? That option causes the steering wheel to move aside a few inches when the driver gets in. (Brad Bowling)*

*Female buyers liked some of the options available for the 1968 Shelby Mustangs, including air conditioning and a tilt steering wheel. (Old Cars Weekly)*

Since the stock 1968 Mustang was little different from the 1967 model, Shelby's GT-350s and GT-500s only received minor cosmetic changes. The most obvious upgrade for 1968 was the hood, which now featured twin scoops running almost to the leading edge of the car. For the first time in Shelby history, the stock Mustang hood lock mechanism was retained, although external turn-knob fasteners were provided for a bit more safety. An all-new fiberglass front valance panel worked with a new upper grille housing to create an even larger "mouth" for the beast. Rectangular Marchal driving lights were perched inside that opening (there was a switch to Lucas units early in the year and a recall to replace the Marchals). The back of the car received wide, sequential taillights from a 1965 Thunderbird.

All Shelbys were again equipped with the Mustang's Deluxe Interior. Some cars had Ford's tilt steering, but it was not possible to specifically order the option; you either got it or you didn't. Cars ordered with air conditioning received tinted glass, as this was the only way Ford would build them. The GT-500 got a special oil cooler.

GT-350s were powered in 1968 by Ford's new 302-cid V-8, which was rated at 250 hp—down 56 hp from the previous model. Early production cars breathed through a 600-cfm Autolite carburetor sitting on a cast iron intake manifold. A 600-cfm Holley four-barrel and aluminum Cobra intake went into the mix once certification was complete. The 302 was another increase of the 260/289 block. The Paxton supercharger option, now boasting a 100 hp increase, was still on the books for the GT-350 but very few were ordered.

*The 10-spoke alloy wheel was a popular upgrade for Shelby owners starting in 1968. (Brad Bowling)*

For 1968, the Shelby Mustang featured two large scoops that sat on the leading edge of the fiberglass hood. Twist pins acted in concert with the stock Mustang hood latch to hold everything in place at speed. (Brad Bowling)

GT-500s got a 428-cid 360-hp version of Ford's Police Interceptor package (although a few 390-cid V-8s were installed when the 428 ran short). The 428 had a single 715-cfm Holley four-barrel carburetor, although it (and the GT-350) had air cleaners sporting two screw-down wingnuts—suggesting there were still two carbs hiding under there.

New for 1968 was a convertible body style for both models. Tops were available in either black or white and the padded roll bar had two small rectangular rings mounted on top—supposedly for surfboards, legend has it. One out of every three Shelby Mustangs sold in 1968 was a convertible.

As if to prove that performance was still a top priority, Shelby introduced mid-year a model known as the GT-500KR as a replacement for the standard GT-500. The KR, whose extra initials stand for "King of the Road," managed to stuff Ford's new 400 hp (unofficial rating) 428 Cobra Jet

Base engine in the 1968 Shelby Mustang GT-500 was the 428-cid engine with 360 hp. (Old Cars Weekly)

*This 1968 GT-350 announces through its personalized plate that it is sporting the rare Paxton supercharger option. (Brad Bowling)*

between the fenders. Other changes were made to the chassis to support such a powerful plant, such as extra bracing on the lower edge of the shock towers and staggered rear shocks when the KR was equipped with the four-speed transmission. Wider rear brake shoes and drums, heavy-duty wheel cylinders and brake line fittings were installed for the sake of safety, as was a freer-flowing exhaust system. As with the standard GT-500, the KR was available in either fastback or convertible body style.

At the end of the year, Shelby's best ever, the company had produced 4,450 cars. The breakdown included 1,253 GT-350 fastbacks (suggested retail $4,116), 404 GT-350 convertibles ($4,238), 1,140 GT-500 fastbacks ($4,317), 402 GT-500 convertibles ($4,438), 933 GT-500KR fastbacks ($4,472), and 318 GT-500KR convertibles ($4,594).

*A rear spoiler and 1965 Thunderbird taillights made the 1968 look different from the stock Mustang. (Old Cars Weekly)*

The padded roll bar was a unique feature of the 1968 Shelby convertibles. (Brad Bowling)

Justifying the $1,000 higher price tags was hard. Shelby Mustangs never came close to the 5,000-cars-a-year goal Ford set. (Volo Auto Museum)

The "King of the Road's" 335-hp V-8 and massive 440 lb.-ft. of torque delivered rapid acceleration from any speed. (Brad Bowling)

*The GT-500KR was "loaded" with all the luxuries and power assists of a Cadillac limo, plus some that the Cadillac didn't even have. (Brad Bowling)*

MUSTANG

*Special touches for the rear of the 1968 fastback included the Shelby name and "Cobra" gas cap. (Brad Bowling)*

*Close-up of the
1968 vent scoop.
(Brad Bowling)*

*Only 4,450 Shelby Mustangs were produced in 1968. (Applegate & Applegate)*

## 1969-70 GT-350 AND GT-500

The third-generation Shelby Mustang was a tragic textbook case of the comedy staple known as "good news/bad news." The good news was that the 1969 GT-350 and GT-500 were the most refined and polished Shelby Mustangs ever. The bad news was that they were the last Shelby Mustangs ever.

Perhaps most striking about the 1969 Shelby Mustang was that it looks nothing at all like the stock Ford on which it was based. Fiberglass was used extensively on the final Shelby design; both for its lightweight quality and the cheapness with which whole body panels could be created and produced.

While the standard Mustang increased in length by four inches for 1969, the Shelby version was extended another three inches past that through the use of an entirely new front end. Shelby once again created a fiberglass hood, this time with a total of five recessed NASA-type hood scoops. The leading edge of the hood was trimmed with a chrome strip that curved around and down at the outer edges to meet the unique-to-Shelby front bumper. The grille was flat black with a chrome strip forming a wide rectangle inside the "mouth." Lucas driving lights were attached to the underside of the bumper.

Fiberglass fenders for the GT-350 and GT-500 were fresh designs whose length helped give the Shelby its lowest and leanest look ever.

The traditional Shelby side stripes were made larger and were raised to the middle of the body, where they now ran the entire length of the car. The rear brakes were once again cooled through an air scoop mounted on the body just ahead of the wheel well; on convertibles it was in line with the body stripe, on fastbacks it sat just behind the door handle.

The rear of the Shelby Mustang received a similar treatment in 1969 as it had in 1968, including the 1965 Thunderbird taillights. A spring-mounted frame displayed the license plate squarely between the two taillights and concealed the fuel filler cap. Directly below the license plate was a pair of rectangular exhaust tips pushed very tightly together. (The proximity of the gas cap to the hot exhaust system outlet was the subject of a fire-hazard recall later in the year.)

Paint colors for 1969 offered the greatest choice in Shelby history, with all of Ford's "Grabber" hues available. Bright Blue, Green, Yellow, Orange, and Competition Orange were added early in the year to Black Jade, Acapulco Blue, Gulfstream Aqua, Candy Apple Red, and Royal Maroon.

*Over a five-year period, Carroll Shelby (seen here with three of his 1969 Mustangs) did more to establish the Mustang's reputation as a high-performance vehicle than anyone. (Shelby American)*

*In 1969, Shelby tried to keep his car line going with a special suspension and exceptional handling, while Ford added "simulated teakwood" interior trim. The GT-500 could still move down a racetrack, though. (Applegate & Applegate)*

Shelby interior colors for 1969 included black and white only, with high-back bucket seats, vinyl-covered "Rim Blow" steering wheel and center console appearing as part of the deluxe Mustang equipment. Door panels and the dashboard contained many imitation wood inserts.

The Mustang's heavy-duty suspension once again provided the GT-350 and GT-500 with their sporty rides. Staggered shocks were standard on the GT-500. Gone were the stamped steel wheels of earlier years and in their place was a five-spoke, 15x7-inch rim that mounted Goodyear belted E-70x15 wide oval tires (F-60x15 tires were optional). Some Shelbys wound up with Boss 302

"Magnum 500" wheels when a defect was discovered in the stock rim, forcing a recall.

Ford's new 351-cid Windsor V-8 was installed in every 1969 GT-350. Rated at 290 hp, it breathed through a 470-cfm Autolite four-barrel carburetor and came standard attached to Ford's four-speed manual transmission. Optional gearboxes included a close-ratio four-speed and the FMX automatic.

The GT-500 (the KR part of the name was dropped for 1969) charged into production with its fire-breathing 428-cid Cobra Jet V-8 in place from the previous year. A close-ratio four-speed was standard, with the C-6 back as an optional automatic.

*"Leftovers" never tasted this good! This 428-cid Cobra Jet V-8 sits under the hood of a carryover 1970 Shelby GT-500. (Brad Bowling)*

In 1969, one writer said, "You can take the latest Shelby and your surfboard to the beach, or let it idle in front of your girlfriend's house in the winter, with the heater on, and not wake up the neighborhood." (Ford)

The 1969 Shelby convertible came in Grabber Blue, Signal Orange, white or red with gold stripes. "Racetrack characteristics of the old Shelby Mustang GT-350 make the new 500 look like a bull in a china shop," Sports Car Graphic said. (Ford)

The 1969 Shelby Cobra GT-500 convertible listed for $5,027. Below its hood was a potent 428-cid 335 hp Cobra Jet V-8. (Ford)

At 3,939 pounds, the GT-500 convertible was about 100 pounds heavier than the SportsRoof version in 1969. Only 535 of these cars were sold. (Ford)

The mesh grille and NASA-scooped hood of the 1969 Shelby-Cobra Mustang were later copied by Ford on the 1971 Mach 1. (Ford)

The 1970 Shelby was really just a 1969 carried over into the next model year. (Brad Bowling)

In spite of their incredible power, performance and potential, the really outstanding feature of the Shelby Mustangs was that they were still "just a plain ol' Mustang" and within the budget of many enthusiasts. (Ford)

*The Shelbys were not at all temperamental or troublesome like a lot of high-performance cars. They didn't leak oil all over your foot or cough and sputter for new spark plugs every few thousand miles. (Applegate & Applegate)*

Sales for 1969 were brisk, with 1,085 GT-350 fastbacks (retailing at $4,434), 194 GT-350 convertibles ($4,753), 1,536 GT-500 fastbacks ($4,709), and 335 GT-500 convertibles ($5,027) going to new owners.

Despite these positive numbers, in the fall of 1969 Carroll Shelby convinced Lee Iacocca to end the Shelby GT program. Shelby could see that the American auto industry and Federal government were tightening the screws on performance cars and that there would soon be no market for the type of vehicles he wanted to produce. Also, Ford Motor Company was mass-producing cars that competed directly with the GT-350 and GT-500, such as the Mach 1, Boss 302, and Boss 429.

With several hundred Mustangs still to be built out, Shelby agreed to update 1969 leftovers into 1970

models with new vehicle identification numbers, a set of black hood stripes and a chin spoiler. The hands-on work of converting from one year to the next was handled by dealers (if the cars had already been delivered) or through Ford's Kar Kraft plant. To fulfill the remaining production, some Mustangs being built as Mach 1s were pulled and turned into 1970 Shelbys, which explains why some of the last GT-350s and GT-500s had certain options not offered by Shelby American.

There is not an accurate count for how many 1970 Shelbys were created, although an educated guess is that 315 GT-350s and 286 GT-500s finished off the 1969 carryovers.

*The Shelby American Automobile Club (SAAC) welcomes enthusiasts of Panteras, Griffiths, Mustangs, and high-performance Fords.*

*SAAC, founded in 1975.*

## The Shelby American Automobile Club

The Shelby American Automobile Club was founded in 1975. Today, it has 6,200 members. Ownership of a Shelby Cobra or Shelby Mustang is not essential. In fact, SAAC is open to all enthusiasts of Panteras, Griffiths, Sunbeam Tigers, Mustangs, and other high-performance Ford-powered vehicles.

The club publishes a professional-quality magazine called *The Shelby American*. Dues are $36.50 per year. Membership information can be obtained from Rick Kopec at P.O. Box 788, Sharon, CT 06069. You can call SAAC at (203) 364-0449 or FAX them at (203) 364-0769. The club's Web site address is www.saac.com.

# CHAPTER 13

MUSTANG

## Saleen—Keeping the
## Edge Razor Sharp (1984-2001)

*Although Steve Saleen produced three of his high-performance Mustangs in 1984, this 1985 model is considered to be part of the first full year of production. (Saleen)*

*This 1988 shows off the sporty lines of the Saleen in convertible form. (Brad Bowling)*

*Taking a chapter from the later Shelby Mustangs, Steve Saleen combined luxury with high-performance. (Brad Bowling)*

For performance junkies, the Shelby years of 1965-70 were magic times when anything was possible. Facing minimal intrusion from the Federal government in terms of safety, emissions and fuel consumption regulations, Carroll Shelby and crew were virtually unrestrained in their attempt to produce high-performance Mustangs.

As was discussed in Chapter 12, Shelby sensed a dark cloud hovering over the American auto industry and took measures to distance himself and his products from the turmoil by bowing out in 1969.

The 1970s produced no high water marks in terms of performance, especially in the Mustang line, where only the 139-hp King Cobra brought any life to the party. American car companies were struggling to keep market share away from foreign companies such as Toyota, Nissan, and Volkswagen; adding a couple of gas crises to the technical hurdles facing the Big Three meant that no one placed high-performance at the top of his priority list.

As Detroit poured money and resources into engine-management computer technologies, the industry was able to turn out a more stable product that was at once fuel-efficient and reliable; tuning for performance was the next logical step.

Although Ford toyed with turbocharging its four-cylinder Mustang off and on between 1979 and 1986, the first real performance pony since 1973 came with the re-introduction of the 5.0-liter V-8 in the 1982 GT.

Steve Saleen, a business school graduate with a racing background in the Sports Car Club of America (SCCA) Formula Atlantic and Trans-Am series, was thrilled by Ford's first assault on the early 1980s horsepower war. Saleen

*Saleen Mustangs have been successful competitors in several racing series. This 1987 fastback, wearing the number 19, won the Sports Car Club of America (SCCA) Showroom Stock GT division championship. (Brad Bowling)*

*This trio of 1989s awaits the transporter truck at Saleen's Anaheim, California, facility. (Brad Bowling)*

*Saleen also built successful race cars for other competitors. John Ames raced his SCC-style Mustang in SCCA's Pro Solo autocross series. (Brad Bowling)*

*The California GT conversion included the Racecraft suspension kit, four-wheel disc brakes with five-lug rotors, Saleen five-spoke wheels and Saleen rear spoiler. (Brad Bowling)*

*Although built by the Saleen factory, the California GT series was not included in the company's regular numbering system. It is one of many special Fords built "on the side" by Saleen over the years. (Brad Bowling)*

(pronounced like the last two syllables of "gasoline") had owned 1965 and 1966 Shelby GT-350s and a 1967 GT fastback with a 390-cid V-8, so he was personally quite aware of how Carroll Shelby's guiding hand had turned a garden-variety Mustang into a world-class performance car. Founding Saleen Autosport in 1984 was the Californian's first step toward carving a place for himself in the Mustang hall of fame.

## 1984: BIRTH AND EVOLUTION OF THE SALEEN "ORIGINAL RECIPE"

Working within the confines of the federally regulated car industry, Saleen established a formula he would apply to all of his high-performance Mustangs—at least initially. Rather than make a faster pony through engine modifications that would require expensive and extensive testing for emissions, fuel consumption and warranty standards, Saleen elected to leave the engines bone stock and enhance performance by concentrating on suspension, brakes, chassis, and aerodynamic improvements.

Saleen Autosport produced only three cars in 1984, each built from 175-hp Mustang hatchbacks. Saleen's own Racecraft suspension components, including specific-rate front and rear springs; Bilstein pressurized struts and shocks; a front crossmember; and urethane sway bar bushings lowered the car and improved the Mustang's handling to near race rack levels. Those first three cars wore some of the largest high-performance rubber available at the time—Goodyear Eagle GTs measuring 215/60-15 wrapped around 15x7-inch Hayashi "basketweave" wheels. A custom front airdam, sideskirts, clear covers for the recessed headlights, and a rather showy spoiler created a smoother aerodynamic package. The interior featured a Saleen-unique gauge package, four-spoke steering wheel and Escort radar detector.

*The SSC prototype (known as the "SA-5") was originally black. When Steve Saleen realized that black cars seldom make the covers of car magazines, he decided to create an all-white series. (Saleen)*

*The SSC was tested thoroughly by the car magazines. Csaba Csere, from* Car and Driver, *wrings out the white fastback on the skidpad at Willow Springs. (Brad Bowling)*

*Some people are never content with perfection. It might look like a stock Saleen Mustang, but under the hood is . . . (Brad Bowling)*

For a sticker price of $14,300 ($4,526 more than a standard Mustang GT), the Saleen was quite reasonable when parked next to a comparably equipped Camaro Z-28 ($14,086), Pontiac Trans-Am ($15,100), or Toyota Supra ($16,853). Even Ford's own SVO Mustang was more expensive at $15,585.

Showing great faith that these would be the first of many cars to bear his name, Saleen took a lesson from the rabid Shelby Mustang culture and began assigning year-specific serial numbers to his Mustangs. Those first three cars were numbered 032, 051, and 052 because Saleen felt having higher numbers than 001, 002, and 003 would suggest a larger, more successful company and encourage orders for more. In succeeding years, Saleen's numbers would never begin with 001 and progress from there, which is why fans of the marque usually become very good detectives when ferreting out information about their particular cars.

Over the next few years, Saleen Mustangs evolved at a fast pace, with more or better equipment being worked into the recipe as it became available.

## 1985

The 1985 Saleen was based on the new 210-hp Mustang, with larger 225/60-15 Goodyear and Fulda tires and a slightly modified aerodynamics package. Metallic pads for the front brakes were standard on the $14,795 Saleen. Sales were definitely improved for the year, with 128 units going to new owners, including one in convertible form.

1985 also marked the year that Saleen gained official factory recognition from Ford, meaning his cars could be sold through the company's established dealer network and were eligible for full warranty protection.

## 1986

1986 saw a return to the racetrack, with Saleen Mustangs competing in SCCA Showroom Stock events. Track testing brought changes to the street car, including an

*. . . a turbocharged 302-cid V-8 custom-built by Ak Miller. The owner of the "Stealth Saleen" estimates its power output at around 450 hp. (Brad Bowling)*

upgrade to 225/50-16 General XP-2000 high-performance radials; a strut-to-tower reinforcement brace (similar to Shelby's Monte Carlo bar); a revised air-dam and spoiler package; a short-throw Hurst shifter; Momo steering wheel; race-style bucket seats; Koni shocks; and a top-line Kenwood stereo system. A race-style "dead pedal" for the driver's left foot, such as what was offered in the SVO Mustang, became standard equipment in 1986.

Magazine testers were impressed with the package's 6.0-second zero-to-60 mph time and top speed of 142 mph. Corvette-caliber handling was a measured .88g of lateral acceleration. At a price of around $15,500, it turns out that 201 customers were also impressed with what they saw.

## 1987

Ford's restyling of the Mustang for 1987 also benefited Saleen. With 225 hp under the hood and a more aerodynamic body, the base 5.0-liter LX was a great starting point for a Saleen Mustang. Saleen's most important refinement to the formula was the decision to replace the standard car's front disc/rear drum, four-lug brake system with a four-wheel-disc, five-lug setup—parts originally designed for the now-defunct SVO Mustang. This labor-intensive change also required the addition of a heavy-duty master cylinder and braided brake lines. When tested, the new brakes showed a five-foot savings when stopping the car from 60 miles an hour and exhibited far less fade under extreme conditions.

Perhaps the greatest boost to acceleration of the Saleen was the introduction in 1987 of the 3.55:1 rear axle ratio as an option. It was available to replace the standard Saleen 3.08:1 gearing and provided a substantial improvement in zero-to-60 mph and quarter-mile times.

Interior upgrades for 1987 included installation of articulated FloFit seats and a new Kenwood six-speaker sound system. Saleen buyers received special commemorative jackets starting this year. The Escort radar detector came off the standard equipment list and became an option as more states were

This 1989 convertible shows the new, blocky Saleen windshield banner. (Brad Bowling)

Scoops and air intakes adorn the 2000 Saleen S281. (Morrison Motors)

A decal on the rear window of the 2000 Saleen S281 coupe boasts of the company's SCCA Manufacturer's Championship in 1987, 1996, 1997 and 1998. (Morrison Motors)

Although they are non-functional, the scoops on this 2000 Saleen help create the illusion of a lower, wider car. (Morrison Motors)

questioning the legality of such products. One two-door coupe was produced in Saleen trim for 1987, adding a third body style to the hatchback and convertible models. Sales of the $19,900 base Saleen were brisk at 280 copies.

1987 was also a good year for Saleen Mustangs on the racetrack, as it marked the company's first (of four) SCCA Manufacturer's championships.

## 1988

1988 Saleens were essentially carryovers from the previous year, with minimal changes. Monroe shock absorbers replaced the Koni units after Monroes helped Saleen racecars turn faster lap times. American-built Pioneer got the nod to replace Kenwood as the official stereo supplier to Saleen Autosport. Factory mufflers were replaced with Walker aftermarket units, which reduced back pressure to provide more horsepower. The Escort radar detector was dropped from the option list for 1988.

With enthusiasm and name-recognition building for Saleen's modified Mustangs, it was no surprise that 708 were sold in 1988, including 137 convertibles.

In an attempt to keep the Saleen production line busy during Ford's annual downtime for Mustang model switchover, the company experimented in 1988 with building a Ranger-based Sportruck for the street. Since Steve Saleen and other drivers were already competing in four-cylinder, short-bed Rangers in SCCA events, a street version built around a V-6, long-bed model seemed like a good marketing idea. Unfortunately, interruptions in the component supply line and a total redesign of the Ranger killed the momentum for this project with only 24 examples produced at a list price of $16,500 each.

## 1989: SALEEN ADDS "HOT & SPICY" TO THE MENU

The year 1989 was the busiest in Saleen history—and also the most productive.

Changes to the 1989 Saleen Mustang package were minimal, as the company was focused on several areas at once, both on and off the track. The SCCA campaign was still successful and continuing to build the high-performance image of the base Saleen Mustang. Saleen tried to move into the open-wheel IndyCar series in 1989 but trouble qualifying for the Indianapolis 500 effectively ended that effort.

The most memorable aspect of the year for fans of the Saleen Mustangs was the introduction, on April 17, 1989 of the SSC (the Mustang's 25th birthday).

The SSC was the second huge step forward for Saleen Autosport as it was built around a 292-hp, EPA 50-states-certified 5.0-liter V-8—no mean feat for a small-volume automaker. Saleen's modifications to the 5.0 included a 65mm throttle body (up from the stock Mustang's 60mm), revised intake plenum, enlarged cylinder head ports, wider rocker arm ratios, stainless steel tubular headers and Walker Dynomax mufflers.

A high-performance version of the Mustang's Borg-Warner T-5 transmission was installed behind the new powerplant and controlled by a Hurst short-throw shifter. Standard rear gears were the 3.55:1 units for ground-scorching acceleration.

Cockpit-adjustable, three-way Monroe shock absorbers were quite an innovation at the time and Steve Saleen had to have them on his flagship SSC. Massive 245/50-16 General XP-2000 rubber sat on the rear, with the slightly narrower front receiving 225/50-16s. SSC wheels were beautiful five-spoke DP models.

Mechanically, the car either benefited from the stock Saleen inventory or, in most cases, went one better with all-new equipment.

Saleen interiors had always been special places; the SSC cabin was a sacred shrine to the marriage of luxury and performance. Leather FloFit seats and matching door panels told the driver he was a very lucky person. There was no back seat in the SSC; that area was taken up with 200 watts of Pioneer sound system, CD player and multiple speakers.

Despite the incredible list of standard equipment, there were no options available. All 161 SSCs produced as 1989-only models were identical; all were white with white wheels and grey-and-white interiors. The asking price for this "unofficial" 25th anniversary Mustang model was $36,500. Four SSC look-alikes built outside the main run were Pioneer promotional cars packed to the hilt with specialized stereo equipment, displayed around the country and eventually given away in contests.

Certifying, building and selling a modified engine package made Saleen customers happy, but it also gave the company a broader product range that now included a constantly evolving "base" model as well as a high-end supercar.

## 1990-93: DARK TIMES FOR SALEEN

Just as things were taking off for Saleen Autosport, the company hit hard times in the form of a national recession and a softening high-performance car market. Displaying the same spirit that won him the 1987 SCCA championship, Saleen worked against the odds to develop and improve his two well-loved products.

In 1990, the upscale SSC became known as the "SC" and continued giving Saleen enthusiasts the power to match the car's handling and looks. Continuous upgrades and changes to the aerodynamic body pieces, wheels and tires, and various other equipment proceeded slowly but surely during this period. The 1991 SC, for example, wore a new 70mm mass airflow sensor, replacing the previous year's 65mm unit. Saleen's "Spyder" convertible package, featuring a soft tonneau cover that turned the rear seats into a convenient storage area, was new for 1992. That same year, Saleen teamed with Vortech to offer one of its superchargers as an option. Seventeen-inch rims became standard Saleen equipment in 1992 at a time when the Mustang GT was still two years away from such rolling stock.

As eager as the team was, though, to put new owners in their cars, the demand for Saleen's products stalled. Only 243 Saleens were built in 1990, just 92 sold in 1991, and a mere 17 in 1992. Outside the regular 1992 Saleen Mustang line were four "entry level" GT Sport hatchbacks modified with the lowered suspension and a few body upgrades, and one Ranger pickup given treatment similar to the 1988 Sportrucks.

Production for 1993 was slow, but a remarkable improvement over the previous year. Saleen sold 87 of its base Mustang packages, five SCs and nine supercharged $37,995 SA-10 models commemorating Saleen's 10th year in business. Sticker for the base, original recipe Saleen hatchback was $27,490; list for the convertible ran $31,690—either model could be pumped up with a $3,200 Vortech supercharger. Ordering the hot and spicy SC with standard supercharger and a never-ending list of high-performance goodies (including a Tremec heavy-duty five-speed transmission) would cost $39,990. Saleen even offered a convertible in the SC for the first time at $44,490.

Comedian Tim Allen's one-off Saleen supercar, known as the "R-R-R" model, was produced in 1993.

## 1994: TURNAROUND TIME

When a rejuvenated Steve Saleen pulled back the covers on his all-new models during the Mustang's 30th anniversary show at Charlotte Motor Speedway in April of 1994, it calmed fears that Saleen Autosport (now Saleen Performance) had gone the way of Shelby American.

Ford's redesign of the Mustang could not have come at a better time for small-volume manufacturer Saleen, who had spent 10 years making the Fox-platform Mustang into an exciting product for performance enthusiasts. The SN-95 (1994-to-present Mustang body), with its better engineering, sportier styling and commitment from Ford to keep the pony fresh, gave Saleen a new canvas on which to create masterpieces into the 21st century.

Saleen showed he could market to a younger crowd with the introduction of the V-6 Sport, a model that combined traditional Saleen equipment with a less-expensive powerplant. Boosted by a standard supercharger, the Sport's 3.8-liter V-6 was rated at 220 hp—just a bit more power than the heavier 5.0-liter V-8—and benefited from Racecraft suspension tuning, 17x8-inch wheels, and Saleen aerodynamic body pieces. A short-throw Hurst shifter and leather-grained shift knob were the only interior modifications.

Listing for less than $22,000 put the V-6 Sport (official name: V-6 Sport by Steve Saleen) in the same price range as a loaded GT Mustang, but without the super-high insurance premium. Saleen saw this as a good entry-level car that would appeal to enthusiasts in their early 20s.

The second 1994 model introduced that day was the S-351, a car that took the previous SSC and SC concepts to the next level. Powered by a 351-cid 371 hp V-8 built and EPA certified by Saleen Performance, the S-351 had the highest Saleen-unique content of any car to date. Ford delivered V-6 coupes and convertibles to the new Saleen factory in Irvine, California, where they were stripped to bare shells (except for certain components such as the dash). The V-8, which featured high-performance cylinder heads with bigger valves; hydraulic roller camshaft and lifters; 65mm throttle body; 77mm mass air sensor; and a slew of other high-tech goodies, was then installed on relocated motor mounts (one inch rearward and one inch lower than stock) and entirely rewired to a new EEC-IV engine management system. Just about every part of the S-351 was replaced or massaged during a period of 120 hours, which made the $33,500 asking price quite remarkable.

Unlike the "no-options" SSC, the S-351 could be outfitted with any number of accessories. The stock 235/40-18 (front) and 245/40-18 (rear) BFGoodrich Comp T/A radials could be upgraded to Dunlop SP8000s measuring 255/40-18 and 285/40-18. Need more power? There was a Vortech supercharger option. Even stronger acceleration could be dialed in with a 3.27:1 rear axle. If stopping was as important as going, larger 13-inch brake discs could be ordered. The Spyder package, first seen as a 1992 option, was again offered, this time with a roll bar-like "sport bar."

If the S-351 was a home run—as several publications described it—then the third all-new Saleen model for 1994 was equivalent to winning the World Series.

The SR ("Supercharged Racer" according to some) was the barely legal equipment package that dressed a Vortech-supercharged S-351 in FIA Group A competition clothing, including a dual-plane rear wing, carbon-fiber hood and scooped bodyside enhancements. Inside, the SR benefited from a rear race tray (taking the place of the back seat), four-point roll bar, four-point safety harness and racing Recaro seats. With its 351-cid supercharged V-8 rated at 480 hp, no one could say the SR was all-show/no-go. Base price for the latest Saleen supercar was $45,000.

Adding to the excitement of the three-model Saleen lineup was the company's announcement that 75 Ford outlets were "stocking dealers," meaning they had agreed to keep a minimum of two cars on the floor at all times. With only a few months of real production time in 1994, those 75 dealers managed to sell 44 S-351s and two SRs.

## 1995

Following Ford's example with the stock Mustang, Saleen made few changes to his offerings for the second year of the new style in 1995. The V-6 GT Sport was dropped from the line so the company could concentrate its resources on further development of the V-8 models.

Sales were picking up in 1995, with 126 S-351s and seven SRs going out the door.

## 1996

In 1996, Saleen started production on yet another all-new Mustang-based model, the S-281. The S-281 marked a return to the original Saleen formula, with only minimal upgrades to the engine and maximum massaging of the suspension, aerodynamics and interior. Built around Ford's new modular 4.6-liter 281-cid V-8 and wearing 245/40-18 BFGoodrich rubber on 18-inch, five-spoke alloy wheels, the S-281 became the entry-level Saleen at $28,990 for the coupe. Options included an 18-inch magnesium wheel and the convertible-only Speedster package (including the hard tonneau, padded roll bar and soft tonneau).

The S-281 proved to be the most popular Saleen model in many years, with 436 examples selling in the first year of production. Twenty S-351s were sold in 1996. The SR model was unofficially blended into the S-351 line on which it was based as the S-351 was now available with the same 500 hp supercharged V-8 as standard equipment.

## 1997

For 1997, Saleen began offering its S-281 with either a 220-hp version of the 4.6-liter SOHC V-8 or a 310-hp 4.6-liter DOHC (the SVT Cobra's 32-valve engine introduced the previous year).

A six-speed manual transmission became standard on the S-351. Optional equipment available on the S-351 included outrageous "Widebody" front fascia, fenders, rear quarter panels, rear valance, a carbon-fiber hood, and dual-plane rear wing.

An extra-cost tire upgrade on the S-281 and S-351 were Michelin Pilots measuring 245/40-18 (front) and a super-wide 295/35-18 (rear).

The company produced 327 S-281s and 40 S-351s in 1997.

## 1998

The 1998 Saleen models, based on a now five-year-old Mustang design, changed little.

Giving the fast-growing SUV and sport truck field another shot, Saleen offered a limited run of Explorer-based high-performance vehicles it called "XP8." Wearing aerodynamic body pieces and suspension components similar to its Saleen Mustang brothers, the Explorer was available with either a 4.0-liter V-6 (211 hp), 5.0-liter V-8 (222 hp), or supercharged 5.0-liter (a dealer-installed option rated at 286 hp). With its lowered ride height and 18-inch magnesium five-spoke wheels, the Saleen Explorer could go around corners as well as any sport coupe. It was available in either two- or four-wheel drive.

The XP8 found a hungry audience, with 57 units selling in its introductory year. Sales of the S-281 slipped to 185 cars, and the super-fast S-351 only found 22 takers in 1998.

## 1999

For 1999, Ford refreshed the stock Mustang's appearance, and Saleen managed to tweak the SOHC 4.6-liter V-8 in its S-281 to produce 285 hp (25 more than stock) through a new premium fuel calibration, special underdrive pulleys and a new exhaust system. Not knowing when to leave well enough alone, Saleen offered a Roots-type supercharger option that boosted horsepower on the S-281 to an advertised 350.

The S-351, again standard with a Vortech supercharger, claimed 495 horses for 1999—down five from the previous year.

While the S-281 came with the standard 15.4-gallon Mustang fuel tank, the 351-equipped Saleens were fitted with 22-gallon race-type fuel cells.

The new Mustang design and more power in its base model gave Saleen a sales spike in 1999, with 373 S-281s, 45 S-351s, and 43 Explorer XP8s finding new homes.

## 2000

Evolution of the species continued at Saleen for the 2000 model year, with the supercharged version of the S-281 now known as the S-281 SC. With a sticker price of $29,900, the S-281 coupe settled in as the lowest-priced Saleen model, but with few other changes. In tests on the dragstrip, the $35,460 S-281 SC coupe bested the zero-to-60 mph time of the normally aspirated 281 by 0.4 seconds (4.8 vs. 5.2) and both models burned up the skid pad at .93g. Even at $55,990, the S-351 was such a desirable car that Saleen was unable to produce enough of the hand-built screamers to satisfy demand that year.

Saleen's version of the Explorer listed for $36,790 with V-8 and four-wheel drive. It registered zero-to-60 mph times of 8.8 seconds and turned .80g of lateral acceleration.

The biggest news for Saleen fans in 2000 was the unveiling of an all-new SR model wearing a $158,000 price tag. The now-familiar 351-cid V-8 was rated at 505 hp and 500 lb.-ft. of torque, with a six-speed transmission sending all that power back to a 3.55:1-geared rear axle by way of a shortened driveshaft. Independent rear suspension components sat where a live axle had been for more than 35 years of Mustang history. Braking was through 14.4-inch front rotors with four-piston calipers in front and 13-inch metallic discs with four-piston calipers in the rear. Beneath the wildly styled, Saleen-unique composite body panels lay a complete roll cage and suspension reinforcement system. The SR, available in coupe form only, was wind tunnel tuned at Lockheed-Martin's full-size tunnel in Marietta, Georgia. Performance figures released by Saleen Performance claim the SR can reach 60 miles an hour from a standstill in 4.0 seconds flat and circle the skidpad at 1.09g.

# A Sample of Saleens

1986 Saleen Mustang

1989 Saleen Mustang

1992 Saleen Mustang convertible

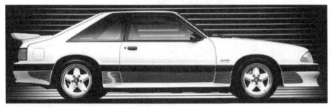

1990 Saleen Mustang convertible

1993 Saleen Mustang R-R-R (Tim Allen's car)

1991 Saleen Mustang

1992 Saleen SC

1993 Saleen Mustang SA-10

1993 Saleen SC

1994 Saleen SR

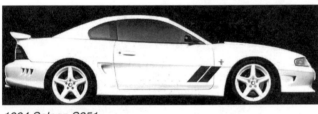

1994 Saleen S351

1995 Saleen SR

1995 Saleen S351 convertible

1996 Saleen S281

# CHAPTER 14

Mustang Prototypes and Specials

*Originally planned for production in 1966, a prototype Mustang retractable was created by Ben Smith, the man who had brought the 1957 Ford Skyliner "hardtop convertible" into the market. (Phil Skinner)*

*The 1966 Bordinat Cobra was an interpretation of what the second-generation Mustang could have looked like. It had a front end treatment that was not unlike that of the Mach II prototype. (Ford)*

*The mid-engined Mach II prototype was around for many years. No wonder! It took two years to build and cost over $150,000. It was started in 1966 and finished in 1968. (Ford)*

Don DeLaRossa was Ford's "Italian connection" as concerned new product development. He negotiated many contracts for concept car development with European design firms in the 1950s and into the 1960s and was instrumental in the Mustang's birth.

"My role in development of the Mustang was to submit proposals of what it might look like, and I (developed) designs for about 16 different cars," said DeLaRossa in a 1994 interview. "The creator of the design that was approved for production was Joe Oros, and there's nothing that I can say—in the face of the Mustang's huge success—to suggest that his design and Lee's (Iacocca) choices weren't right."

Of course, new concepts for the Mustang did not cease when the production car hit the showrooms. Factory stylists in Detroit, designers in Europe (especially in Italy), customizers, street rodders, car magazines, and racing buffs continued to dream up concepts for the pony car.

The following is a sampling of Mustang prototypes and specials that appeared after the 1963 Mustang I started the pony car era rolling:

## 1963 Mustang II

The 1963 Mustang II was a running prototype of the production Mustang that was completed in the fall of 1963. It was a much more conventional car than its predecessor, the mid-engine Mustang I. Based on Joe Oros' car, it was closer to the actual production version of the Mustang than most people realized at the time. Ford brought the car to the sports car races at Watkins Glen, New York that fall. It created quite a stir. A lower roofline, bumperless front and rear styling, and louvered headlamps gave it slightly racier styling than the car that hit the showrooms seven months later. However, it was so close to the real thing that even the pony-and-bars fender badges and grille "corral" with galloping pony were part of its design.

## 1964 Two-Seater Mustang

Photos show this car in the courtyard of the Ford Design Center on June 11, 1964. It looks like a production Mustang convertible with its body "sectioned" to fit a several-inches-shorter wheelbase.

## 1965 Mustang III

Early in the Mustang's genesis, Ford was experimenting with ways to alter the basic car without losing its "magic." Andy Hotten, of Dearborn Steel Tubing Company, a Ford supplier who built the famous "Thunderbolt" lightweight drag racing cars, took delivery of a 1965 Mustang 2+2. He shortened the wheelbase by 16 inches to create a semi-factory prototype. It had a fiberglass body with the rear quarter windows permanently fixed in place. Up front, Lucas "Flame Thrower" road lamps were installed. Even though Ford didn't market the car, which was shown as the "Mustang III," Hotten did sell a few copies of the front valance panel.

## 1966 Mustang Retractable

Originally planned for production in 1966, a prototype Mustang with retractable top was created by Ben Smith, the man who had brought the 1957 Ford Skyliner "hardtop convertible" into the market. It had its roof "break line" just in front of the C-pillar, requiring the addition of three inches to the quarter panels, behind the rear wheel openings. Market studies showed a lot of interest in the Mustang retractable concept. Only a disagreement between management and Smith caused this model to miss production. The company wanted the top to be electrically-operated and Ben Smith favored manual operation. "I felt that automating it would be too complicated, and eventually cause maintenance headaches for the company," Smith said in a 1994 interview. "I wanted to keep it simple and efficient."

## 1966 Bordinat Cobra

This car was Eugene Bordinat's interpretation of what the second-generation Mustang should look like. It had a front end treatment that was not unlike that of the Mach II prototype in its overall appearance. The basic shape was that of the first production Mustang: smooth and round. It was a very handsome machine with a look that suggested it might reach production.

## 1966 *Car and Driver* Mustang Wagon

A beautiful 1966 Mustang station wagon was featured on the cover of *Car and Driver* magazine in October 1966. The sports car periodical commissioned the station wagon conversion as a promotional item and conversation piece. It set lots of tongues wagging with suggestions that Ford should produce such a model. Some time ago, there were rumors that the car had surfaced in a Northeastern state.

## 1966 Mustang Aspen Wagon

The factory designers weren't too far behind the staff of *Car and Driver*. This prototype was photographed at the Ford Design Center on October 28, 1966. The wagon styling did not look as nice on a modified 1967-68 Mustang 2+2 body as it did on the original 1965-66 body that was converted for the car buff magazine.

## 1966 Mustang Maverick

This was a styling mock-up completed at the Ford Design Center in July 1966. It looked something like a

Mustang body mated with the front end of an Oldsmobile Toronado. The back seemed to be copied from an AMC product. Overall, the car was larger than first-generation Mustangs—closer in size to the 1971-1973 Mustang.

### 1966/1968 Mach II

This mid-engine prototype took two years to build and cost more than $150,000. A bright red fiberglass body was "glued" on a shortened and modified Mustang chassis with adhesive. The Mach II was just 47-inches high and accommodated two passengers only. Twin recessed scoops accented the front fenders, while full wheel openings highlighted the Firestone racing tires and Magnum 500 wheels. The powerplant was a Mustang V-8 and German-built five-speed ZF transaxle. The radiator was front-mounted. A center-mounted tunnel was used for the routing of water hoses, wiring and brake lines. Ford engineer Ed Hull worked out most of the technical details. The Mach II was studied extensively for several years, but ultimately judged to be of no potential sales volume. It did, evidently, open a few eyes at General Motors, because it wasn't too long before mid-engined Corvette prototypes were developed.

### 1967-1968 Mach 1

This was a customized version of the 1967 Mustang 2+2 with a competition image. It had rectangular, competition-style headlamps, with large scoops attached to the body behind the side cove. Large, round competition-style

flip-open fuel fillers were seen on both sail panels. The rear had four exhaust extensions exiting in the center of the car, just below the bumper. It had wide performance tires and five-spoke mag wheels and sported a red, monotone finish. Body-colored racing mirrors were affixed directly to both side windows. The car looked quite a bit like the production version Mach 1, introduced in 1969.

### 1968 Mustang Mach 1

Ford Division's experimental 1968 Mustang Mach 1 was reported to have many design features of the production Mustang and the Ford GT competition vehicles. Up front, it had a recessed grille and rectangular headlights set horizontally in the fenders. The twin-louvered hood and 64-degree windshield angle accentuated the racing look of the car. Air intakes in the body, just behind the doors, provided extra cooling for the rear brakes. The wheel openings were flared to accept special, Wide-Oval low-profile racing tires mounted on cast-aluminum alloy wheels. Side marker lights were mounted on the front and rear fenders. The prototype was styled at the Ford Design Center in Dearborn, Michigan.

### 1968 Mustang Cobra

The Mustang Cobra was photographed at the Ford Design Center on Oct. 14, 1968. The prototype car's front end looked like a boat and the rear looked like a Cougar Eliminator. It gave a hint of how the production model would look in the early 1970s.

*The 1968 Mach 1was a customized version of the 1967 Mustang 2+2 with a competition image. It had rectangular, competition-style headlamps. Large scoops were attached to the body sides, behind the coves. (Ford)*

The 1972 Mustang Milano was a sleek, two-passenger grand touring car. It was made by "chopping" the top of a stock 1970 Mustang SportsRoof model. This gave the windshield a 67-degree rake. The car was only 43-inches high. (Ford)

### 1969 302 Mustang

This was a low-slung, Kammback design that resembled a cross between a Pantera and a Corvette. It looked much more "European" than most Mustang styling cars. It was photographed, inside the Ford Design Center, in July 1969.

### 1972 Mustang Milano

The Milano was a sleek, two-passenger grand touring car whose profile was established by "chopping" the top of a stock 1970 Mustang SportsRoof. This gave the windshield a 67-degree rake. The car was only 43 inches high. Concealed headlamps, a hood with NASA-style scoops, an electrically operated rear hatch, and multi-color tail lamps were some of the gimmicks on the dream car. The tail lamps were white when not in operation, green when accelerating, amber while coasting and red during braking. The Milano also had cast aluminum wheels with "laced" spokes and F60x15 Firestone tires. A wild purple color called "Ultra Violet" was used on the show car. Blue-violet fabric upholstery with light purple trim and dark purple mohair carpeting made the interior eye-catching. Ford promoted it as "similar to those (cars) seen cruising the countryside, near Milan, Italy." The hood of this Ford Division show car contained air scoops for increased power through ram-air induction. The back window and rear deck lid raised electrically, to provide generous access to the luggage compartment.

### 1980 Mustang IMSA

The Mustang IMSA, a Ford concept car, was highlighted at major auto shows in 1980. It was designed to project the image of cars competing on the International Motor Sports Association (IMSA) racing circuit. The car's impressive .418 aerodynamic drag coefficient was obtained through body modifications that included a front air dam with smoked plastic covers, clear plastic covers for the quad halogen headlamps, special wide fender flares, plastic covers on Gotti modular wheels, flush-fitting windows and a rear deck lid spoiler. It had a unique hood with air-extractor louvers and a "shaker" scoop. It was finished in shimmering Pearlescent White, with bold orange and gold accent striping. The engine was a turbocharged 2.3-liter four. The concept car became a sort of pilot model for the limited-edition McLaren Mustangs and Capris of the early 1980s.

### 1982 Motorcraft Image Mustang

Inspired by Ford's Daytona and Sebring racing cars, the Marketing Corporation of America built a pair of Image Mustangs for the automaker's Motorcraft parts and services division. The special street/competition models featured a 302-cid H.O. V-8, a four-speed manual competition gearbox. Inside, they had Recaro seats, special Stewart-Warner instrumentation and a competition steering wheel. Firestone HPR tires were mounted on Gotti wheels. Unique body details included a massive hood scoop, a front air dam, flared front and rear fenders and a "whale-tail"-type rear spoiler. The cars had air conditioning and custom factory red paint. Other features included competition power steering and rear axle "limit" straps. One car toured as part of the Ford Motorcraft display and remained with Ford Motor Company. The other car was purchased by Larry Dobbs, the founder of *Mustang Monthly* and Dobbs Publishing, in Lakeland, Florida.

*The 1993 Mustang Mach III had an oval grille, a smoothly-styled carbon fiber roadster body, a rounded front end, a low riding height, and a rakishly-slanted windshield. (Ron Kowalke)*

## 1993 Mustang Mach III

The Mustang III concept car appeared in early 1993. It had an oval grille, a smoothly-styled carbon fiber roadster body, a rounded front end, a low riding height and a steeply raked windshield. The body sides were scooped out, not unlike those of the 1994 Mustang, but ended in large, gloss-black air ducts. A galloping pony grille emblem and three-bar tail lamps hinted at the line's heritage. The engine was an ultra-high-tech 4.6-liter supercharged V-8 that produced 460 hp. It was linked to a six-speed manual transmission. The suspension featured front struts, with quad shocks at the rear. Anti-lock brakes with 13-inch front and 12-inch rear vented rotors were

*The 1980 Mustang IMSA concept car had Recaro buckets and a four-point safety harness designed for competitive driving. A special hub in the padded, leather-wrapped steering wheel had switches for the controls. (Ford)*

incorporated. The rotors were made of a composite material and the system featured dual-piston calipers. The 245/40R19 front and 315/40R19 rear tires were mounted on 19-inch diameter, chromed-aluminum wheels. Rack-and-pinion steering was used. The Cobra III had a 101.25-inch wheelbase. Overall length was 188.605 inches; overall height 46.268 inches, overall width 76.63 inches. It was finished in a color called "Hot Poppy Red."

## 1999 Razzi Mustang

Modern car companies like to cruise the Specialty Equipment Manufacturers Association (SEMA) booths in Las Vegas every year looking to see what the aftermarket has done with certain popular models. Ford apparently took notice of this muscular concept put together by the Alpharetta, Georgia-based Razzi Corp. as it won the Ford Design Award for Best Car of the 1999 SEMA Las Vegas Show. The green convertible is equipped with a Razzi ground effects kit, Ultra wheels, Eibach springs, Borla exhaust, and Kar Kraft Engineering's Euro Dual Sport Arch, functional ram-air kit, and Sport Tonneau Cover.

## 2000 Bullitt Mustang

This rolling reference to the finest chase scene ever filmed might be headed for production, according to Ford. Mustang enthusiasts have replayed the 1968 Steve McQueen detective drama *Bullitt* so many times that they dream about GT fastbacks chasing Dodge Chargers through the hilly streets of San Francisco. The prototype that made the rounds of the auto shows starting early in 2000 (shown here) has many features that were "dream-only," such as the modified trunk lid, rear spoiler and valance panel that mimicked the 1968 Mustang design but would be too expensive to see production. Due to the show car's popularity, a second version was prepared for Ford to consider producing as a 2001-1/2 model. Expected standard equipment would include a 275-hp 4.6-liter SOHC V-8; vintage-looking, 17-inch five-spoke wheels; a racing-style aluminum gas cap; 1960s-style gauges and special "Bullitt" brushed-aluminum scuff plates. Rumors have it the car will be offered in Highland Green (similar to the dark hue of the McQueen car) or black (like the Charger it chased and, ultimately, destroyed).

*A galloping pony grille emblem and three-slot tail lamps hinted at the Mustang III's 30-year heritage. The engine was a high-tech 4.6-liter supercharged V-8 of 460 hp linked to a six-speed manual gear box. (Ron Kowalke)*

*This muscular concept put together by the Alpharetta, Georgia-based Razzi Corp. won the Ford Design Award for Best Car of the 1999 SEMA Las Vegas Show.*

*Designed as a tribute to the hard-charging 1968 Mustang fastback driven by Steve McQueen in the movie "Bullitt," this rough-and-ready styling exercise is being considered for limited production.*

*Notice the "Bullitt" Mustang's side-mounted pop-open gas cap.*

# CHAPTER 15

## How to Buy a Mustang

*Classic car auctions are operated in different cities by over a dozen companies. Vintage Mustangs are consigned to many sales. Inspecting and evaluating an auction car prior to purchase is essential. (Old Cars Weekly)*

When it comes to purchasing a used Mustang—whether it's 35 years old or still under warranty—it's a good idea to do some homework. As with any car, boat, house, or other major purchase, a missed detail here or there can be the difference between a good buy and a miserable money pit.

What follows is a good, common sense approach to picking a pony car, but the best advice for a first-time buyer is to join a Mustang club and seek advice from its members. While the Mustang nameplate has endured since 1964, many thousands of components, powertrains, and unique body panel designs have come and gone and experts on particular year models or body styles can offer invaluable insight. Another recommendation is to buy several magazines devoted to Mustangs and Fords.

*Evaluating a car prior to purchase entails inspection and a test drive. It doesn't matter whether you're making the purchase on the street, from an ad, at a swap meet, or (in this case) at a car show. (Old Cars Weekly)*

## CHECK THE "WANT ADS"

Whether you use the local publications or the national hobby magazines, you're going to see lots of Mustangs for sale. That's good. It means you don't have to rush out and buy the first available car. It means it will be easier to determine fair prices and bargain more competitively. It also means that you'll find parts available when you begin restoring the car.

## SHOWS AND AUCTIONS

In many cases, larger car shows include "car corrals" where vehicles can be bought and sold. A swap meet (automotive flea market) will also be part of some shows and may offer additional cars for sale. Classic car auctions are operated, in different cities, by over a dozen companies. Vintage Mustangs are consigned to many of these sales. Inspecting and evaluating a car prior to purchasing it, entails the same procedure. It doesn't matter whether you're making the purchase on the street, from an advertisement, at a swap meet, during a car show, or through an auction.

## PRICE GUIDES

As a buyer, the first thing that you'll want to know is whether the prices being asked for different Mustangs are high, low, or fair.

Krause Publications (700 E. State St., Iola, WI 54990) prints a bi-monthly magazine called *Old Cars Price Guide*, which can help you determine the "collector value" of Mustangs greater than seven years of age. Each Mustang listing shows all models made each year. Individual models are listed with six values: 1) Excellent; 2) Fine; 3) Very Good; 4) Good; 5) Restorable; and 6) Parts Car. Illustrated instructions inside *Old Cars Price Guide* tell you how to gauge the condition of a particular car using the 1-to-6 scale.

For newer Mustangs, several used car price guides are offered on most newsstands, listing cars and telling what they sold for new, what their wholesale value is today, and what their average retail price is estimated to be. One such reputable guide is produced by Pace Publications (1020 N. Broadway, Milwaukee, WI 53202).

Both collector car price guides and used car price guides give *estimated* values for cars. They are only guides and should be used as such. They indicate fair market values, but individual cars can sell for way less or far more than "book" value. When you get very serious about buying a particular Mustang, you may want to get second and third opinions about its value. The more sources you use, the better picture you'll get of the car's true value. In addition, when different sources list estimated values in the same general range, it's your best indication that the estimated prices are pretty accurate.

## HIGH MILEAGE

Armed with an idea of the value of the Mustang you want to buy, it's now time to get down to the task of contacting the car's owner. Always ask the seller how many miles the car has traveled. Many cars are advertised as "XX miles on new engine," but may have 300,000 miles on the chassis and running gear. That doesn't necessarily mean the car isn't worth buying, but it should raise a red flag that suspension components, the brake system or body integrity could be compromised. Always press the owner to state total mileage, not just the miles driven with a new engine. Mileage of 10,000 to 12,000 per year is considered "normal."

*If you want to go racing, buy yourself a race car. If you want a stock, restored Mustang, avoid vehicles built solely for competition. It's not wise to start an original restoration with a highly modified drag machine. (Old Cars Weekly)*

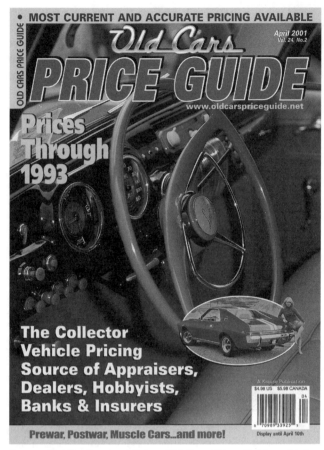

*Krause Publications publishes* Old Cars Price Guide, *which can help you determine the collector value of Mustangs. (Old Cars Weekly)*

If you've ever traded in a used car with 100,000 miles on the odometer, you know that such vehicles lose value. However, a classic 1965 Mustang with "normal" (10,000 miles per year) use would now have some 350,000 miles on it! On any car that has that high an odometer reading, the suspension, brakes, and body will usually have some degree of "restoration" work done. In inspecting the vehicle, you'll have to determine if repairs were done properly.

High mileage does scare away many buyers, and with good reason. Most motorists don't maintain cars very well. A six-figure odometer total usually equates to extreme wear and tear, but there may be some cream-puffs out there as well.

## MAKE THE SELLER "SING"

Asking if the seller is the original owner of the Mustang you want to buy can be an important question. For example, an odometer showing 30,000 miles might have gone around two or three times, which makes a big difference in the car's market value. Gauges may have been replaced in the car, and the odometer might reflect mileage from a completely different car!

Buying from an original owner is the ideal situation, as you can get a good picture of its "medical history." Was

the oil changed every 3,000 miles? What repairs has it had? At what mileage intervals was service completed? Who did the work? Knowing the answers to such questions can tell you how well the car has been maintained as well as whether it has 20,000 miles or 200,000 miles.

If the car had other owners, did the current owner obtain past records from them? Ask to see any documentation of the vehicle's service history. Also ask the owner if the car is titled and insured. Possibly, it has been off the road, sitting in storage. Low-mileage cars that are improperly stored can have more hidden problems than a well-maintained 300,000-mile vehicle. Special note, if the Mustang is a 1980s or later model, computerized records of all service done at Ford dealers should be available. Check with local dealers on how to access such information from Ford Motor Company.

## SERVICE MILEAGE

Let's assume that you obtain a maintenance history or written records. Don't look only at mileage intervals between service. Check the dates when the oil was changed and the chassis was lubricated. If the car got serviced at 3,000 mile intervals, but only once a year, you'll know it wasn't driven too much. In that case, it should have at least had the oil changed every three months. If it was serviced every 3,000 miles and every 30 days, it was driven more than normal each month.

The ideal is a regularly-driven car with modest mileage (let's say 8,000 to 9,000 miles annually) that was serviced every three months. That would equate to lower-than-average mileage, with enough use to avoid "over-storage" problems, combined with adequate maintenance.

Naturally, there are mitigating circumstances with many cars. For example, the 1966 Mustang, with 20,000 original miles, that has been stored in a climate-controlled building since 1970, might not have the normal problems that a car stored in a small, uninsulated, wooden garage would have.

While the owner is on the phone, ask for a personal evaluation of the car. What you hear and how it's said might reveal enough to help you decide to take the next step. If you like what the owner says—if he or she sounds confident and honest—grab a flashlight, a screwdriver, a pair of pliers, and a felt-covered magnet (to use as a gauge for body filler). It's time to see the car and inspect it.

## RAISE THE CAR

With an old Mustang, the first thing to check is under the body. If at all possible, get it up on a lift. It's worth the time to pay a local service station for lift time. In cities, you can sometimes rent a lift at a "fix-it-yourself" facility. Check under the battery for corrosion caused by acid leaks. Look for loose parts, especially on cars with heavy-duty or competition suspensions. Shelby Mustangs were known for shaking many small parts loose. Many sloppy electrical wiring connections can also be seen from below.

Check the rocker panels. On unit-body cars (as all Mustangs are), this is especially important, because the rockers serve a structural purpose. Look for pinholes in the metal. Then gently poke corroded areas with your screwdriver to see how far the flakiness extends out from the pinhole. Reproduction rocker panels for Mustangs are available, but you will be far ahead to buy a car with a solid body.

While the car is in the air, inspect the fuel tank for odors or wetness. Leaky tanks shouldn't be tolerated; they're dangerous! Use your flashlight to look up into the wheel wells. Crimped-over sheet metal can form pockets for dirt and salt to cling to and cause corrosion. With your light and screwdriver, inspect any areas where road gook can set up. Rust-prone areas include the cowl vent and under-cowl area (where water was supposed to drain); the top of the windshield (prone to leaking, which causes rust); the headlamp "buckets" the front fender tips; the lower rear fender panels; and the convertible top boot area in open cars. Cars of the 1960s also tended to rust around and on the bottom of the rear window opening.

Collision damage most often shows up as twisted metal behind the grille, since front end accidents are the most common type. Check around the hood, doors and rear deck lid for signs of paint overspray. While the doors are open, inspect the door hinges for integrity and alignment. Make sure that the doors swing freely on them and that they fit flush to the body. Check to see that the door seam openings are straight and that the door gap is uniform. Sloppy door gaps are signs of an accident or a poor-quality restoration.

## CHECK EVERY NOOK AND CRANNY

Open the deck lid and check the trunk. Roll back the mat or carpet (there should be one and it should be clean). Inspect the trunk floor for corrosion. Check weather-stripping around doors, windows, and the rear deck lid. While it's true that weatherstripping is readily available, it's not exactly cheap to replace all the rubber in a Mustang. The less required work, the better off your budget will be.

Car doors have drain holes with plastic plugs along their bottom edge. If you want to know if the car was repainted, pry out one of these plugs and look at the metal under the lip of the plug. Few refinishers bother to replace these plugs. In addition, if water drips out of the door when the plug is removed, you'll know you have a problem with rust inside the door. On 1974 and later Mustangs, inspect the gas filler door to see that it opens and closes readily. Inside the fuel door is another place to check for overspray, if you suspect the car was repainted.

## CHECK THE PAINT

Check the overall quality of the paint, too. There is a tool that professionals use to "measure" the depth of paint covering a metal surface. It reveals how many millimeters of top coatings remain. If you can borrow one of these from a body shop or auto parts store (a few have them), you can determine if the car has very thin paint. This is important. Thin paint might look nice when buffed out by the owner, but the next time you wax the car, the paint may start to vanish. A good paint job can cost $3,000 or more these days!

A repainted car isn't necessarily something that you should reject out of hand, but it does pay to ask questions if you spot one. Who painted the car? What kind of paint was used? How long ago was it done? Some painters use very "hard" paint that covers flaws very well, but tends to chip when stones fly against it. If you want to know more about the characteristics of different kinds of paint, visit your local paint supplier. They will have manufacturer contacts you can write to or call to get more information.

## A GLASS ACT

It's important to look the glass over for cracks, discoloration or cloudiness. Flat glass is easily replaceable, but curved glass can be more difficult to renew.

If the car is a late-model Mustang with a sunroof, check its operation. Manual sunroofs should open and close easily and seal tightly. Electrically-operated sliding roofs should be tested for proper functioning. If the car has a T-roof, check the rubber weather-stripping around the edges of the removable panels. Any damage could permit rain to leak into the car. Many Mustang convertibles have glass rear windows. Don't forget to raise the top. That way, you can check the rear window, while you make sure the top-raising mechanism works correctly.

Excessive use of plastic body filler should not be tolerated in a vintage Mustang. There is no reason for doing so, as so many of the Mustang body panels are readily available from hobby suppliers. A "friendly" car that "waves" at you (with wavy panels that should be straight) has very little eye appeal. It also has minimal collector value.

A simple magnet can be used to determine if what you're looking at is plastic or metal. However, there are sliding magnet tools available from hobby vendors. They incorporate a gauge that tells you the depth of the plastic filler on the car body. One of these is marketed as the "Spot Rot" tool.

## INTERIOR TOO

Part of inspecting a Mustang's body should be examining the interior. Look for water stains on the upholstery and carpets. Check the bucket seats, the console and the headliner. Do all of the windows lower and raise the way they should? Make sure that all the controls and gauges function properly. Check all the lights for proper functioning; head, tail, brake, back-up, directional, and courtesy. Look inside the glove box. Check the dashboard. It is very difficult

*Talking about Mustangs is fun. Armed with an idea of Mustang values, you'll want to discuss the purchase of the car with the owner. Ask why he's selling it and how many miles the car has traveled. (Old Cars Weekly)*

to replace cracked padded dashes on older models. Late-model Mustangs will probably have dash overlay panels available for them. A very good source to listing sources of dash pads, door panels, carpets, upholstery materials, and replacement convertible tops.

## ACCESSORIES

Extra-cost accessories play an important role in the purchase of a Mustang. Many accessories offered for the early models are desirable because they are neat to have on a car. Some are also rare and valuable.

A Rally Pac gauge cluster is one of the most desirable options for 1965-66 models, adding several hundred dollars to the value of a car. Six different types have been identified. The 1965 type used on both 1965 and 1966 cars is the most common to find. The low-profile 1966 versions generally are worth slightly more. The 8,000-rpm type offered in 1966 is the most valuable of all.

*While the doors are open, inspect the door hinges for integrity and alignment. Do the doors swing freely? Do they fit flush to the body? Check to see that the door seam openings are straight and that the door gap is uniform. (Old Cars Weekly)*

*If the car has a T-roof, check the rubber weatherstripping around the edges of the removable panels. Any damage could permit rain to leak into the car. (Old Cars Weekly)*

Styled steel wheels were always popular and remain so today. Used on nearly 50 percent of all early Mustangs, they used to be plentiful and bargain-priced. The styled wheels used on the earliest Mustangs, made in both 1964 and 1965, are the most valuable. The 1966 and 1967 styles, with trim rings, are about 10 percent less costly.

Mustang GT grille parts are very desirable today. They include the fog lights, grille, grille bar, and light switch. Values for all of these run in the same vicinity as the more expensive Rally Pacs and the less expensive styled wheels.

Front seat center consoles are another item that Mustang collectors go for. From time to time you'll see ads for a Mustang with the "rare bench seat option." The bench seats may be rare, but there was a good reason for this. Everyone preferred bucket seats and a console. They still do today. In 1965 and 1966, two different consoles were used. One was longer than the other. The "short" consoles are worth a bit more, since air conditioned cars used them.

AM/FM radios for early Mustangs were very valuable years ago. They brought as much as $1,000 not so long ago. Today, you can buy modern, high-tech radios with original-looking replica face plates. This has tended to "cap" the wild inflationary spiral, but the factory AM/FM radios are still an expensive "must have" for serious buffs. If the car you are buying has one of these, keep it in the vault.

Other accessories to look for when buying a Mustang include the scissors jack for 1965-66 models; the 1965-66 Deluxe steering wheel; the 1967-68 illuminated grille emblem; 1969-70 Sportslats; 1965-67 hi-po cylinder heads for the 289-cid V-8; 1965-66 Shelby 6-1/2x14-inch 10-spoke wheels; Detroit-Locker axles; 1969-70 Boss 302 cylinder heads; 1969-70 31-spline rear axles; 1971-73 mini consoles and 8-track stereos; and the 1969 "Cross-Boss" intake manifold.

Accessories should not prompt you to buy a car that's in poor condition. However, a good Mustang with any of the above accessories on it will be worth more than the "book value" for the base car. In some cases, the accessories could make it thousands of dollars more valuable.

## KEY POINTS

Start your mechanical evaluation of the Mustang by obtaining the keys from the owner. Are all of the keys available? Do all the locks work? Does the owner have extra locks for items like wheels? Does he or she use any other passive or active theft-deterrent devices? An owner who has a well-organized keyring and a concern for security probably took good care of the car all its life.

## ENGINE OFF

Checking under the engine is important. Hopefully, you did this when the car was on the lift. Start with the ignition off. Look for oil leaks and greasy deposits. Is the engine painted nicely? Was it painted to look good at a show or to hide problems? Shiny metal on the oil pan might indicate impact with a rock or curb damage. Belts and hoses should be inspected while the engine is turned off. Check the oil level, power steering fluid level, and brake fluid. Probe the exhaust system with your screwdriver, looking for pinholes that become craters when you hit them.

Accessories (notice the luggage rack and GT package gas cap and trumpet exhaust) play an important role in the purchase of a Mustang. Many accessories for early models are highly desirable to collectors. (Old Cars Weekly)

Don't forget to raise the top. That way, you can check the rear window, while you make sure the top-raising mechanism works correctly. (Old Cars Weekly)

Part of checking a Mustang is examining the interior. Look for water stains on upholstery and carpets. Check the bucket seats, console and headliner. (Old Cars Weekly)

## ENGINE ON

Start the motor. Allow it to run and warm up for several minutes.

If the Mustang has an automatic transmission, pull the dipstick and check the automatic transmission fluid (ATF) level. Look for blue smoke (oil burning), black smoke (air/fuel mixture too rich) or white smoke (coolant in the cylinders). On a later-model, fuel-injected Mustang, white smoke can be a sign of high fuel consumption.

Place a rubber hose or solid stick between your ear and the engine's surface to listen for engine noises. Either method will provide a "stethoscope" to help you hear clicks, taps and knocks better. Does the engine idle smoothly? Does the exhaust system snap, crackle or pop? Backfires are a sure sign of problems. Also, a car stored for years may have an exhaust system that a chipmunk or squirrel has packed up with acorns.

Move to the inside of the Mustang with the engine running. Check the fuel, temperature, oil pressure, and electrical system gauges. "Bump" the accelerator rapidly. Does the engine speed up immediately or does it stumble and bog down? If installed, does the air conditioner work properly? How about the heater and defroster? On cars that have been stored for a while, a noisy blower or a working ventilation system with no airflow could indicate vermin or insect nests in the air ducts. This is common on cars stored in rural areas.

## BRAKES

For safety's sake, before you do a test drive of the vehicle, make sure the brakes work. Start with the emergency brake. It should function easily and positively. It should be able to hold the car on an incline, without the regular (service) brake being applied. After testing the emergency brake on an incline, release it and apply the service brake with your foot. If the brake pedal starts to give way under pressure, there's a brake fluid leak or the brakes have been improperly bled. If the pedal generates more pressure each time you apply it, there is air in the brake lines. If the brakes (especially disc brakes) are noisy, you need new linings, pads or other parts.

## TEST DRIVE

Start with the owner driving the car in his or her normal manner. If the owner is used to taking unusual steps to work around a problem (for example, revving the engine at stops to prevent its dying), this will show up as you observe the driving procedure.

Now, you drive. Try all gears in the transmission, including reverse. Difficulty entering a gate or a chattering noise could suggest clutch problems. Does the automatic transmission "clunk" into gear? This could mean repairs are in order. Transmission noise and driveshaft vibration are other things to listen for. A recurring vibration can probably be traced to an unbalanced propeller shaft or worn universal joints.

"Pull" the steepest hill you can find with the Mustang. As you crest the incline, let off the gas. While coasting like this, look in the mirror. Blue smoke (or black, sooty smoke with newer models) will indicate oil burning. When you get up to 55 miles an hour, put the car in neutral and coast along with your ears open. Any humming noises from the transmission or rear end will indicate repairs are going to be needed. Now shut the car off. Does it restart easily? If not, you may have electrical system or fuel system problems that adversely affect hot starts.

## SUSPENSION

Find (or create) a large puddle of water on the ground. Drive the car through the water and look at the tire tracks carefully. You'll be able to see if the front or rear wheels aren't tracking properly. This would indicate wheel alignment problems. Find a level floor or spot of ground. Measure the distance between the ground and the bumpers on both sides of the car. The measurements should be about equal, on one side and the other, at both the front and the rear. However, they may not be the same front and rear.

The suspension can be tested by pushing the front/rear of the car strongly up and down. If the shocks or struts are working properly, the car will not continue bouncing up and down very long. Replacing these parts isn't difficult, but you should figure any needed repairs into the deal you're making.

## TIRES

Tires should all be of the same brand, size and condition. Inspect the sidewalls for heavy scrubbing, tears, breaks, punctures and abrasions. Insert a Lincoln penny into the tread to see if it's deep enough to hide Abe's hairline. Check to see that the tread wear patterns on all of the tires look about the same.

## FINAL POINTS

If your inspection of the Mustang turns up no problems and it performs "A-1" during your test drive, you have found a pretty good car. Now you will have to start using your price guides to determine if the owner will sell the vehicle at a price that you can afford and are willing to pay. Good luck with your purchase.

# MUSTANG TRIVIA

**Q:** What was the only model year that the Mustang was not available with a V-8 engine?

**A:** 1974, the introductory year of the down-sized Mustang II.

**Q:** What was the smallest displacement engine ever available in a Mustang?

**A:** The 2.3-liter four-cylinder, introduced in the 1974 Mustang II, stayed in regular production until '93.

**Q:** What was the largest displacement engine ever available in a Mustang?

**A:** Ford's first use of a 429-cid V-8, the largest ever put in a Mustang, was the 1969 Boss 429. It was a race-bred "semi-hemi" design that was also utilized in the 1970 Boss. In 1971, a different 429 was available, although it was a de-stroked "wedge head" version of the 460 found in Thunderbirds and Lincolns.

**Q:** Who is Stanley Tucker and what is his place in Mustang history?

**A:** Tucker was a commercial airline pilot who accidentally bought the display-only white 1965 convertible Mustang that happened to be the very first production unit. Ford Motor Company managed to retrieve the car after a year in Tucker's ownership—the cost was a new Mustang. Mustang No. 1 resides in the Henry Ford Museum in Dearborn, Michigan.

**Q:** What years did Ford not offer a GT model?

**A:** The GT ran from the Mustang's introduction through 1969, then returned in 1982.

**Q:** What was the first year for a factory, stand-up hood ornament on a Mustang?

**A:** In 1975, this un-sporty option was available on Mustang IIs.

**Q:** What is the least powerful Mustang ever?

**A:** The 1978 Mustang II's 2.3-liter four-cylinder was rated at a lethargic 88 horsepower.

*1997 Cobra (Brad Bowling)*

# Index

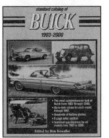